PQ 1441

TWO OLD FRENCH
GAUVAIN ROMANCES

TWO OLD FRENCH GAUVAIN ROMANCES

PART I

LE CHEVALIER À L'ÉPÉE

and

LA MULE SANS FREIN

Edited with Introduction, Notes and Glossary

by

R. C. JOHNSTON and D. D. R. OWEN

PART II

Parallel Readings with

SIR GAWAIN AND THE GREEN KNIGHT

by

D. D. R. OWEN

BARNES & NOBLE
BOOKS
10 East 53d St., New York 10022
(a division of Harper & Row Publishers, Inc.)

Published in the U.S.A. 1973 by
Harper & Row Publishers, Inc.
Barnes & Noble Import Division

ISBN 06-495323-8

Printed in Great Britain by
R. & R. Clark, Ltd., Edinburgh

CONTENTS

PART I

PART II

PREFACE

We present our work on *Le Chevalier à l'épée* and *La Mule sans frein* in two parts. Part I grew out of the joint efforts of both of us, and we are equally responsible for the Introduction, Texts, Notes and Glossary. Part II is entirely the work of D.D.R.O.

Part I was read through in typescript by Professor B. Woledge of University College, London, and by Dr. I. Short of Westfield College, London, and we have greatly profited from the suggestions and criticisms they kindly made. We are grateful to the photographic services of the Stadt- und Universitätsbibliothek in Berne for providing photographs of the manuscript. For Part II much helpful advice and comment has been offered by Professor J. MacQueen and by Mr. T. G. Duncan of the Universities of Edinburgh and St Andrews respectively. We wish also to express our appreciation of the many services rendered over a number of years by the St Andrews University Library staff, of all the typing and re-typing so patiently executed by Miss J. Henderson, and of the valuable help given by Mrs Berit Owen and Mr N. R. E. Johnston in the checking of proofs and references.

Grants towards the cost of publication have been made by the University of St Andrews, Westfield College, London, and the Marc Fitch Fund. To them too we wish to record our thanks for their generous assistance.

R.C.J.
D.D.R.O.

INTRODUCTION

A. LITERARY

Preserved together in a single manuscript (Berne, Bibliothèque de la Ville, MS 354) are the two short Gauvain romances, *Le Chevalier à l'épée* and *La Mule sans frein*.[1] Real though their literary qualities are, judgments have in the past been vitiated to some extent by being based on a misunderstanding of their true nature. Moreover, all considerations of artistic merit apart, they occupy a place of some importance in the history of medieval literature, and not only in that of France.

Who composed them? The question may be unanswerable, but the possibilities are intriguing.[2] The *Mule* (of the *Chevalier* we shall speak later) purports to be the work of a certain Paien de Maisières, but this has been shown to be almost certainly a pseudonym, playing on the name of the master of French romance, Chrétien de Troyes himself.[3] We present below linguistic evidence to suggest that both texts were composed in approximately the same area, probably Champagne; and this raises at least the possibility of common authorship. What can be said of the dating takes us little further. In each work the influence of Chrétien is very apparent and points to a *terminus a quo* at least after

---

[1] The MS is of the late 13th or early 14th century (for the language of the scribe see below, pp. 13–16). As well as an incomplete prose version of the *Sept sages de Rome* and Chrétien's *Conte du Graal*, it contains 74 relatively short poems, mainly fabliaux, but including didactic works, the *Cort mantel* (*Mantel mautaillié*), the *Folie Tristan* and our two romances. It once belonged to and is autographed by Henri Estienne, but whether this is the famous humanist or his grandfather is not clear (the latter is known to have worked for Geoffroy Tory: see S. L. Smith's edition of *La Mule sanz frain*, pp. 2–3). Our romances are copied consecutively on fol. 16b–26c (*Chevalier*) and 26c–36b (*Mule*). For the second we adopt the traditional title found in the rubric, though the text itself speaks of the *aventure* 'de la damoisele a la mure' (ll. 18, 1134). On the MS see H. Hagen, *Catalogus Codicum Bernensium* (Berne, 1875), pp. 338–45.

[2] The question of possible authorship is treated more fully in D. D. R. Owen, 'Two More Romances by Chrétien de Troyes?', *Romania* XCII (1971), pp. 246–60.

[3] See Owen, 'Païen de Maisières—A Joke That Went Wrong', *Forum for Modern Language Studies* II (1966), pp. 192–6. See also note to *M* (= *Mule*), ll. 1–16.

his *Yvain* and *Lancelot*, and either after or contemporary with his un-
finished *Conte du Graal*, as we shall see. Features of the language (in
most respects strikingly similar to Chrétien's) confirm the late twelfth
or perhaps early thirteenth century as the period of composition. One
is encouraged to think in terms of a single poet by the similarity in
tone and inspiration as well as in the organisation of the subject-matter.
On the other hand, there do seem to be some divergences, as in the
extent to which the two-case system is retained.

*   *   *

To all appearances *Le Chevalier à l'épée* is a composite romance and
cannot be taken as derived from any single coherent tale, Celtic or
otherwise. It comprises essentially one main and one subsidiary adventure. Gauvain, having lost his way in the forest, strikes up an acquaintance with a mysterious knight, who offers hospitality in his castle.
There the host makes over his daughter to Gauvain, supposing that,
as the two lie together at night, the sword that has hitherto protected
the girl's chastity will make an end of the hero. But in the morning
Gauvain is still in good shape, and the host recognises him as the finest
of all knights and therefore worthy of his daughter's hand. So ends the
main tale, with Gauvain and his 'bride' setting out for Arthur's court.
Then the action takes another turn. The girl abandons Gauvain for a
newcomer; but he is slain in a dispute with the hero over her dogs,
who are more steadfast than she in their attachments. Leaving the
faithless hussy to her fate, Gauvain returns to his uncle's court.

It will be seen from our Notes[4] that the core of the main action,
namely the temptation scene, has been ingeniously derived from two
episodes in Chrétien's *Lancelot*, an amusing twist being the transformation of the unwilling bedmate Lancelot into the too ardent lover
that is Gauvain. This central scene has been placed in a context (the
huntsman host and his perilous hospitality) most probably culled from
Chrétien's 'Gauvain', as we shall call the second part of his *Conte du
Graal*.[5] We refer to Gauvain's encounter with the young King of
Escavalon and his sister. There is a further clear debt to Chrétien in

---

[4] See especially notes to *Ch* (=*Chevalier*), ll. 78 ff. and 454 ff.

[5] In this Introduction the two parts of the *Conte du Graal* will be referred to as
the 'Perceval' and the 'Gauvain'. For an investigation of the bipartite nature of
the romance and arguments for its two main sections being originally independent,
see Owen, *The Evolution of the Grail Legend* (Edinburgh & London, 1968),
ch. VII.

the shepherd's warning, taken almost verbatim from the passage in *Erec* where fears are expressed for the hero's safety as he affronts the dangers of the Joie de la Cort.[6]

The subsidiary plot, with its strong anti-feminist tone, appears to have its main source in a different tradition, whether a lost *lai*, as Gaston Paris suggested,[7] or some popular, fabliau-type tale that has failed to survive.

* * *

La Mule sans frein seems similarly composite in its structure. A maiden arrives at Arthur's court seeking a knight who will recover the lost bridle of her mule. The animal will carry him to his destination. Kay volunteers; but, having safely passed through a wild forest, whose denizens do obeisance to the mule, and a foul and verminous valley, and having revived body and spirits at a lovely fountain, the sight of a slender bridge spanning a river of fearsome aspect proves too much for him. He returns to court and forfeits the quest to Gauvain. The king's nephew braves the perils of the way and arrives at a revolving castle, where he is called upon to undergo a beheading test and vanquish a mysterious knight as well as lions and serpents, before receiving the bridle from the mistress of the castle, the maiden's sister. He quits the place and its now joyful inhabitants to ride back in triumph to the court.

There is no doubt that much of this tale derives from some lost legend of ultimately Celtic provenance, in which figured at least the beheading test and probably the whirling fortress. But here again, Chrétien has been put to liberal use. Apart from the direct modelling of the prologue on that of *Erec*, apparent reminiscences of every one of his romances are to be found.[8] More curious is the fact that at several points the poet appears to show knowledge of Chrétien's own likely sources;[9] and this is a circumstance to which we shall return later.

As with the *Chevalier*, the author of the *Mule* has used some subsidiary material from outside the normal bounds of the *matière de Bretagne*, in this case from the field of pious, eschatological narrative. We notice it at two junctures. Firstly there is the picture of the hideous

---

[6] See note to *Ch*, ll. 160–3.

[7] *Histoire littéraire de la France* XXX (Paris, 1888), pp. 63–4.

[8] See especially notes to *M*, ll. 1–16, 391–400, 433–7, 465–70, 676, 714, 758–9, 760–5, 800 ff., 931–8.

[9] See notes to *M*, ll. 147–59, 160 ff., 214 ff., 258 ff., 678–741, 946–9, 968–71.

valley, with its bitter cold and wind, stench, and fire-breathing reptiles, which would appear to have been elaborated from descriptions of the places of infernal torment as found in such legends as the *Vision of St Paul*, *St Patrick's Purgatory* or the *Vision of Tundal*. If there were any doubt, the appearance of the testing bridge of Hell and the demon-infested river would dispel it. Certainly there are to be found in Celtic literature analogues to both valley and bridge, as well as to the beautiful spring. But we believe the poet had the vision of the Christian otherworld clearly in mind as he composed, especially when we recall that the fountain in its flowery meadow is also a common feature of the pious tradition, normally visited after the regions of Purgatory and Hell.[10]

The second instance of borrowing from religious writings occurs when the inhabitants of the revolving castle express their joy at Gauvain's victory in terms echoing a verse from *St Luke* and, moreover, reminiscent of those used by the imprisoned souls in many an account of Christ's spoliation of Hell.[11]

Surprisingly, even this incongruous use of Christian material turns our thoughts back to Chrétien de Troyes who, in his *Cligés* and *Lancelot*, had indulged in much the same practice. Into the first he had inserted a near-parody of Christ's Passion and Resurrection, and into the second a diffuse rehandling in profane terms of the story of the Harrowing as found in the *Gospel of Nicodemus*.[12]

*   *   *

From the point of view of subject-matter and composition the *Chevalier* and the *Mule* have, then, much in common; and the same could be said of their tone, which we would characterise as predominantly burlesque.[13] For the *Mule* the key is already set in the prologue by the sly mimicry of Chrétien together with the play on his name. Then the humour is turned against the craven Kay before it is brought to flicker round Gauvain himself, as this illustrious figure launches forth on the mule in quest of a mislaid bridle, leaps through the gateway of a spinning castle, plays the beheading game with an uncouth *vilain*,

---

10 See notes to *M*, ll. 160 ff., 214 ff., 238 ff.

11 See note to *M*, ll. 1030-3.

12 See Owen, 'Profanity and its Purpose in Chrétien's *Cligés* and *Lancelot*', *Forum for Modern Language Studies* VI (1970), pp. 37-48 (reprinted in *Arthurian Romance: Seven Essays*, ed. D.D.R.O., Scottish Academic Press, 1970).

13 For the *Mule* cf. Owen, 'Païen de Maisières ...'.

proves his valour in combat against beasts and a knight recuperating, it would seem, from a previous wound, and spurns in uncharacteristic fashion the lady's offer of her love (as well as of one of her thirty-nine castles!). In the end, at least as the story stands, we are left with the impression that Gauvain has been put to a deal of trouble to find the missing piece of harness, considering it was in the safe-keeping of its owner's sister all the time. The maiden for her part slips secretively from the story at the end, prompting us to suspect some family collusion in the whole affair, which would appear quite pointless were it not for the deliverance brought to the common folk of the castle (though why they were in such a plight in the first place we can only guess). One is left to wonder if all this mystery and ambiguity, rather than being a mark of the author's slackness, does not serve as a legitimate comic device reflecting the hero's own bewilderment.

The prologue of the *Chevalier*, of which more will be said, is touched by a quizzical ambiguity not unlike that at the beginning of the *Mule*. For the rest, as with its companion romance, most of the humour is applied to a slight deflation of Gauvain. He loses his way in the forest in a fit of absent-mindedness and enters upon the adventure dressed like a dandy, though not entirely unarmed. His subsequent trials may single him out as the best knight on earth, but his role in the story scarcely demonstrates the fact. First he is caught by his sinister host like a fly in a web; then he is thwarted in his amorous endeavours; and when he does finally win the girl, she is not so impressed by his qualities as a spouse as to be unwilling promptly to abandon him for a total stranger. The upshot is Gauvain's hardly chivalrous dispatching of the helpless knight and his subsequent misogynistic tirade. And the story of his experiences as he tells them at court is 'laide ct anuiose' at the end. The main humorous point bears, of course, on Gauvain's reputation as the ladies' man *par excellence*, showing him less than invincible in this sphere of knightly activity. The poet is carrying further a lesson that can be read into Chrétien's 'Gauvain'.

* * *

The suggestion that our two romances serve to continue what by now has become a tradition of the affectionate burlesquing of Gauvain has been made elsewhere.[14] The first, almost casual, hint of his philandering disposition was dropped by Wace in his *Roman de Brut*

[14] Owen, 'Burlesque Tradition and *Sir Gawain and the Green Knight*', *Forum for Modern Language Studies* IV (1968), pp. 125–45.

(based on Geoffrey of Monmouth's *Historia Regum Britanniae* and completed in 1155). There, in a passage foreign to his source, he expresses through Gauvain's mouth his own pacific sentiments:

> 'Bone est la pais emprés la guerre,
> Plus bele e mieldre en est la terre;
> Mult sunt bones les gaberies
> E bones sunt les drueries.
> Pur amistié e pur amies
> Funt chevaliers chevaleries.'[15]

This was the characteristic that Chrétien was to submit to a playful probing in his later romances, shedding some doubt at the same time on the notion of chivalric perfectibility as personified by Gauvain.

Already in *Yvain* there may be a touch of criticism. There we see Gauvain, having engaged in amorous dalliance with the lively Lunete, whose mistress Yvain had just wed, luring that knight away from his bride of a few days with warnings of uxoriousness and talk of tournaments to visit. He had assured Lunete that he would be at her service whether she needed him or not (l. 2434); and later we learn that no distressed damsel ever sought his aid in vain (ll. 3700-1); so it comes as no surprise to find him some time afterwards championing a girl in a cause that is manifestly unjust.

At about the same time, it seems, as he composed *Yvain*, Chrétien was working on his *Lancelot*. Here too we catch a glimpse of the flirtatious Gauvain;[16] but he is also seen in a situation of unusual discomfiture—having to be fished out of a river into which he had fallen and where he wallows, all but drowned. Now there is more than a touch of burlesque about this whole romance, and it is tempting to see Chrétien at this point deliberately indulging in a little wry humour at our hero's expense.

In 'Gauvain' he goes much further. Indeed it is possible to see this good-humoured deflation of King Arthur's nephew as the key to the whole romance, or at least to as much of it as Chrétien completed. He shows his august hero tumbling from one liaison into another, progressively being deflected from the course of duty and losing his freedom of action, until he ultimately finds himself in a castle peopled by women and maidens from which (supreme irony) he would fain

---

[15] Ed. I. Arnold, Paris (SATF), 1940, ll. 10767-72.

[16] As in ll. 544-9, where we see him in intimate conversation with a girl 'ne sai de quoi' (ed. M. Roques, Paris, C.f.m.â., 1958).

escape, but cannot. And in the course of his rovings he has suffered other indignities, on one occasion being left to ride a broken-down nag, on another taking a splash, as in *Lancelot*, into a raging torrent. Even worse, perhaps, he has meekly to suffer the withering tongue of that embittered maiden, the Orgueilleuse de Nogres.

The *Chevalier* and the *Mule* were composed very much in the spirit of Chrétien's 'Gauvain', of which they betray a detailed knowledge, and with which they share many features. For instance, involvements with members of the fair sex land the hero in situations of acute embarrassment and in which he sometimes falls short of the highest ideals of knightly behaviour; however, despite various humiliating experiences, he succeeds in each case in establishing his pre-eminence among knights; his triumphs result in his being offered the lordship of the castle where his main trials have taken place, and public rejoicing ensues; in none of the romances, though, is he interested in accepting the honour, nor is he able to form a permanent liaison with any of the women concerned. And in all three works, the humour comes to the surface only in isolated passages, being for the most part merely implicit in situations which could be taken quite seriously by the uninitiated.

The *Chevalier* and the *Mule* lie, then, directly downstream from Chrétien's later romances and follow a current of burlesque that he himself had initiated. More than this, they share a purpose and method so strikingly similar to that of his 'Gauvain' that one is forced seriously to consider not merely whether the two short works could be by the same author, but even whether they could have been produced by Chrétien himself, taking time off, as it were, from his more serious labours.[17]

* * *

In our view, the prologue to the *Chevalier* makes sense as it stands only if the author is naming himself in l. 18 as 'Crestïen de Troies'. If this is so, and remembering that 'Paiens de Maisieres' must be taken as a pseudonym playfully derived from 'Crestïens de Troies', we might say that each of the short romances is prefaced by a more or less oblique ascription to Chrétien. Is it possible that he wished in this cryptic way

[17] For a fuller investigation of this possibility see Owen, 'Two More Romances . . .?'

[18] See note to *Ch*, ll. 18–28.

to set his mark on them, but without too openly avowing himself their author?

That Chrétien wrote the *Chevalier* is implied by whoever copied his name into the margin of the manuscript (in the early sixteenth century, perhaps) and is stated by Geoffroy Tory in his *Champ Fleury* (1529) and by various other writers up to the late eighteenth century. Only then was the attribution called into question, and that, curiously enough, on the sole evidence of the prologue. A more reasonable objection might seem to be that if, as we suppose, Chrétien was still at work on his 'Perceval' and his 'Gauvain' when he died, he would scarcely have produced another romance that appears to show knowledge of both of them. Against this one might propose that he was composing all three simultaneously, but only completed the *Chevalier*. That would also account for the statement (l. 24) that Chrétien never told a story about Gauvain: though he had a full romance in preparation, he was not yet ready to proclaim and present it to his public.

The *Mule*, too, apparently owes a debt to 'Perceval' and 'Gauvain', and again we might think in terms of simultaneous composition—not now of three, but of four romances, two major and two minor. There is in this case a different argument that might be offered in favour of the ascription to Chrétien. As we have observed above, as well as familiarity with all Chrétien's acknowledged romances, the *Mule* seems to show knowledge of certain of his sources (the Owein and Fair Unknown stories). Who more likely than Chrétien himself to have this material at his disposal?

One must not overlook the possibility that one, or two, of his pupils had the idea of continuing their master's work in this light-hearted fashion, using his own texts as well as others from his 'library'. If this was the case, we might think the author of the *Chevalier* singularly perverse when he stated that Chrétien had never told of Gauvain, knowing full well that he had bequeathed over four thousand lines of the hero's adventures. But the possibility cannot be ruled out.

It might well be claimed that our texts lack the polish of Chrétien's other works, that the descriptions are less fully developed, the psychology and motivation rudimentary—the work, surely, of an apprentice, not of the master at the height of his powers. To this, however, there is a ready answer. As Orłowski has already suggested[19] and as the opening lines of the *Chevalier* strongly imply, these short romances were in all likelihood intended to be memorised and recited, not read

[19] *La Damoisele a la Mule*, p. 29.

privately or aloud like the full-scale works. Seen in this light, the terseness and economy of the narrative as well as the occasional appeals to the audience and repeated lines are not blemishes but the recognised techniques of oral literature. And why should Chrétien not have turned an honest penny by composing in a less demanding genre while waiting for the time and inspiration to complete his two long romances on Perceval and Gauvain?

But when all is said, the debate must still remain open. If not the author, then Chrétien was the inspirer of our texts; and they develop further the particular line of burlesque that he began. It was to bear remarkable fruit.

Although the *Chevalier* and the *Mule* have survived in only one manuscript, they must have been more widely diffused in the Middle Ages, and may often have been transmitted together and thought of as a pair. Both were put to extensive use by the Carinthian poet Heinrich von dem Türlin in his prolix romance *Diu Krône*, composed in about 1220.[20] Rather later, perhaps, the Picard author of *Hunbaut* drew liberally from them; and they seem also to have been known to the poet of the *Chevalier aux Deux Épées*.[21] On the other hand Raoul (de Houdenc?), who wrote his *Vengeance Raguidel* in the early part of the same century, made free use of the *Chevalier à l'épée* alone; and an apparent echo from the same text is even found to be in the *Queste del saint Graal*.[22] Our tales evidently enjoyed quite wide currency, and not only in France, in the thirteenth century.

But it was towards the end of the fourteenth that they underwent by far their most exciting transformation, when a great but anonymous English poet combined the two plots and expanded them into a unified whole to produce his masterpiece, *Sir Gawain and the Green Knight*.

[20] Ed. G. H. F. Scholl, Stuttgart, 1852. See also L. L. Boll, *The Relation of 'Diu Krône' of Heinrich von dem Türlin to 'La mule sans frain': A Study in Sources*, Washington, 1929; E. K. Heller, 'A Vindication of Heinrich von dem Türlin, based on a Study of his Sources', *Modern Language Quarterly* 3 (1942), pp. 67 ff.

[21] *Hunbaut*, ed. J. Stürzinger & H. Breuer, Dresden, 1914; *Li Chevaliers as Deus Espees*, ed. W. Foerster, Halle, 1887.

[22] *La Vengeance Raguidel*, ed. M. Friedwagner, Halle, 1909; *La Queste del saint Graal*, ed. A. Pauphilet, Paris (C.f.m.â.), 1923. In the *Queste* (pp. 109–10) Perceval is tempted by the devil in the form of a beautiful *damoisele*. He goes to bed with her after a surfeit of wine, and his chastity is preserved only by the sight of his sword engraved with a cross. In his remorse, he strikes and wounds himself with the weapon. Similarities of detail suggest borrowing from *Ch.* This *Queste* episode was used in turn by Malory in *The Tale of the Sankgreal* (*The Works of Sir Thomas Malory*, ed. E. Vinaver, 2nd edn. 1967, vol. II, pp. 918–19).

Part II of the present edition is devoted to an investigation of his treatment of the material. As late as the sixteenth century, Geoffroy Tory saw and handled our texts, apparently in a manuscript that is now lost;[23] and two hundred years later Sainte-Palaye made available a transcription from Berne 354, which had at one time been in the possession of Henri Estienne.[24] In 1777 the German poet Wieland turned the story of the *Mule* into his gay and charming 'Verserzählung' *Das Sommermärchen, oder des Maultiers Zaum*—'nach einem Fabliau des Chrétien de Troyes'![25]

★   ★   ★

How, then, are we to assess the value of these romances? Seen as isolated texts, they are not outstanding literary monuments, nor were they intended to be. And if they are full of Arthurian cliché, this was no doubt deliberate. For we interpret the intention behind them as the production not of model romances to vie with Chrétien's major works, but of playful skits on a genre that was in danger of becoming a little too stereotyped and self-important. Or if even this be thought too serious a purpose, then let us say they were designed to provide a few hours' carefree entertainment for a courtly audience; and this they surely did. With their rather bare but crisp and lively style they would give a reciter scope for his histrionic talents and even for a measure of interpretation. The underlying humour could in places be advertised by the droll expression and conniving wink, or else be overlaid by an unsmiling tone, serious and dramatic. Our hero might be presented as our hero or as an amiably luckless knight in slightly tarnished armour: an imposing or a gently comic figure.

When viewed from the longer perspective, our tales seem to mark a significant stage in the development of the romance. With them one

---

[23] 'On porroit aussi vser dez oeuures de Chrestien de Troyes, & ce en son Cheualier a lespee, & en son Perseual quil dedia au Conte Phelippe de Flandres. On porroit aussi vser pareillement de Hugon de Mery, en son Tornoy de Lente-crist. Tout pareillement aussi de Raoul en son Romant des Elles. Paysant de Mesieres nest pas a depriser, qui a faict maintz beaux & bons petitz coupletz, & entre les aultres, en sa Mule sans frein. Iay nagueres veu & tenu tous ces susdictz reuerendz & anciens Autheurs escriptz en parchemain, que mon seigneur & bō amy Frere Rene Masse de Vēdosme, Chroniqueur du Roy ma liberallement & de bon cueur monstre.' (Geofroy Tory, *Champ Fleury*, Paris, 1529, fol. iiiᵛ-iiiiʳ.)

[24] See above, note 1, and Armstrong's edition of *Ch*, pp. 37-8.

[25] *Christoph Martin Wieland: Epen und Verserzählungen*, ed. F. Beissner, Darmstadt, 1964, pp. 669-705.

feels that a critical look is being taken at a relatively new and much favoured genre, and at one of its most illustrious characters, in order to see where their weaknesses lay. This is part of the process of rejection, renewal and re-creation that runs throughout the course of literary history, but which does not always receive the attention it deserves from students of the medieval period. That the ultimate destiny of our texts was to provide the English *Gawain*-poet with the main stuff of his own masterpiece was not, perhaps, mere chance. One senses that his was a mind well attuned to their strain of humour with its implied criticism of those brittle ideals of the chivalric world. And his achievement was to move beyond the phase of criticism and rejection to that of re-creation, and by so doing to provide one of the jewels of medieval literature.

B. LINGUISTIC

Versification

Both poems are written in octosyllabic couplets[26] about whose syllable count there appear to be no features which are not generally known elsewhere.[27]

Occasional recourse is had to the appropriate short or long form of the same few words available to all poets: *el, ele; c', ce, ice;* (*i*)*tel;* (*i*)*tant; or, ore; encor(e); iluec, ilueques; avec, aveques; por coi, por qu'*. Such differences as can be observed, e.g. *itel, itant, por qu'* in *Ch* only, *iluec, ilueques, avec, aveques* in *M* only, are, by themselves, of limited significance in view of the small number of examples involved, or, as in the case of the 18 instances of *el* in *Ch* compared with only 5 in *M*, can be explained by differing circumstances, in this instance the important role played by the host's daughter in *Ch*, in the two texts.

There is no sure instance of the dropping of an internal *e* in hiatus in either poem, *cranté* for *creanté*, *Ch* 331, being almost certainly scribal. The final -*e* of polysyllables is normally elided, the only examples to the contrary being 5 in *Ch* (413 *sachë*, 515 *celë*, 666 *espaulë*, 991 *druë*, 1030 *escrië*) and 5 in *M* (301 *demoinnë*, 626 *domachë*, 656 *porchacë*, 765

---

[26] The errors in the very few lines that are metrically faulty (*Ch* 125, 143, 172, 321, 808, 835; *M* 178, 366, 619, 713, 1126) can safely be laid at the door of the scribe.

[27] The occurrence of hiatus or elision in *je, li* (article and pronoun), *si* and *se* is treated on pp. 21–3. A partial count of *que* and *qu'*, whether conjunction or pronoun, indicated that they were so freely interchangeable that separate figures for the two poems were meaningless.

conbatrë, 823 *iaumë*). The scribe may have eliminated a few other examples by writing *-es*, as in *Ch* 477 where *cierges* may stand for the poet's correct nominative plural *ciergë*. A few examples of *jusquë* have been regarded as part of the very common *que*, *qu'* alternations.

Broken couplets are common in both poems. There is a certain subjective element in the detection of these, and our figures for *M* are higher than those given by Orłowski (pp. 24–5). Taking Chrétien's *Conte du Graal* as our standard, we may summarise our findings by saying that *Ch* shows about 3% and *M* 12% more than Chrétien. The consideration of bold enjambement presents even greater difficulties of definition; but considering the same texts, we find it in *Ch* slightly less and in *M* rather more frequent than in Chrétien.[28] It is safe to say, then, that *M* takes noticeably more liberties in this aspect of versification than does *Ch*, though it is doubtful how much significance should be attached to the fact in view of the relative brevity of the texts.

Rhymes between simple words and their compounds or between different compounds of the same simple words are used in substantially the same numbers in both poems. A count of identically spelled words, not distinguishing between identical and homonymic rhymes, reveals fewer cases in *Ch* than in *M*.[29]

Consecutive couplets with the same rhyme never occur in *M*. In *Ch* on the other hand we find three certain cases: 527–30 *vivant* : *demant* : *desfent* : *talent*, by this time original *-ant* and *-ent* are identical and rhyme constantly together; 935–8 *conquerre* : *gerre* : *fere* : *aire*; 1091–4 *joie* : *oie* : *moie* : *aconplisoie*, by ca. 1200 A.D. *-oi*<AU+yod and Ē tonic and free are both reduced to [u̯ę]; and in addition 783–6 *estoit* : *voloit* : *tret* : *fet* would rhyme [u̯ęt]<*-oit* and [ęt]<*-ait*, while 1077–80 link *gré* : *Maïsté* : *faudrai* : *lessai* involving final [e]<*-a* tonic and free and <*-a*+yod. Plainly there is something to be said about the antecedents of all five occurrences; no such question arises about any four consecutive rhymes in *M*.

The following 14 rhymes, seven each in *Ch* and *M*, are in fact assonances only (not allowing for editorial corrections except for the

---

[28] We detect in *Ch* 17 instances (the first line of the couplet involved being: 118, 124, 222, 276, 278, 297, 393, 498, 683, 734, 878, 900, 923, 1034, 1058, 1096, 1152), as opposed to 28 in *M* (47, 102, 103, 133, 134, 143, 147, 148, 276, 320, 468, 488, 584, 590, 604, 662, 710, 735, 736, 744, 822, 837, 842, 864, 871, 964, 972, 1024).

[29] *Ch* 9 cases (23, 137, 147, 199, 227, 543, 551, 603, 1187); *M* 20 cases (15, 59, 105, 133 in MS, 185 in MS, 193, 229, 269, 389, 447, 573, 615, 671, 713, 745, 793, 925, 1017, 1089, 1115).

last example): in *Ch decopees*: *ovree(s)* 39–40; *riches*: *lices* 217–8; *porte*: *estorde* 545–6; *maintenant* : *branc* 561–2 (the grammatically correct *branz* would be no better); *Artu(r)* : *seür* 743–4; *sage* : *resnable* 1005–6; *païs* : *ami* 1195–6; and in *M il* : *peril* 251–2; *diz* : *hardi* 523–4; *maniere* : *armeüre* 655–6; *autre* : *faudre* 799–800; *ovraigne* : *painne* 1025–6; *aessent* : *baisent* 1051–2 (but in view of the scribe's confusion of single and double *s* both spellings may indicate [z]); *ot* : *veno(i)t* 1069–70.

The Language of the Scribe

One assumes that when given a text to copy a scribe normally regarded his task as the reproduction of what was before his eyes, but that he might well introduce some of his own spellings and forms of speech, particularly as medieval 'silent' reading actually involved the mouthing and muttering of what was being read. If the text were dictated this personal contribution, unchecked by the sight of his exemplar, would be greater. We can safely say, because of the number of occasions on which this scribe's eye strayed to adjacent lines, that MS Berne 354 was not written from dictation.

The manuscript version of *Ch* and *M* is basically written in what is conventionally called Francien (i.e. the standard literary language, in the form it had reached by the end of the twelfth and the beginning of the thirteenth centuries) plus a number of dialectal features. Theoretically this could represent (i) exactly the language of the author, if in the first place his work was so written down by himself or another, and if all subsequent copies reproduced this without change, or (ii) the original text with alterations introduced by a later copyist or later copyists. Supposition (ii) is the more likely because of the extent of the varieties of spellings and forms which seem unlikely to belong all to the same individual, although there is no means of ascertaining exactly the contributions of author and scribe(s) to the final mixture. After all the same person could use traditional graphies, e.g. *ai* and *en* and phonetic ones *e* and *an*, and early forms, e.g. *faz*, alongside later *fais* if he lived in the period of transition.

Accepting the assumption at the beginning of this section we may say that a scribe is more likely to give his personal colouring to words in the body of a line of verse that do not affect syllable count than to make changes which involve creating rhymes in a dialect which is not that of the author or to rewrite a line in order to introduce a shorter or longer word—though the possibility cannot be ruled out.

Dialectal Features

Both texts contain a number of spellings which indicate non-Francien pronunciations and forms. We give a selection of them,[30] preceded by their Francien counterparts, in an order suggested by M. K. Pope's treatment in the 'Conspectus of Dialectal Traits' to which the numbers in brackets refer.

Northern and North-Eastern

1. **iee : ie** mesnie *M* 949, haitie *M* 950 (N v).
2. **uee : ue** püent *M* 155 (N v).
3. **ieu : iu** liue *Ch* 122, liuee *M* 816 (N vi).
4. **eau : iau** oisiaus *Ch* 50, biaus *Ch* 85, piaus *M* 706 (N vii).
5. **ndr : nr** venré *Ch* 846, revenrai *M* 578 (N xiii).
6. **eł > eu : au** aus *Ch* 108, *M* 45, solaus *Ch* 60, viaut (< VOLET) *Ch* 293, *M* 616 (N xvii, E ix).
7. **z = [ts] : s** fruis *Ch* 443, girois *Ch* 499, viés *M* 16, miaus *M* 248 (N xxi).
8. **vostre : vo** *Ch* 1035 (N xxv) Once only.
9. **poüst : poïst** *Ch* 320, *M* 138.
10. **prendre : penre** *Ch* 1149 The only example.

North-Eastern

11. **ue : o** voil *Ch* 198, *M* 104 (N-E i).
12. **eu : o, ou** sol *Ch* 586, sole *Ch* 1190, chevous *M* 299 Pope, §230, Fouché, *Phon.* p. 306.

Eastern

Features 1, 2, 5, and 6 above.

13. **eu + r : o + r** Tonic, free ǫ in this position > [ou] and later reduced to [ǫ] > [u]. saignor *Ch* 8, plusor *Ch* 116, anor *Ch* 1155, *M* 151, plusors *M* 865 (E xviii) but much more wide-spread (Fouché, *Phon.* p. 307).
14. **labial + ei > ai + n : labial + oi + n** moinne *Ch* 137, 1028, avoinne *Ch* 237, poinne *M* 179, demoinne *M* 301 (E xix).
15. **ł > u** : effaced piez (< PALOS) *M* 782 (E xx).
16. **le : lo, lou** (def. art. and pron.) *Ch* and *M passim* (E xxv(a) and S-C xxi).
    je : jo *Ch* 507, 531.
17. **del, du : do, dou** *Ch* 20, 221, *M* 190 (Pope §843).

---

[30] For a longer discussion, as far as the text of *Ch* is concerned see Armstrong, pp. 51–8.

18. **age** : **ache** domache *Ch* 195.

19. **ei + n'** : **ai + n'** saignor *Ch* 8, ensaignié *Ch* 9, taing *Ch* 1037.

South-Centre

20. **-ons** : **-on** avon *Ch* 175, *M* 63, savon *Ch* 188 (S-C xvi also W xv).

South-Western

21. **pou, peu** : **poi** *Ch* 659, *M* 650 (S-W v) See Fouché, *Phon.* p. 310.

Western

22. **ele** : **el** *Ch* 284, *M* 70 (W xiv) but this form of the f.sg.pron. is much more widespread.

Conclusion

Looked at geographically these features appear to show the influence of dialects spread in a circle all round the Île de France; but the completeness of the circle is illusory. Feature 21, *poi*, crops up sporadically in twelfth- and thirteenth-century texts from many regions. It would be as absurd to attribute a Western origin to the scribe on the strength of the use of *el* beside *ele* as to call him an Anglo-Norman on the ground that this form is very frequently found in texts produced or copied in England; in reality this useful monosyllabic form found its way into Francien from the West, and can be regarded as available to writers of texts in the standard language. It is, however, noteworthy that according to Foerster, p. 213*, *el* was not used by Chrétien de Troyes.[31] We are inclined to think that Foerster, having standardised the language of his author, as nineteenth-century editors were wont to do, was apt to lean a little heavily on his reconstruction when formulating opinions about Chrétien's language.[32]

What we are left with, apart from *-on* for *-ons*, is an arc of Northern, North-Eastern, and Eastern features from which the more extreme are entirely lacking, no *waumoner, destrir*, unstable *e* in hiatus, *le vile, taule, -omes, apries, giteir*, imperfects in *-eve, vaiche, maleide*, 3rd pers. pl. pret. in *-arent*, etc. This reduces us to the consideration of a relatively narrow band of the arc, close to the border of the Île de France, i.e. the western region of Champenois, of which M. K. Pope writes: 'In its linguistic development Champagne shows the lack of unity that

---

31 '*ele* : *el* (öfter in [MS] A, schlecht gestützt) kommt nicht vor.'

32 P. Jonin in *Prolégomènes à une édition d'Yvain* (Gap, 1958) accepts *el* in his specimen reconstruction, l. 5903.

characterises its cultural history. The speech of the northern part of the province is linked with the northern and north-eastern region; the speech of the eastern with Lorraine, of the southern with Burgundy and the western is but little differentiated from the Île de France' (p. 497).

The Language of the Author(s)
Sounds

The amount of phonological information that can be gleaned from the study of 1171 rhyming couplets, when allowance has been made for the inevitable rhyming of infinitives, present and past participles with each other and similar uninstructive rhymes, is necessarily small. A dialectal form of a tonic vowel or a final consonant developed from the same source in two rhyming words does not prove anything about authorial pronunciation, since the scribe could have altered both as easily as he could have altered a single word in the interior of a line. Thus *perillose* : *anuiose* Ch 1201–2 and *perillouse* : *tenebrose* M 171–2 tell us something about the development and orthography of the French suffix <Latin -OSUM, but do not forbid the assigning of the pronunciation [ö] to the author. Nevertheless such spellings, if in the majority, do lend some support to the belief that the scribe found them or something like them in his exemplar.

The vast majority of the rhymes, like the vast majority of the scribe's spellings, go to prove the basically Francien or Western Champenois nature of the language employed. The extreme N, N-E and E dialectàl features absent from the graphies are also absent from the rhymes; also absent from the rhymes are all the features listed above except 11, 12, 13, 14, 18 and 21; 22 is abundantly attested by syllable count. This means that the likelihood of any northern Champenois influence is far less on authorial than on scribal language, unless, of course, the rhymes reveal other features which cannot be seen from internal scribal graphies only.

We deal first with the five possibly dialectal features common to scribe and author(s).

(1) FEATURES 12 AND 13

Latin [ǫ] tonic and free normally gives [ö]. This is shown by the predominant spellings *deus* Ch 730, M 150, 367 etc., *eure* Ch 88, *preu* Ch 308, 382 etc., M 929, *seus* Ch 88, M 118, 561, *seul* M 43, 436, *seule*

M 39, 1135, *oiseuse M* 253, *perilleuse M* 254, and the rhyme *eus*<ILLOS : *seus*<SOLUS *Ch* 891–2 and *angoiseus* : *jeus*<JOCOS *M* 323–4.

Contrary evidence, apart from special cases (for which see below), is provided by the spellings *soe Ch* 251, *M* 87, *sol Ch* 586, 628, 929, 983, and the rhyme *vos* : *anguissos Ch* 677–8.

The suffix <-OREM and the words *amour* beside *ameur* and *jaloux* beside *jaleux* constitute special cases and are examples of *tolérances* of which poets from many regions take advantage. If *amour* and *jaloux* are not remodelled on *amoureus, jalouser, jalousie*, they are borrowed forms into the vocabulary of love from Provençal or Champenois.[33] They occur as a graphy, *amor*, in *M* 91, 369, and as a rhyme *jalous* : *vos* in *Ch* 289–70. The pronunciation (ǫr) or (ur) is undoubtedly dialectal in origin but is an accepted element in the literary language. In *Ch jor* rhymes with *anor* 5, *valor* 253, *plusor* 417, and *dolor* 681 and in *M* with *puor* 211; *Ch* also shows *flor* : *retor* 871–2, *anor* : *tor* 1177–8. On three occasions *M* rhymes two <-OREM words together, 141, 185 and 275; this, as also the rhymes *corent* : *anorent* 67–8 and possibly *dedesor* : *peor* 415–6, might indicate an (ör) pronunciation, keeping them apart from *jor*-type words.

Taken all together the total evidence shows that scribe and poet(s) use (ö) and special cases of (o)/(u) as in the standard literary language but add some familiarity with the dialectal practice east of the Île de France, which familiarity may be slightly greater in the case of *Ch*.

(II) FEATURE 14

Francien -*ein* (cf. the belated spelling *freinc M* 103) lowering to -*ain* is attested for the scribe by occasional spellings, e.g. *mainne M* 359, for *Ch* by the rhymes *fain* : *Gauvain* 237–8, *Gauvain* : *amain* 277–8, *vilainne* : *painne* 321–2, *premerainne* : *painne* 1175–6, and for *M* by the rhymes *painne* : *certainne* 419–20 and *ovraingne* : *painne* 1025–6.

The presence of the Eastern differentiation -*ein*>-*oin*[34] is not seen in any rhymes of the type *foint*<FINGIT : *point*<PUNCTUM, but *M* shows a tendency to isolate *moinne* : *poinne* (with or without -*oin* spellings) so frequently[35] against only the two examples of -*ain* : -*ein*, that

---

[33] See Fouché, *Phon.*, p. 307.

[34] This feature is not restricted to cases where a labial consonant precedes, cf. *ploins*, Fouché, *Phon.*, p. 376, remarque I. However there is no trace of this in our scribe or author(s) and Francien forms only are seen: graphy *fainte Ch* 1186, *frains M* 79 and rhyme *Gauvain* : *frain Ch* 907–8.

[35] *painne* : *moinne* 71–2, *mainne* : *painne* 165–6, *moinne* : *painne* 539–40, *amoinne* : *mainne* 679–80, *peine* : *mainne* 753–4, *demoine* : *amoinne* 989–90, *painne* : *amainne* 1125–6.

a slight presumption of the *-oin* pronunciation after the labial consonant, contrasted with *-ain* after other consonants, must be allowed for and opposed to the freer mixing characteristic of the rhymes in *Ch*.

(III) FEATURE 11

The uniform occurrence of the spellings *voil, voille, voillent,* no examples to the contrary, could indicate that the scribe was never presented with *vueil* etc. in his exemplar and therefore that the author(s) too employed the dialectal form.

(IV) FEATURES 21 AND 22

PAUCUM and Germanic **blao* regularly give *po, pou* and *blo, blou* in Francien. *Ch* 303–4 rhymes *bloi : poi* and these forms are undoubtedly Western and South-Western. But they are used in other regions; *poi* by Gautier d'Arras and Chrétien de Troyes for example.

Similarly *el* is not confined to its Western place of origin, nor are poets who use it to be assigned on that account only to that region.

(V) FEATURES 16 AND 17

The forms *lo, lou, jo, do* and *dou* being unstressed cannot occur in rhymes, but, as with (iii) above, these graphies so largely preponderate that they may well go back to the author(s).

(VI) FEATURE 18

Dialectal *-ache* in the scribe's *domache Ch* 195 occurs also in the rhyme *rage : arrache M* 681–2, but is not further supported: *domages : sauvages M* 923–4, *rage : langage M* 1029–30.

The remaining features, most of them confined to single instances, not shown in the interior of lines, are revealed by rhymes.

(VII) The linking of *e* and *ie* is seen in *armez : sorquidez* for *sorquidiez Ch* 917–8 and *pere : Pere* for *Pierre M* 745–6. *M* also gives us *mestier : deslier* 677–8, *anuié : detrïé* 819–20, and *deslïer : depecier* 1027–8. Here the explanation may be that between *i* and *e* a palatal glide developed, so that *li-er* in fact is pronounced *li-jer*. The pronunciation without a palatal glide occurs once in *M* at line 285, *Gueherïez : Girflez*, and it is the only one attested for *Ch* in *oblïer : reconter* 25–6, *pensé : oblié* 93–4, *creanté : mercïé* 463–4, *volenté : mercïé* 773–4, *obliee : contree* 865–6, *retornez : obliez* 877–8. One example of *M*'s pronunciation is cited by Foerster, p. 212*; it occurs in *Yvain* 135.

(VIII) The Francien development of **USTIUM* is *(h)uis* and this is the form in the interior of lines, *Ch* 513, *M* 439, and at the rhyme *huis*: *reduis M* 755–6. The poet of *Ch* who twice, 500 and 821, rhymes *us* with *plus* is therefore on his own; this is perhaps more important to us than to try to decide whether his form is Western or North-Eastern dialect[36] or one of those that has slipped into the standard language as a licence of which poets make occasional use.

(IX) Certainly to be attributed to the language of the poet of *M* are two by-forms, both Eastern, both in Chrétien de Troyes. They are *mure* for *mule*, on which see the note to *M* 18, and *jame* for *jambe*. The syllable count also assures the Northern *renderai* for *rendrai* in *M* 584.

Declension

1. The Two-Case System

The breakdown of this system is shown when the poet achieves a correct rhyme between words in different cases which would be rendered incorrect by perfecting the accidence. Thus at *Ch* 47–8:

> *Puis s'en est de la ville issu*   (for *issuz*)
> *Tot lo droit chemin a tenu*   (correct oblique)

and at *M* 333–4:

> *Que Gauvains li a creanté*   (correct oblique)
> *Que li frains sera aporté*   (for *aportez*).

Rhymes between words in the same case, whether correct or incorrect, prove nothing, because the scribe could have altered both. Syllable count is sometimes decisive, as at *Ch* 455 *Les liz conmanda l'oste a fere* where the poet could not have written *l'ostes*, still less *li ostes*, without wrecking his octosyllabic line.

(a) Masc. obl. sg. for the nom. sg. form in -*s* or -*z*:

Chevalier 47 instances:

> 34 *talent*, 46 *atorné*, 47 *issu*, 63 *issu*, 74 *alé*, 94 *oblïé*, 104 *descendu*, 194 *chevalier*, 219 *entré*, 224 *joiant*, 225 *vaslet*, 228 *oste*, 238 *Gauvain*, 263 *vilain*, 343 *acointié*, 427 *Gauvain*, 430 *hasté*, 448 *certain*, 453 *haitié*, 480 *atorné*, 521 *alé*, 562 *branc*, 570 *garni*, 605 *esperdu*, 607 *esbahi*, 616 *mort*, 622 *morne*, 635 *honi*, 652 *tret*, 653 *vilain*, 670 *mort*, 698 *dolant*, 708 *mort*, 785 *tret*, 850 *repairié*, 920 *hardi*, 942 *garni*, 954 *desarmé*, 956 *fet*, 980 *certain*, 987 *vaillant*, 1003 *marri*, 1051 *certain*, 1076 *saisi*, 1110 *plait*, 1116 *eslessié*, 1173 *sage*.

Mule 4 instances:

> 334 *aporté*, 449 *recreant*, 510 *Marcel*, 513 *Gauvain*.

[36] See M. K. Pope, §183, §315, W x, and Fouché, *Phon.*, p. 287.

Four doubtful instances, three in *Ch* and one in *M*, remain. At *Ch* 120 *lo chevalier* could be either subject or object of *esvella*; 180 *retorné* should have a final -*z*, but so could 179 *mené*, if *mout* were treated as plural; and at 742 we have no knowledge of the author's practice with *avoir non*, which in Old French in general is as frequently followed by the nominative as by the oblique. At *M* 921–2 the rhyme *venu* : *avenu* is correct if *vos* is treated as plural, as it can be, and *avenu* agrees with neuter *il*; it would be equally correct if *vos* and *venuz* were treated as singular and *avenuz* were made to agree with *anuiz*.

Syllable count reveals three instances of *oste* for *ostes*, at *Ch* 277, 360 and 455; one instance of *delivre* for *delivres*, *Ch* 702; and, in a different category, *nului* for *nus*, *Ch* 1038.

The final totals for instances of masc. obl. for nom. are thus 52 in *Ch* against only 4 in *M*.

There is a strong presumption that the scribe is not responsible for every instance of incorrect oblique cases in rhyming pairs of words and in the interior of lines. Such mistakes are far more common in *Ch* than in *M*. It must be quite safe to affirm with Orłowski that the author of *Mule* 'a observé assez exactement le système de la déclinaison à deux cas',[37] whereas in *Chevalier* the breakdown is almost complete.

(b) Incorrect neut. nom. form with -*z*:

Chevalier 1 instance:

    582 *celez*

Mule no instance.

(c) Masc. obl. pl. for nom. pl.:

Chevalier 5 instances:

    477 *cierges*, 833 *amis*, 869 *biaus*, 1056 *esloigniez*, 1148 *provez*.

Mule 2 instances:

    135 *Lïons et tigres*, 878 *fiers et granz*.

2. Analogical Forms

(a) Extension of -*s* to masc. nouns and adjectives:

Chevalier 2 instances:

    400 *peres*, 758 *miaudres*. Both of these could be attributed to the
    scribe if we corrected to *perë* and *miaudrë* with hiatus.[38]

Mule no instance.

---

[37] Orłowski, p. 11.

[38] Such forms are more frequent in preconsonantal position in the interior of lines, where syllable count is unrevealing, in *Ch* (e.g. 680, 791, 801) than in *M*; but they are probably authorial rather than introduced by a Champenois scribe.

(b) Extension of -s to fem. nouns and adjectives:

No example attributable to the author of either text. At the most suspicion could be aroused by spellings, affecting neither rhyme nor syllable count. There are two cases in *Ch* (308 *preuz*, 1181 *pitiez*), six in *M* (40 *avenanz*, 172 *crüeus*, 229 *granz*, 392 *bruianz*, 414 *moitiez*, 1015 *Quieus*).

(c) Extension of -e to fem. of uniform adjectives:

Chevalier no instance.

Mule 3 instances:

111 *Quele* (could be attributed to scribe if we alter *voille* to *voillë* with hiatus), 277 *grande*, 389 *grieve*.

(d) Incorrect forms of imparisyllabic nouns and adjs.:

The scribe could be responsible for *Ch* 761 *miaudre* for *meillor* and *M* 11 *miaudres* for *meillors*; the author(s) come under suspicion only.

Conjugation

There are very few significant forms to glean.

(a) In the imperfect indicative all the -er and -ier verbs have -oie etc. forms except for a single instance at *Ch* 983 where *porpensot* is assured by its rhyme with *sot* (<SAPUIT); *estre* shows *ert* and *erent* alongside *estoit* and *estoient* in both texts; the extraordinary form *venot*, *M* 1070, is to be attributed to the scribe and corrected to *venoit* as in *M* 41 etc., whether we accept a poor rhyme with *ot* (<AUDIT) or correct this to *oit*.

(b) Although -oiz is frequent in the interior of lines in both texts, the ending of the 2nd pers. pl. of the future simple is -ez at the rhyme (e.g. *Ch* 124 and *M* 292) with the single exception of *orroiz M* 330 rhyming with *foiz*. The same text supplies a unique example of the dialectal fut. *renderai* at 584.

(c) Only in the choice of the auxiliary in the compound tenses of *aler* and *venir* do the two texts notably differ. *Ch* uses *estre* throughout, while *M* has *avoir* with *alé* at 132, 164, 168, 232, 238 and 914 and with *venu* at 842, a total of 7 instances.

Other Parts of Speech

(a) The -e of the weak subject pronoun *je* is always elided except for 4 instances in *Ch* at 143 g[e] i envoi, 147 je irai, 864 je ai droit, 1069 je ain. One possible instance in *M* 90, Et je orendroit . . . feroie, is more likely to be a scribal spelling for *gié*, the tonic form.

(b) The weak dative pers. pron. *li* normally retains its -i in hiatus.

Elision is found twice in *Ch* at 383 and 550 both times in *l'estuet* (unless *l'* is accusative, as with *estovoir* it may possibly be), and once in *M* 549 *Et cil l'en done* (which could be eliminated by the simple correction *Cil li en done*).

The tonic oblique fem. <*ILLAEI is the expected Francien form *li*; there is no trace of the north-eastern *lei*, nor of the western *lie*. The masc. <*ILLUI is in *Ch* reduced to *li* four times (99, 459, 1148, 1152). Rhyme can of course only attest the (earlier) shift in *lúi*>*luí* of a descending to an ascending diphthong (*li* : *qui* 459–60), but the spellings may be frequent enough to incline us to think that this eastern form was used by the author of *Ch*. *M* prefers *lui*, 20 times, to one dubious case (493) of *li*.

(c) The masc. nom. pl. *vo* for *vostre*, which in addition to being a Picardism is unusual in pronominal use, occurs once only, at *Ch* 1035. The scribe could conceivably be responsible for altering *quant vostre ne sont* to *quant il vo ne sont*.

(d) The form of the impersonal subj. pron. is always *l'en* or *en* except for one instance of *l'on*, *Ch* 184 where it rhymes with *non*, and one of *on* in the interior of *M* 1076.

(e) Forms of the relatively late pronoun *lequel* occur in both texts: *Ch* 312, 976, 1044 and *M* 569 and 581.

(f) Elision is the rule with the *-e* of the obl. sg. pers. pron. *le*; hiatus occurs once only in *Por prendre le et por oster* at *Ch* 564.

(g) The masc. nom. sg. form of the def. art. shows both hiatus *li* and elision *l'* before a noun beginning with a vowel. Because its story necessitates the use of the word *oste(s)* we know more about the practice in *Ch* than in *M*. *Ch*. uses *li ostes* 9 times (240, 263, 372, 426, 435, 684, 817, 849, 882), *li oste* twice (277, 360), *li uns* 4 times (108, 160, 174, 799); *l'ostes* 5 times (388, 471, 721, 746, 874), *l'uns* twice (680, 1116) and *l'autres* once (680). This proportion, 15 instances of hiatus to 8 instances of elision, is maintained in *M*, but in view of the small number of instances there involved the fact is of little or no significance. *M* has *li un* (799) and *li uns* (1011) against *l'uns* (818). Both texts invariably elide *li* before the impersonal pronoun *en* or *on*.

(h) *Si* 'and' develops a weakened form *se*, which may by elision be reduced to *s'*. We find no unequivocal instance of this in *M*, but:

    Chevalier 5 instances:

        se+*en*>*s'en* 773; *se*+*lo*>*sel* 106, 599, 1088, and >*sou* 105. At 405 we print *S'il* = *Si*+*il*, but this may be a scribal spelling for *Si* with mute and redundant *-l*.

(i) *Se* 'if' usually shows elision to *s'* before a vowel. Hiatus is more than twice as common in *Ch* as in *M*:

Chevalier 10 instances:

183, 214, 287, 311, 380, 431, 563, 612, 636, 675. There is one doubtful instance at 469 where the MS reads *sil contredit*. If this means 'if he contradicts' we understand *s'il* with a perfectly normal *se* elided. It if means 'if he contradicts him', then either we have an abnormal *si + le* or more likely *se + il + le > s'ill > s'il*.

Mule 4 instances:

86, 252, 736, 784.

(j) Both texts know the slightly archaic negative *nen* and use it occasionally, instead of *n'*, before a vowel: *Ch* 505 and *M* 449, 476, 713.

Authorship

As the earlier part of this Introduction shows, the subject-matter and handling of possible sources and the general tone of the two romances make single authorship a distinct possibility, which the result of their being written out by the same scribe does not diminish. The linguistic examination has revealed certain differences which may or may not indicate two different authors or one author in differing circumstances, such as we see in the earlier and later language of Chrétien de Troyes and Frère Angier for example. The differences may not be decisive. The following summing up makes, we think, the maximum case against single authorship.

1. Bold enjambement less common in *Ch* than in *M*.
2. Two successive couplets with the same rhyme likely on five occasions in *Ch* but never in *M*.
3. *Ch* rather less Francien than *M* in the treatment of -osum, solum, and -orem.
4. *Ch* perhaps more Francien than *M* in the development of *-ein* preceded by a labial consonant.
5. Some slight difference in the pronunciation of *-ier* verbs.
6. *Ch us* against (*h*)*uis* in *M*.
7. Breakdown of the case-system considerably more advanced in *Ch* than in *M*.
8. Rather more possibility of the extension of analogical *-s* and *-e* to feminine adjectives in *Ch* than in *M*.
9. *Aler* and *venir* never conjugated with *avoir* in *Ch*, but seven instances in *M*.
10. *Ch* possibly knows *li* for *lui*, but *M* does not.

11. Hiatus with *je* and *se* commoner in *Ch* than in *M*.

12. *Ch* knows the reduced form *se* for *si* 'and'; *M* does not.

The purely linguistic evidence may be summarised thus. Both texts have passed through the hands of the same Champenois scribe. Any changes that he made would have tended to make the texts linguistically more alike and thus to diminish any original differences between them. Nevertheless our evidence would support the conclusion that both texts were composed in the language spoken near the western border of Champagne, with *Ch* characterised by a more western flavour than *M*. Armstrong (edition pp. 50-1), probably placing too much weight on negative evidence such as the absence of imperfect indicatives in *-eve*, went so far as to consider *Ch* a Francien text.

That the localisation of literary texts is a delicate task no one would doubt. Three authorities have come to three different conclusions about the language of Chrétien de Troyes: A. Ewert in *The French Language*, p. 365, opts for East Champagne; Foerster, p. 210*, for West Champagne; and M. K. Pope, §1324 for South Champagne. Prudence makes us do no more than put forward our conclusion in favour of the western border of Champagne for *M* and somewhere further west for *Ch* as tentative and the best that can be offered in the circumstances of the case.

Another scruple in the balance may come from the following scraps. In the matter of vocabulary the argument *ex silentio* is particularly feeble, because the non-appearance of even a favourite word in eleven or twelve hundred lines is not very surprising. Nevertheless we note that *M* does not use *demaintenant, demanois, eneslopas, forment*, which are in *Ch*, and on the other hand uses three times each *des mois, ladedenz*, and phrases involving the well-known *soz ciel* (833, 845, 873), which also shows that once *M* has a word in his head he is apt to return to it. It is perhaps a commentary on the doubtful value of such observations that *Ch* uses the words *cortois, cortoisement* or *cortoisie* on thirteen occasions (37, 136, 261, 274, 300, 314, 326, 382, 571, 826, 933, 938, 1006), whereas *M* does not appear to know them!

The repetition of whole lines verbatim is a striking feature of both texts: we find ten instances in *Ch* and thirteen in *M*, as well as a number of near-identical or very similar pairs.[39] In both romances these include

---

[39] Identical lines (discounting orthographical variants): *Ch* 89/110; 96/1046; 215/792; 274/300; 292/366; 367/795; 516/690; 590/1165; 694/1036; 894/1164.— *M* 18/1134; 32/1059; 89/560; 94/428; 141/276; 150/1050; 158/361; 244/406; 269/1047; 336/372; 545/949; 634/1014; 725/821.

some personal interjections by the author. While the repetitions might be thought a personal stylistic feature and be used to support the theory of common authorship, they could as plausibly be explained as the mark of poems designed for oral performance.

Any consideration of authorship must take into account this 'oral' nature of our texts and the consequent strong likelihood of oral transmission as well as delivery. It is significant that most of the works preserved in MS Berne 354 are fabliaux, and that a number of these are extant elsewhere in variant forms. Indeed, in his study of the transmission and adaptation of fabliaux, Jean Rychner used our manuscript for most of his examples.[40] We cannot assume, therefore that we have our romances in the state in which they left the pen of the author: changes may have crept into the texts, possibly even more into the one than the other. For the advocate of common authorship the most difficult point to overcome is the variation in the handling of the case-system. Even with this, however, one might well maintain that the similarities are more interesting than the differences. As it is, the verdict for us must be 'not proven'.

*   *   *

The closeness of the language of *M* to that of Chrétien de Troyes has been commented on by most of the scholars who have dealt with the text. Hill, edn., p. 9, says that it is 'written in a dialect similar to that used by Chrétien de Troyes'. Jeanroy, in the *Revue critique d'histoire et de littérature* LXXI (1911), p. 429, regards *M*'s language as 'calquée sur celle de Chrétien de Troyes'. Orłowski, p. 15, considers that 'les ressemblances de sa langue avec celle de Chrétien de Troyes par exemple sont frappantes'. Smith, p. 35, concludes: 'Written in a language that is in no way distinguishable from that of Chrétien, the *Mule sanz frain* could well have been written during the same period in which Chrétien was writing, or it could just as well have been written later.'

For us the comparison with Chrétien's language is another way of

---

Similar lines: *Ch* 35/281; 153/389; 166/494, 982; 187/470; 215/355, 482; 286/316; 291/329; 314/326; 337/550; 479/639; 489/895; 498/781; 508/640; 582-4/626-8; 601/731; 696/732; 833-4/838-9; 893/1163; 935/945; 1026-7/1068-9. —*M* 71/166; 93/427; 100/343; 115/674, 1127; 130/167; 132/168; 140/1066; 150/367; 215/386; 228/1133; 232/1042; 238/402; 243/405; 333/568; 382/607; 609/675; 635/849; 637-8/871-2, 889; 757/915; 779/785; 943/961; 1041/1045.

[40] *Contribution à l'étude des fabliaux: variantes, remaniements, dégradations*, 2 vols., Neuchâtel/Genève, 1960.

pointing to the geographical area we have specified and the period of composition we consider likely for *M*. What is known about literary western Champenois at this time is so largely influenced by evidence gathered from Chrétien that the two categories of language must considerably overlap. As evidence of some slight differences between Chrétien and *M* we may mention the case-system, which is even better observed by Chrétien than in *M*[41] and perhaps the rhyming of *męs* with *męs* at ll. 713–4.

The author of *Ch* is linguistically further from Chrétien in respect of his handling of the declension system, his use of *peüst* (rhyming with *aperceüst*) instead of *poïst* at l. 719, his freer use of the pronoun *el* before consonant (17 cases against 6 and 3 respectively in Mario Roques's editions of *Yvain* and *Charrete*), and his use of *vo* at l. 1035 for *vostre*.

Like the literary evidence, the facts of language bring us into a close relationship with Chrétien de Troyes but do not permit us to advance further than a statement of their considerable similarities.

[41] Professor Woledge allows us to quote the result of his computerisation of the case-system of nouns in Guiot's copy of *Yvain*, which revealed 'no clear case of declension breakdown, either rhymes or elsewhere'.

EDITORIAL PROCEDURE

Both texts are preserved in a single manuscript written by a scribe who is reasonably competent, but does have a tendency to let his eye occasionally be caught by similar forms in neighbouring lines. We have introduced as few changes as possible. Wherever we have been able to defend the MS we have followed it without trying to improve upon it or to discern behind it better readings that the author might have intended.

There are very few places where the MS is difficult to read. The great similarity between *n* and *u* causes no hesitation in determining the word intended. The scribe's abbreviations are the normal ones and have been resolved without trouble. The proper names Gauvain (usually), Keu (frequently) and Yvain (once, in *M* 286) are represented by their initial letter. Except where the rhyme dictates otherwise, *-s* forms have been employed for the nominative and vocative uses in resolving these abbreviations. In the following instances the scribe has written these names in full: *Ch* 31 *Gauuaī*, which rhymes with *Yvain* and would be correctly oblique if *ot* be the verb assumed, or incorrect if the missing verb was *estoient*; *Ch* 466 *Gauuains*, *M* 285 *Gauuaīs* are correct nominatives; *M* 50, 56, 96, 108 *Kex*, where in the first instance *Keus* is vocative and in the other three the subject. All the other proper names are given in full.

The editors are responsible for the punctuation, use of capital letters, distinction between *i* and *j*, *u* and *v*, and the acute accent which distinguishes between the full vowel *e* and feminine *e*, the diaeresis, the word-division, the writing as words of the numerals given in figures, and the indentations denoting new sections of the story.

Every rejected reading is recorded in the list preceding the Notes. Where an addition has been made to the text, it has been done within square brackets.

BIBLIOGRAPHICAL NOTES[1]

MODERN EDITIONS

Le Chevalier à l'Épée: An Old French Poem, ed. E. C. Armstrong, Baltimore, 1900 (=Armstrong).

La Mule sanz frain: An Arthurian Romance by Paiens de Maisieres, ed. R. T. Hill, Baltimore, 1911 (=Hill, edn.).

La Damoisele a la Mule (La Mule sanz Frain): Conte en vers du cycle arthurien par Païen de Maisières, ed. B. Orłowski, Paris, 1911 (=Orłowski).

Paien de Maisieres' 'La Mule sanz frain': An Edition. University of Pennsylvania Ph.D. dissertation, 1968, by Stephen Lawrence Smith (=Smith).[2]

REVIEWS, STUDIES AND WORKS ON LANGUAGE

P. FOUCHÉ, *Phonétique historique du français*, 3 vols., Paris, 1952–61 (=Fouché, *Phon.*).

—— *Le Verbe français: étude morphologique*, nouv. éd., Paris, 1967 (=Fouché, *Verbe*).

L. FOULET, *Petite syntaxe de l'ancien français*, Paris (C.f.m.â.), 1930.

R. T. HILL, review of Orłowski's edn. of *La Damoisele a la Mule* in *Romanic Review* IV (1913), pp. 392–5 (=Hill).

T. A. JENKINS, review of Hill's edn. of *La Mule sanz frain* in *Modern Language Notes* XXVI (1911), pp. 148–51 (=Jenkins).

R. LEVY, '*La Damoisele a la mure*: étude textuelle', *Medium Ævum* IV (1935), pp. 194–8.

A. MICHA on *M* and *Ch* in R. S. Loomis, ed., *Arthurian Literature in the Middle Ages*, Oxford, 1959, pp. 362–5.

J. MORAWSKI, *Proverbes français antérieurs au XVe siècle*, Paris (C.f.m.â.), 1925 (=Morawski).

J. ORR, '*La Demoiselle a la mure*: étude textuelle', *Medium Ævum* V (1936), pp. 77–8.

[1] We list only the principal works used in the preparation of this edition. We give in round brackets the abbreviated references used in the Introduction and Notes.

[2] This unpublished edition came to our notice when our typescript was ready for the printers, but still in time for us to include some references to it. Its Introduction contains a useful section on sources and analogues.

G. PARIS, review of Armstrong's edn. of *Le Chevalier à l'Épée* in *Romania* XXIX (1900), pp. 593–600 (=Gaston Paris).

M. K. POPE, *From Latin to Modern French with Especial Consideration of Anglo-Norman*, Manchester, 1934 (revised edn. 1952) (=M. K. Pope).

M. ROQUES, review of edns. of *M* by Hill and Orłowski in *Romania* XLI (1912), pp. 144–7 (=Mario Roques).

CHRÉTIEN DE TROYES: EDITIONS

Erec et Enide, ed. Mario Roques, Paris (C.f.m.â.), 1955 (=*Erec*).
Cligés, ed. A. Micha, Paris (C.f.m.â.), 1957.
Le Chevalier de la Charrete, ed. Mario Roques, Paris (C.f.m.â.), 1958 (=*Lancelot*).
Le Chevalier au Lion (Yvain), ed. Mario Roques, Paris (C.f.m.â.), 1964 (=*Yvain*).
Le Roman de Perceval ou le Conte du Graal, ed. W. Roach, Genève/Lille (TLF), 1956 (=*Conte du Graal*).

DICTIONARIES, ETC.

L.-F. FLUTRE, *Table des noms propres avec toutes leurs variantes figurant dans les romans du moyen âge*, Poitiers, 1962.

W. FOERSTER, *Kristian von Troyes: Wörterbuch zu seinen sämtlichen Werken*, Halle, 1914 (=Foerster).

L. FOULET, *Glossary of the First Continuation (The Continuations of the Old French 'Perceval' of Chrétien de Troyes*, ed. W. Roach, Vol. III.2), Philadelphia, 1955 (=Foulet in Roach).

F. GODEFROY, *Dictionnaire de l'ancienne langue française*, Paris, 1881–1902 (=Godefroy).

R. GRANDSAIGNES D'HAUTERIVE, *Dictionnaire d'ancien français*, Paris, 1947.

A. J. GREIMAS, *Dictionnaire de l'ancien français*, Paris, 1969.

A. TOBLER & E. LOMMATZSCH, *Altfranzösisches Wörterbuch*, in progress, Berlin, 1925 ff., now Wiesbaden (=Tobler-Lommatzsch).

LE CHEVALIER À L'ÉPÉE

Cil qui ainme desduit et joie 16b
Viegne avant si entende et oie
Une aventure qui avint
4 Au bon chevalier qui maintint 16c
Loiauté, proëce et anor,
Et qui n'ama onques nul jor
Home coart, faus, ne vilain:
8 Je cont de monsaignor Gauvain,
Qui tant par ert bien ensaigniez
Et qui fu des armes prisiez
Que nus reconter ne savroit.
12 Qui ses bones teches voudroit
Totes retrere et metre en brief,
Il n'en vendroit onques a chief.
Se je nes puis totes retrere,
16 Por ce ne me doi je pas tere
Que je ne die totes voies.
L'en ne doit Crestïen de Troies,
Ce m'est vis, par raison blasmer,
20 Qui sot dou roi Artu conter,
De sa cort et de sa mesniee
Qui tant fu loee et prisiee,
Et qui les fez des autres conte
24 Et onques de lui ne tint conte.
Trop ert preudon a oblïer.
Por ce me plest a reconter
Une aventure tot premier
28 Qui avint au bon chevalier.

Li rois Artus en un esté
Estoit a Cardoil sa cité,
O lui la roïne et Gauvain,

32 Keu lo seneschal et Yvain
   Et des autres vint solement.
   A Gauvain prist tot jorz talent   *16d*
   D'aler desduire et deporter.
36 Lors fist son cheval aprester,
   Cortoisement s'aparrella.
   Uns esperons a or chauça
   Sor unes chauces decopees
40 De drap de soie bien ovree[s];
   Si ot unes braies chauciees
   Mout tres blanches et mout dougiees,
   Et chemise gascorte et lee
44 De lin menuement ridee,
   Et un mantel vair afublé:
   Mout richement fu atorné.
   Puis s'en est de la ville issu.
48 Tot lo droit chemin a tenu
   Tant que en la forest entra.
   Lou chant des oisiaus escouta,
   Qui mout chantoient doucement.
52 Tant i entendi longuement,
   Por ce qu'il en oï plenté,
   Que il entra en un pensé
   D'une aventure qu'il savoit,
56 Qui avenue li estoit.
   Tant longuement i demora
   Qu'en la forest se desvoia
   Et que il perdi son chemin.
60 Li solaus torna a declin,
   Si conmença a porpenser;
   Et il prenoit a avesprer
   Quant de cel penser fu issu;
64 Mes onques ne sot ou il fu.   *17a*
   Lors quida retorner arriere.
   Puis entra en une charriere
   Qui toz jorz avant lou mena;
68 Et il plus toz jorz anuita,
   Si que il ne sot ou aler.
   Il conmença a esgarder
   Devant lui aval une voie

72 Parmi une clere fustoie
    Si vit un grant feu alumé.
    Cele part est son pas alé,
    Car il quida que il trovast
76 Aucun home qui l'avoiast,
    Ou boscheron ou charbonier.
      Lors vit lez lou feu un destrier
    Qui fu a un arbre aresnez.
80 Il est desci au feu alez
    Si vit un chevalier seant.
    Salüé l'a demaintenant:
    'Cil Dieus,' fet il, 'qui lo mont fist
84 Et les ames es cors nos mist,
    Vos doint, biaus sire, en lui grant part.'
    'Amis,' fait il, 'et Dieus vos gart.
    Car me dites don vos venez,
88 Qui a tel eure seus alez.'
    Et Gauvains li a tot conté,
    De chief en chief la verité:
    Conment il en desduit ala,
92 Et puis conment il esgara
    En la forest por un pensé
    O il se fu trop oblïé,   17b
    Si que il en perdi sa voie.
96 Et li chevaliers li otroie
    Qu'il lou remetra lou matin
    Mout volentiers en son chemin,
    Ne mes qu'o li se demorast
100 Et conpaignie li portast
    Tant que cele nuit fust passee.
    Ceste proiere est creantee.
    Jus mist sa lance et son escu,
104 De son cheval est descendu
    Sou lia a un aubrisel
    Et sel covri de son mantel,
    Puis s'est delez lou feu assis.
108 Li uns d'aus a a l'autre enquis
    Conment il ont lou jor erré.
    Et Gauvains li a tot conté,
    C'onques mentir ne li daigna;

112 Et li chevaliers li fausa,
    Onques mot de voir ne li dist:
    Assez orroiz por coi lo fist.
    Quant il orent assez vellié
116 Et de plusors choses plaidié,
    Lez lo feu se sont endormi.
    A l'ajornement s'esperi
    Messire Gauvains tot premier,
120 Puis esvella lo chevalier.
    'Ma meson de ci est mout pres,
    Deus liues i a et non mes;
    Si vos pri que vos i venez,   17c
124 Et sachiez que vos i avrez
    Ostel mout [tost] et volentiers.'
    Lors monterent sor lor destriers,
    Lor escuz et lor lances pristrent
128 Et lor espees, si se mistrent
    Tantost en un chemin ferré.
    N'orent mie granment erré
    Quant de la forest sont issu
132 Et au plain païs sont venu.
    Li chevaliers l'araisona:
    'Sire,' fet il, 'entendez ça:
    Toz jorz est costume et usage,
136 S'uns chevaliers cortois et sage
    En moinne un autre aveques lui,
    Que il envoie devant lui
    Fere son ostel atorner,
140 Que il i porroit tost trover,
    Qui lor venue ne savroit,
    Tel chose qui li desplairoit;
    Et je n'ai cui g[e] i envoi,
144 Ce veez vos bien, ne mes moi.
    Si vos pri, qu'il ne vos desplaise,
    Venez belement a vostre aise
    Et je irai grant oirre avant.
148 Lez un plesseïz ça avant
    En un val verrez ma meson.'
    Gauvains set bien que c'est raison
    Et afaitement que il dit;

152 Por ce se mist o pas petit,
    Et cil s'en va grant aleüre.   *17d*
        Messire Gauvains a droiture
    A quatre pastoriaus trovez
156 Delez lo chemin arestez.
    Salüé l'ont mout doucement,
    El non Dieu lor salu lor rent,
    Trespassa les, ne lor dist plus.
160 'Ahi,' fet li uns, 'tant mar fus,
    Biaus chevaliers genz et adrois!
    Certes il ne fust mie drois
    Que fussiez bleciez ne laidiz.'
164 Gauvains en fu toz esbahiz,
    Qui les parroles bien entent.
    De ce se mervella forment,
    Par quel raison il lo plaingnoient
168 Quant il de rien nel connoissoient.
    Vistement a aus retorna,
    Tot derechief les salua,
    Docement lor a demandé
172 Qu'il li dïent la verité,
    Por coi il ont dit que mar fu.
    Et li uns li a respondu:
    'Sire,' dist il, 'pitié avon
176 De ce que sevre vos veon
    Ce chevalier qui la devant
    S'en va sor cel cheval ferrant.
    Mout en a veant nos mené,
180 Mes nus qui en soit retorné
    N'avons nos pas encor veü.'
    Et Gauvains dist: 'Amis, sez tu
    Se il lor fet rien se bien non?'   *18a*
184 'Sire, par cest païs dist l'on
    C'ome quil contredit de rien,
    Que que ce soit, o mal o bien,
    En son ostel lo fet ocire.
188 Nos nel savon que d'oïr dire,
    Car onques encore ne vit
    Nus hom qui de la revenist;
    Et se vos croire nos volez,

192 Ja avant plain pié no sivrez
Se vos avez vostre cors chier.
Tant par iestes biaus chevalier
Que domache iert s'il vos ocist.'

196 Et messire Gauvains lor dit:
'Pastorel, a Dieu vos conmant.
Ne voil por lou dit d'un enfant
Leissier l'oirre de son païs.'

200 S'il fust seü en son païs
Que il l'eüst por tant lessié,
A toz jorz li fust reprochié.
    L'anbleüre de son cheval

204 Erra pensant deci al val
Que cil ensaignié li avoit.
Delez un grant plesseïz voit
Sor une mote un bel chastel,

208 Qui estoit fermez de novel.
Lou fossé voit lé et parfont,
Et el baille devant lo pont
Avoit mout riche herberjage;

212 Onques Gauvains en son aage
Nus plus riche n'ot mes veü,
Se a prince o a roi ne fu.
Mes je ne me voil demorer

216 Au herberjage deviser,
Mes que mout estoit biaus et riches.
Il est venuz desci q'as lices,
Ainz est parmi la porte entré

220 Et a lou baille trespassé
Et est au chief do pont venu;
Encontre lui est acouru
Li sires, qui fait grant sanblant

224 Qu'il soit de son venir joiant.
Les armes reçut un vaslet,
Uns autres prist lou Gringalet,
Li tierz les esperons li oste.

228 Lors l'a par la main pris son oste
Si l'a lo pont amont mené;
Et ont un mout biau feu trové
En la sale devant la tor,

18b

232   Et mout riche seoir entor
       Covert d'une porpre de soie.
       A une part, que il lo voie,
       Li ont son cheval establé,
236   Et si li a l'en aporté
       A grant plenté avoinne et fain.
       De tot lo mercia Gauvain,
       Que de rien no voust contredire.
240   Li ostes li a dit: 'Biaus sire,
       L'en atorne vostre disner,
       Et sachiez que de l'aprester
       Se hastent forment li serjant.

18c

244   Or vos deduisiez a itant,
       Soiez toz liez et a vostre aise;
       Se rien i a qui vos desplaise,
       Si lou dites seürement.'
248   Gauvains dist que a son talent
       Est l'ostel do tot atorné.
         Li sire est en la chanbre entré
       Por une soe fille querre,
252   Qu'il n'ot en trestote la terre
       Damoisele de sa valor.
       Je ne vos porroie a nul jor
       La biauté tote ne demie
256   Don ele estoit plainne et garnie
       Ne je ne la voil trespasser,
       Si la voil a briés moz conter.
       Quanc'onques Nature sot fere
260   Qui a cors d'ome deüst plere
       De cortoisie et de biauté
       Ot tot entor li asanblé.
       Li ostes, qui n'ert pas vilain,
264   L'a prise par la destre main
       Si l'a en la sale amenee.
       Et Gauvains, qu'il a esgardee
       La grant biauté qui ert en li,
268   A bien pou qu'il ne s'esbahi,
       Et neporquant si sailli sus.
       La damoisele encore plus,
       Quant ele ot Gauvain esgardé,

272 S'esbaï de sa grant biauté
    Et de son grant afaitement.   *18d*
    Et neporcant cortoisement
    Et a briés moz la salua.
276 Tantost par la main la bailla
    Li oste a monsaignor Gauvain,
    Si li a dit: 'Je vos amain
    Ma fille, qu'il ne vos anuit;
280 Car je n'ai nul plus bel desduit
    A vos deduire et deporter.
    Ele vos savra bien porter,
    S'ele vialt, bele conpaignie:
284 Je voil qu'el no desvoille mie.
    Tant a en vos sens et valor
    Que s'el vos amoit par amor
    Ja n'en avroit se anor non.
288 Endroit moi vos en fais un don,
    Que ja de vos n'iere jalous,
    Ançois li conmant oiant vos
    Que ja de rien ne vos desdie.'
292 Gauvains bonement l'en mercie,
    Qui contredire no viaut pas;
    Et cil s'en ist enesloupas
    Vers la cuisine demander
296 S'en porroit a pieces disner.
      Lez la pucele s'est assis
    Gauvains, qui mout ert entrepris
    Por l'oste qu'il dote forment;
300 Et neporquant cortoisement
    Et sanz un point de mesprison
    Mist demaintenant a raison
    La damoisele o lou chief bloi.   *19a*
304 L'en ne li dist ne trop ne poi:
    Sajement l'a a raison mise.
    Mout li offre bel son servise,
    Et tant li dist de son corage
308 Que cele, qui preuz ert et sage,
    Aperçut et entendi bien
    Qu'il l'ameroit sor tote rien,
    Se il li venoit a plaisir.

312 Lors ne se set auquel tenir,
    A l'escondire ou au graer:
    Tant l'ot cortoisement parler
    Et tant lo voit de bones mors

316 Que ele l'amast par amors,
    S'ele descovrir li osast;
    Mes por neiant li creantast
    A faire li vers li entendre,

320 Quant il n'i poïst ja plus prendre.
    Bien set qu'el feïst que vilainne,
    S'el lou meïst d'amors en painne
    Don il ne traissist ja a chief;

324 Mes l'escondire li est grief,
    Tant a vers lui son cuer torné.
    Lors a cortoisement parlé:
    'Sire,' dist el, 'j'é entendu

328 Que mes peres m'a desfendu
    Que je de rien ne vos desdie.
    Or ne sé je que je vos die,
    Que se vos avoie cranté

332 A fere vostre volenté,
    Ja mes a bon chief n'en trairoie   *19b*
    Et mort et traï vos avroie;
    Mes d'une chose vos chasti

336 Et par bone foi le vos di,
    Que vos gardez de vilenie;
    Ne rien que mes peres vos die,
    Que que ce soit, o mal o bien,

340 Mar lou contrediroiz de rien,
    Que morz serïez a itant;
    Ne ja mar ferïez sanblant
    Que soiez de rien acointié.'

344   Estes vos l'oste repairié,
    Qui vers la cuisine ert alez;
    Et li mengiers fu aprestez,
    Si a l'en l'eve demandee.

348 Ne voil ci fere demoree.
    Quant lavé orent, si s'asistrent,
    Et li serjant les napes mistrent
    Desus les dobliers blans et biaus,

352 Les salieres et les coutiaus,
Aprés lou pain, et puis lo vin
Es copes d'argent et d'or fin.
Mes je ne voil plus demorer

356 As mes un a un aconter,
Mes mout orent char et peson,
Oisiaus rostiz et venoison,
Et mout mengierent lieement.

360 Et li oste efforça forment
Gauvain de boivre et la pucele,
Et si dist a la damoisele
Qu'ele efforçast lou chevalier;

364 Et dist: 'Mout vos poëz prisier
Que je voil qu'el soit vostre amie.'
Gauvains bonement l'en mercie.
Quant mengié orent a plenté,

368 Lors furent serjant apresté,
Qui dobliers et napes osterent
Et qui l'eve lor aporterent
Et la toaille a essuier.

372 Li ostes dist aprés mengier
Qu'il vialt aler ses bois veoir;
Et si rova Gauvain seoir
Et deduire o la damoisele.

376 Endementres Gauvain apele
Et li a dit et conmanda
Qu'il ne s'en aut jusqu'il venra;
Et conmanda a un serjant

380 Que, se il fait de rien sanblant,
Que il lou preignent demanois.
Gauvains, qui preuz ert et cortois,
Voit bien que remanoir l'estuet

384 Et q'autrement estre ne puet;
Si li avoit dit erranment
Que il n'avoit d'errer talent,
Por qu'il lo voille herbergier.

388 L'ostes monta sor son destrier,
Si s'en va mout grant aleüre
Et va querre une autre aventure,
Que de ceste est il a seür

19c

392 Qui l'a enclos dedenz son mur.
        La damoisele a Gauvain pris   *19d*
     Par la main, si se sont assis
     A une part por deviser
396 Conment il se porra garder.
     Docement et bel lou conforte,
     Mes de ce est traïe et morte
     Qu'ele ne set la volenté
400 Que ses peres a en pensé.
     S'ele seüst, el li mostrast
     Par quel engin il eschapast,
     Mes onques n'en vost nule dire;
404 Or se gart de li contredire,
     S'il porra par tant eschaper.
     'Or laisons,' fet il, 'ce ester;
     Ja ne me fera se bien non.
408 Il m'amena en sa meson
     Si m'i a fet mout bel sanblant;
     Ne ja des ici en avant,
     Quant il m'a fet anor et bien,
412 No doteré de nule rien
     De si que je sachë et voie
     Par quel raison doter lou doie.'
     Ele li dist: 'Ce n'a mestier;
416 Li vilains dist en reprovier,
     Si lou dïent encor plusor,
     Q'au vespre loe l'en lo jor,
     Quant l'en voit que bele est la fin,
420 Si fet l'en son oste au matin;
     Et Dieus, si con je lo desir,
     Vos en doint a joie partir
     De vostre oste sanz mautalant.'   *20a*
424   Quant parlé orent longuement
     Et mout parlé de ce et d'el,
     Li ostes revint a l'ostel.
     Encontre lui sailli Gauvain
428 Et la pucele, main a main;
     Mout l'ont doucement salüé.
     Il lor dist qu'il s'est mout hasté,
     Qu'il cremist, se il demorast,

432 Que Gauvains ainz ne s'en alast;
Por ce ne vost plus demorer.
Il conmença a avesprer,
Et li ostes si demanda
436 As serjanz que il soupera.
Sa fille li dist: 'Par deduit
Poëz demander vin et fruit
Et nule autre chose par droit,
440 Qu'assez menjastes orendroit.'
Il a maintenant demandé.
Il ont premierement lavé,
Puis lor fu mis li fruis devant;
444 Lou vin aportent li serjant
A plenté de mainte maniere.
'Sire, car fetes bele chiere,'
Fet il a monsaignor Gauvain.
448 'D'une chose soiez certain:
Il me coste sovent et poise
Quant j'é oste qui ne s'envoise
Et qui ne dit sa volenté.'
452 'Sire, sachiez de verité,'
Fet Gauvains, 'que je sui haitié.'
Quant il orent lo fruit mengié,
Les liz conmanda l'oste a fere,
456 Et dist: 'Je jerré en ceste aire,
Et cist chevaliers en mon lit.
No faites mie trop petit,
Car ma fille jerra o li—
460 A si bon chevalier lo qui
Qu'ele est en lui bien enploiee.
Ele doit estre mout haitiee
De cen qu'en lor a creanté.'
464 Amedui l'en ont mercïé
Et font sanblant que mout lor plese.
Or est Gauvains mout a malaise,
Que il crient s'il s'i va cochier
468 Qu'il lou face tot detrenchier,
Et si set bien s'il contredit
En son ostel que il l'ocit.
    L'ostes de cochier se hasta;

20b

472 Par la main lo prist si mena
Dedenz la chanbre demanois.
La damoisele o lo vis frois
I est ensanble o lui alee.
476 La chanbre est bien encortinee
Et doze cierges i ardoient,
Qui tot entor lo lit estoient
Si gitoient mout grant clarté;
480 Et li liz ert bel atorné
De riches coutes, de blans dras.   20c
Mes je ne voil demorer pas
En la richece deviser
484 De dras de soie d'outremer,
De Palerne et de Romenie,
Dont la chanbre estoit enbelie,
De sebelins, de vair, de gris.
488 Tot a un mot le vos devis:
Quanque convient a chevalier
Et a cors de dame atillier
Et en iver et en esté
492 I avoit a mout grant plenté;
La ot maint riche garnement.
Gauvains s'en mervella forment
De la richece que il vit.
496 Et li chevaliers li a dit:
'Sire, ceste chanbre est mout bele;
Entre vos et ceste pucele
I girois, ja n'i avra plus.
500 Damoisele, fermez les us,
Si faites son conmandement,
Que je sai bien que itel gent
N'ont mie de presse mestier.
504 Mes d'itant vos voil chastoier
Que les cierges nen estaingniez,
Que j'en seroie mout iriez.
Jo voil, por ce l'ai conmandé,
508 Qu'il voie vostre grant biauté
Quant vos giroiz entre ses braz,
Si en avra graignor solaz,
Et que vos veoiz son gent cors.'   20d

512 Lors se mist de la chanbre fors,
    Et la pucele l'uis ferma.
        Messire Gauvains se coucha,
    Celë est o lit revenue,
516 Si s'est lez lui cochiee nue,
    Onques proiere n'i estut;
    Et cele tote la nuit jut
    Entre ses bras. Mout docement
520 La bese et acole sovent;
    Et si est tant avant alé
    Qu'il en feïst sa volenté,
    Quant ele dist: 'Sire, merci!
524 Il ne puet pas aler issi;
    Je ne sui pas o vos sanz garde.'
    Gauvains de totes parz esgarde
    Si n'i vit nule rien vivant.
528 'Bele,' fait il, 'je vos demant
    Que me dites qui me desfent
    A fere de vos mon talent.'
    Ele respont: 'Jo vos dirai
532 Mout volentiers ce que j'en sai.
    Veez vos cel branc qui la pent
    Qui a cel entrecor d'argent
    Et lou pon et lou heu d'or fin?
536 Ceste chose pas ne devin
    Que vos m'orroiz ja ci conter,
    Ainz l'ai veü bien esprover.
    Mes peres l'ainme durement,
540 Que il li ocist bien sovent
    De mout bons chevaliers de pris;
    Sachiez bien qu'il en a ocis
    Solement çaienz plus de vint—
544 Mes je ne sai don il li vint.
    Ja n'entrera en ceste porte
    Chevaliers qui vis en estorde.
    Mes peres biaus sanblant lor fet,
548 Mes ja a si petit forfet
    Ne lou prendra qu'il ne l'ocie.
    Garder l'estuet de vilenie,
    Mout lou convient charroier droit.

21a

552 Maintenant an a pris lo droit
     S'i[l] l'entreprent de nule rien;
     Et se cil se garde si bien
     Qu'il ne soit de rien entrepris,
556 La nuit o moi cochier est mis.
     Lors est il venuz a sa mort.
     Savez por coi nus n'en estort?
     S'il fait sanblant en nule guise
560 De volenté qui li soit prise
     De faire lo moi, maintenant
     Lou fiert parmi lou cors lo branc.
     Et se il viaut vers lui aler
564 Por prendre le et por oster,
     Tot par lui salt do fuerre fors
     Si li done parmi lou cors.
     Et sachiez de voir que l'espee
568 Est en tel maniere faee
     Qu'ele me garde toz jorz si.
     Ja par moi ne fussiez garni,
     Mes tant iestes cortois et sages   *21b*
572 Que ce seroit mout granz domages,
     Si m'en peseroit mais toz dis,
     Se por moi estïez ocis.'
       Or ne set Gauvains que il face.
576 Onques mais de si grant manace
     N'oï parler jor de sa vie,
     Et si dote qu'ele lou die
     Por soi meïsmes garantir,
580 Que il n'en face son plaisir.
     D'autre part si s'est porpensez
     Qu'il n'en porroit estre celez,
     Que il ne fust partot seü,
584 Que il avroit o li geü,
     Tot sol, nu a nu, en son lit,
     Et si avoit por sol son dit
     Laissié a faire son pleisir.
588 Miaus vient il a anor morir
     Qu'a honte vivre longuement.
     'Bele,' fet il, 'ce est neient.
     Puis que venuz sui jusque ci,

592 Enfin voil estre vostre ami:
Vos n'en poëz par el passer!'
'Vos ne m'en poëz pas blasmer,'
Fet ele, 'des or en avant.'
596 Il est de li aprimiés tant
Que ele en a gité un cri.
Et li brans do fuerre sailli,
Sel fiert res a res do costé
600 Si qu'il li a do cuir osté,
Mes ne l'a pas granment blecié;   *21c*
Outre a lou covertor percié
Et toz les dras desci au fuerre,
604 Puis se fiert arriers en son fuerre.
Gauvains remest tot esperdu
Si a son talant tot perdu,
Lez li se jut tot esbahi.
608 'Sire,' fet el, 'por Dieu, merci,
Vos quidïez que jou deïsse
Por ce que de vos me vousisse
Desfendre por tel achoison.
612 Onques certes se a vos non
A chevalier ne lou conté,
Et sachiez que grant mervelle é
Que vos n'iestes sanz nul resort
616 Trestot au premerain cop mort.
Por Dieu or vos gisiez en pes
Et si vos gardez desormés
De tochier a moi en tel guise.
620 Uns sages hom a tost enprise
Tel chose qui a mal li torne.'
Gauvains remest pensis et morne,
Qu'il ne set conment se contiegne.
624 Se Dieus done qu'il s'en reviegne
Jamés arriere en sa contree,
Ja ceste chose n'iert celee,
Que il ne soit partot seü
628 Qu'il avra sol a sol jeü
A nuitiee o une pucele
Qui tant est avenanz et bele,   *21d*
Si que onques rien ne li fist,

632   Ne de rien ne li contredist
  Fors la manace d'une espee
  Qui de nelui n'ert adesee;
  Si seroit mes toz jorz honi
636   Se el li eschapoit issi.
  Et si li font mout grant anui
  Li cierge qu'il voit entor lui,
  Qui rendoient mout grant clarté,
640   Par que il voit sa grant biauté.
  Lou chief ot bloi, et plain lo front,
  Et ses sorcis qui dogié sont,
  Les iauz vers, lo nés bien assis,
644   Et fres et coloré lo vis,
  La boche petite et riant,
  Et lou col lonc et avenant,
  Les braz lons, et blanches les mains,
648   Et les costez soués et plains,
  Soz les dras la char blanche et tendre.
  Nus n'i seüst riens que reprendre,
  Tant ot lo cors jent et bien fet.
652   Il s'est vers li doucement tret
  Conme cil qui n'ert pas vilain.
  Ja li feïst lou jeu certain,
  Quant l'espee do fuerre salt,
656   Lors li a fet un autre asalt:
  Do plat lo fiert parmi lo col—
  A poi qu'il ne se tient por fol.
  Mes l'espee un poi chancela,   *22a*
660   Sor la destre espaule torna,
  Que do cuir li trencha trois doie;
  Et fiert en la coute de soie,
  Que une piece en a trenchiee,
664   Puis s'est en son fuerre fichiee.
  Quant Gauvains se senti navré
  En l'espaulë et ou costé
  Et voit qu'il ne puet a chief traire,
668   Mout est dolanz, ne set que fere,
  Et anui a de son deport.
  'Sire,' fet ele, 'iestes vos mort?'
  'Damoisele,' fet il, 'je non;

672 Mes anuit mes vos doin un don,
Que vos avez trives de moi.'
'Sire,' fet ele, 'par ma foi,
Se eles fussent lors donees
676 Que eles furent demandees,
Il fust or plus bel endroit vos.'
Mout par fu Gauvains angoissos,
Et la damoisele autresi.
680 Ne l'uns ne l'autres ne dormi,
Ainz vellierent a tel dolor
Tote la nuit desi au jor.
  Vistement et tost se leva
684 Li ostes des qu'il ajorna,
Puis est en la chanbre venuz.
Ne fu mie taisanz ne muz,
Ainz apela mout durement,
688 Et la damoisele erranment   22b
Ovri l'uis et puis est venue,
Si s'est lez lui couchiee nue,
Et li chevaliers vint aprés.
692 Andeus les vit gesir en pes
Si lor demande que il font,
Et messire Gauvains respont:
'Sire, bien ja, vostre merci.'
696 Quant li chevaliers entendi
Que il parla si hautement,
Sachiez que il fu mout dolant,
Que mout estoit fel et eschis.
700 'Conment,' fet il, 'iestes vos vis?'
'Par foi,' fet messire Gauvains,
'Je sui trestoz delivre et sains.
Sachiez que je n'ai chose fet
704 Par coi je doie estre a mort tret,
Et se vos en vostre meson
Me feïssiez sanz achoison
Mal et anui, ce seroit tort.'
708 'Conment,' fet il, 'si n'estes mort?
Mout m'anuie quant vos vivez.'
Puis est avant un poi alez
Si a a descovert veü

712 La coute qui trenchiee fu,
Et les linciaus ensanglentez.
'Vasaus,' fait il, 'or me contez
Delivrement dont cest sanc vint.'

716 Et messire Gauvains se tint,
Qui pas mentir ne li voloit,   *22c*
Que nule achoison ne savoit
Don il bel covrir se peüst

720 Que cil ne s'en aperceüst.
L'ostes de parler se hasta:
'Vassaus,' fait il, 'entendez ça.
Por droit noient lo me celez.

724 Vos vousistes vos volentez
De cele damoisele faire
Mes n'en peüstes a chief trere
Por lou branc qui lo contredist.'

728 Et messire Gauvains li dist:
'Sire, vos dites verité:
Li branz m'a en deus leus navré
Mes ne m'a pas blecié forment.'

732   Et quant li chevaliers entent
Que il n'est pas navrez a mort,
'Biaus sire,' fait il, 'a bon port
Iestes venuz; mes or me dites,

736 Se vos volez eschaper quites,
Vostre païs et vostre non.
De tel jent et de tel renon
Poëz estre et de tel afere

740 Que toz vos bons m'estouvra faire—
Mes j'en voil estre bien certain.'
'Sire,' fet il, 'j'é non Gauvain
Et sui niés au bon roi Artu[r].

744 De ce soiez tot a seür,
Que onques mon non ne chanjai.   *22d*
'Par foi,' fait l'ostes, 'bien lo sai,
Qu'en vos a mout bon chevalier

748 De nul mellor parler ne quier.
N'a vostre per jusc'a Maogre,
N'en tot lou roiaume de Logre
Ne seroit il mie trovez.

752 Savez conment j'é esprovez
Trestoz les chevaliers do mont
Qui aventures querre vont?
Peüssent en cest lit gesir

756 Et toz les convenist morir,
Un et un, tant qu'il avenist
Que toz li miaudres i venist.
Li brans lo me devoit eslire,

760 Car il no devoit pas ocirre,
Lou miaudre, quant il i vendroit:
Et si est esprovez a droit,
Qu'il vos a choisi au mellor;

764 Et quant Dieus vos a fet anor,
Ne sai ne choisir ne veoir
Qui miaus doie ma fille avoir.
Je la vos otroi et creant,

768 Ne ja mal desci en avant
Avroiz nule garde de moi,
Et si vos doins par bone foi
A toz les jorz de vostre vie

772 De cest chastel la saignorie;
S'en faites vostre volenté.'
Lors l'en a Gauvains mercïé,
Qui mout en fu joianz et liez.   *23a*

776 'Sire,' dist il, 'bien sui paiez
De la pucele seulement;
De vostre or ne de vostre argent
Ne de ce chastel n'ai je cure.'

780 Lors se leverent a droiture
Entre Gauvain et la pucele.
    Par lou païs vait la novele
C'uns chevaliers venuz estoit

784 Qui la pucele avoir voloit,
Sor qui li branz s'ert deus foiz tret,
Que point de mal ne li ot fet.
Et qui ainz ainz i vienent tuit.

788 Mout ot o chastel grant deduit
De dames et de chevaliers,
Et fu mout riches li mengiers
Que li peres fist atorner.

792 Mes je ne me voil demorer
     A aconter quel li mes furent,
     Mes assez mengierent et burent.
     Quant mengié orent a plenté
796 Et li doblier furent osté,
     Cil lecheor, dont mout i ot,
     Mostra chascuns ce que il sot.
     Li uns atenpre sa vïele,
800 Cil flaüste, cil chalemele,
     Et cil autres rechante et note
     Ou a la harpe o a la rote;
     Cil list romanz et cist dist fables;
804 Cil chevalier jeuent as tables
     Et as eschés de l'autre part,   *23b*
     O a la mine o a hasart.
     Issifaite vie ont menee
808 Tot lo jor jusq'a la vespree.
     Puis souperent a grant deduit.
     Assez i ot oisiaus et fruit,
     Et de bon vin a grant plenté.
812 Quant a grant joie orent soupé,
     Delivrement cochier alerent.
     La pucele et Gauvain menerent
     En la chanbre demaintenant
816 Ou il jurent lou soir devant.
     Et li ostes o aus ala,
     Qui de son gré les esposa;
     Puis mist ensanble sanz dongïer
820 La pucele et lo chevalier,
     Si s'en issi et ferma l'us.
     Que vos en diroie je plus?
     La nuit a sa volenté fete,
824 Onques espee n'i ot trete.
     S'il recovra, pas ne m'en poise,
     A la damoisele cortoise,
     A qui il ne greva noient.
828   Issi demora longuement
     A tel joite e a tel revel
     Monsaignor Gauvains o chastel.
     Puis si s'est de ce porpensé

832   Que lonc tens i ot demoré,
      Que si parent et ses amis
      Quidoient bien qu'il fust ocis.
      A l'oste ala [lo] congié querre: 23c
836   'Sire,' dist il, 'en ceste terre
      Ai demoré tant longuement
      Que mi ami et mi parent
      Quident que je soie peri;
840   Si demant, la vostre merci,
      Lou congié de l'aler arriere.
      Et si fetes en tel maniere
      Cele damoisele atorner
844   Que j'aie anor de li mener,
      Et vos qui la m'avez donee,
      Quant je venré en ma contree,
      Qu'en die que j'ai bele drue
848   Et qu'ele est de bon leu venue.'
      Li ostes li done congié,
      Et Gauvains s'en est repairié
      Et la damoisele ensement.
852   Ses palefrois fu richement
      Atornez de frainc et de sele.
      Sus est montee la pucele,
      Et Gauvains sor son cheval monte.
856   Que vos feroie plus lonc conte?
      Ses armes prist qu'il aporta;
      Au congié de l'oste s'en va,
      Liez et joianz de s'aventure
860   .   .   .   .   .   .
      Et quant fors de la porte vint,
      La damoisele son frainc tint.
      Il li demande ce que doit.
864   'Sire,' fet ele, 'je ai droit,
      Que j'é fet trop grant oblïee.   23d
      Sachiez que de ceste contree
      Je m'en irai mout a enviz
868   Sanz mes levriers que j'ai noriz,
      Qui mout par sont et bons et biaus,
      Ainz ne veïstes si isniaus,
      Et sont plus blanc que nule flor.'

872 Lors s'est mis Gauvains el retor
Si va por les levriers poignant;
Et l'ostes li va au devant
Qui bien lo vit venir de loing.

876 'Gauvains,' dist il, 'por quel besoing
Estes vos si tost retornez?'
'Sire,' dist il, 'que oblïez
A vostre fille ses levriers,

880 Si me dist qu'el les a mout chiers
Et que sanz aus ne s'en ira.'
Et li ostes les apela
Si les bailla mout volentiers.

884 Et Gauvains a toz les levriers
S'en revet mout delivrement
A la pucele qui l'atent.
Lors se resont acheminé

888 Et sont en la forest entré
Par ou il estoient venu.
    Lors ont un chevalier veü
Qui lou chemin venoit contr'eus.

892 Li chevaliers venoit toz seus,
Mes il ert armez mout tres bien,
Qu'il ne li failloit nule rien
De quanqu'estuet a chevalier,

896 Et seoit sor un bai destrier
Fort et isnel et remuant.
Li chevaliers venoit errant
Tant que il vint d'aus auques pres.

900 Et Gauvains lou quida en pes
Salüer et puis lui enquerre
Qui il estoit et de quel terre.
Mes cil, qui ot autre pensé,

904 A lou cheval esperroné
Si durement qu'il se lança—
Et onques un mot ne sona—
Entre la pucele et Gauvain,

908 Si l'a prise parmi lo frain.
Puis si revet mout tost arriere,
Et cele sanz autre proiere
S'en vet delivrement o lui.

24a

912 Se Gauvains ot ire et anui
　　Quant il l'en voit issi mener
　　Il ne fet mie a demander,
　　Car il n'ot arme o lui portee
916 Fors escu et lance et espee,
　　Et cil qui bien estoit armez
　　E[r]t forz et granz et sorquidez,
　　Si ot vers lui mal jeu parti;
920 Et neporquant conme hardi
　　Point Gauvains vers lui lo destrier
　　Por la pucele chalongier.
　　　'Vasaus,' fet il, 'grant vilenie
924 Avez fet qui avez m'amie　　　　　　　　24b
　　Saisie si estroitement;
　　Mes or fetes un hardement
　　Tel conme je deviserai.
928 Vos veez mout bien que je n'ai
　　Fors sol ma lance et mon escu
　　Et lou branc au costé pendu.
　　Je vos conmant a desarmer
932 Tant que nos soions per a per,
　　Si ferez mout grant cortoisie.
　　Et se vos par chevalerie
　　La poïez vers moi conquerre,
936 Si soit vostre sanz autre gerre.
　　Et se vos ce ne volez fere,
　　Soiez cortois et debonaire,
　　Si m'atendez desoz ces charmes.
940 G'irai enprunter unes armes
　　Ça arrier a un mien ami,
　　Et quant g'iere d'armes garni,
　　Je revenrai demaintenant;
944 Et se vos d'iluec en avant
　　La poëz conquerre vers moi,
　　Sanz mautalant la vos otroi:
　　Issi de voir lo vos creant.'
948 Et cil respont demaintenant:
　　'Ja a vos n'en iert congié pris,
　　Et se g'i ai de rien mespris,
　　Ja ne vos en querrai pardon.

952 Se vos dou mien me faites don,
    Mout par avez grant poësté.   *24c*
    Por ce que iestes desarmé,
    Que vos no taigniez a forfet,
956 Vos iert ja un jeu parti fet.
    Vos dites qu'ele est vostre drue
    Por ce qu'ele est o vos venue,
    Et je redi que ele est moie.
960 Or la meton en cele voie,
    Si aille chascuns de sa part,
    Puis soit do tot en son esgart
    Loquel ele ainme plus de nos;
964 Et s'el s'en vialt aler o vos,
    Je la vos creant et otroi:
    S'ele s'en vialt venir o moi,
    Donc est il droiz qu'ele soit moie.'
968 Gauvains bonement li otroie,
    Qui tant la creoit et amoit
    Qu'a escïent de voir quidoit
    Qu'el nou laissast por tot lo mont.
972   Atant la lessent, si s'en vont
    Et se traient un poi en sus.
    'Bele,' font il, 'or n'i a plus:
    Do tot est a vostre plaisir
976 Auquel vos vos voudroiz tenir,
    Car nos l'avons acreanté.'
    Ele a l'un et l'autre esgardé,
    Primes celui et puis Gauvain,
980 Qui bien quidoit estre certain
    D'avoir la tot seürement,
    Et si se mervelloit forment
    Sol de ce qu'el se porpensot.   *24d*
984 Mes la pucele, qui bien sot
    Conment Gauvains se puet aidier,
    Revialt savoir do chevalier
    Conment il est preu et vaillant.
988 Sachiez trestuit, petit et grant,
    Qui qu'en rie ne qui qu'en gronde,
    N'a gaires nule feme o monde,
    S'ele estoit druë et moillier

992 A tot lo mellor chevalier
   Qui soit jusqu'en Inde Major,
   Ja par lui n'avroit tele amor
   Que, s'il n'estoit preuz en l'ostel,
996 Qu'el lou prisast un dor de sel—
   Vos savez bien de quel proëce.
   Or oëz de si grant laidece
   Que cele damoisele fist:
1000 En la garde celui se mist
   Qu'ele de rien ne conoissoit.
   Quant messire Gauvains ce voit,
   Sachiez qu'il en fu mout marri
1004 Qu'ele l'ot de son gré guerpi;
   Mes tant estoit et preu et sage
   Et si cortois et si resnable
   Que onques mot ne li sona,
1008 Ja soit ce que mout li pesa.
   Et li chevaliers li a dit:
   'Sire,' fet il, 'sanz contredit
   Doit la damoisele estre moie.'
1012 'Ja Dieus,' fet Gauvains, 'ne me voie
   Quant je contredit i metrai,   *25a*
   Ne quant je ja m'en conbatrai
   De chose qui de moi n'a cure!'
1016 Adonc s'en vont grant aleüre
   La pucele et li chevaliers;
   Et Gauvains a toz les levriers
   S'en va en la soe contree.
1020 La pucele s'est arestee
   Tantost enz o chief de la lande,
   Et li chevaliers li demande
   Por qu'ele s'est aresteüe.
1024 'Sire,' fet el, 'ja vostre drue
   Ne serai a jor de ma vie
   Desi que je soie saisie
   De mes levriers que je la voi,
1028 Que cil vassaus en moinne o soi.'
   Et il li dist: 'Vos les avrez.'
   Puis s'escrië: 'Estez, estez,
   Sire vassus! Je vos conmant

1032 Que vos n'ailliez plus en avant!'
      Puis vint a lui toz abrivez.
      'Vassaus,' dist il, 'por coi menez
      Les levriers, quant il vo ne sont?'
1036 Et messire Gauvains respont:
      'Sire,' fait il, 'jes taing a miens,
      Et se nului i clainme riens,
      Conme miens les m'estuet desfendre;
1040 Et se vos en volïez prendre
      Lou jeu parti que me feïstes
      Quant enmi lo chemin meïstes
      La damoisele por choisir   25b
1044 Auquel el se voudroit tenir,
      Volentiers le vos souferroie.'
      Et li chevaliers li otroie
      Que volentiers cel jeu prendra,
1048 Car conme fel se porpensa,
      Se li levrier o li vendront,
      Que sanz estor li remandront,
      Et si pot estre bien certain,
1052 S'il s'en aloient a Gauvain,
      Que delivrement les toudroit
      Ausi con il ore feroit.
      Lors les ont o chemin lessiez.
1056 Quant il se furent esloigniez,
      Si les a chascuns apelez,
      Et il sont droitement alez
      A Gauvain, que il conoissoient
1060 Por sol tant que veü l'avoient
      Chiés lou pere a la damoisele.
      Gauvains joïst et apele,
      Car mout est liez que il les a.
1064   Et la pucele araisona
      Lo chevalier enesloupas:
      'Sire,' fet ele, 'ja plain pas
      N'irai o vos, se Dieus me voie,
1068 Desi que je saisie soie
      De mes levriers que je ain tant.'
      Et il respont: 'Sanz mon creant
      Nes en puet il mie mener.'

1072 Puis avoit dit: 'Lessiez ester,
Vasaus, que vos n'en menrez mie.'   *25c*
Et Gauvains dist: 'C'est vilenie
Se vos en desdites ensi;
1076 Mes je sui des levriers saisi,
Si vindrent a moi de lor gré.
Ja li Sires de Maïsté
Ne m'aït quant je lor faudrai!
1080 La damoisele vos lessai
Por sol tant que a vos se tint,
Qui moie estoit et o moi vint;
Dom me devez vos sanz dongier
1084 Par raison les levriers laissier,
Quant il sont mien et o moi vindrent
Et de lor gré a moi se tindrent.
Une chose sachiez de voir,
1088 Et sel poëz par moi veoir:
Se vos volez tot son plaisir
A cele pucele aconplir,
Vos avroiz de li corte joie—
1092 Je voil mout bien que ele m'oie!—
Que sachiez, tant con el fu moie,
Que ses bons li aconplisoie.
Or voiez con el m'a servi!
1096 Il ne va pas de chien issi
Con de feme, ce sachiez bien.
Une chose sachiez de chien:
Ja son mestre qui norri l'a
1100 Por estrange ne changera.
Feme a mout tost guerpi lo suen
S'i[l] ne li conplist tot son buen;
Si est mervelle de tel change   *25d*
1104 Qui lou suen laisse por estrange.
Li levrier ne m'ont pas gerpi,
Dont puis je bien prover issi—
Ja n'en seré desdiz de rien—
1108 Que nature et amor de chien
Valt miauz que de feme ne fait.'
'Vassaus,' fait il, 'li vostre plait
Ne vos puet ici rien monter.

1112 S'orendroit nes lessiez ester,
    Gardez vos, que je vos desfi.'
    Lors a Gauvains l'escu saisi
    Si l'a devant son piz sachié.
1116 Puis s'est l'uns vers l'autre eslessié
    Tant con chevaus li pot randir,
    Si lou feri par tel aïr
    Desus la bocle en l'escu taint
1120 Que peçoié li a et fraint
    Si qu'en volerent li tronçon
    Loing et haut lo giet d'un bozon.
    Et Gauvains l'a aprés feru
1124 O premier qartier de l'escu
    Si durement, si con moi sanble,
    Que lui et lou cheval ensanble
    Abati en une charriere.
1128 Cil chaï en une toiere,
    Entre les cuisses son destrier.
    Et Gauvains trait lou branc d'acier,
    Tot maintenant sor lui guenchi,
1132 A l'ainz que il pot descendi
    Si l'a contre terre as poinz pris.   *26a*
    Grant cop lou fiert parmi lo vis
    Et o chief si que tot l'estone:
1136 Tote sa force i abandone,
    Car mout lou het por lo meffet
    Et por l'anui qu'il li a fet.
    Mout lou laidist et mout lo grieve:
1140 Lou pan do hauberc li solieve
    Si li a maintenant botee
    Parmi les flans sa bone espee;
    Lors lou let, quant vengiez se fu.
1144 Cheval ne hauberc ne escu
    Ne voust il onques regarder,
    Ainz va les levriers apeler,
    Que il avoit forment amez,
1148 Que bien se sont vers li provez.
    Et puis cort penre son destrier,
    Qui par lou bois vet estraier;
    Vistement l'a ataint et pris.

1152 Onques par li ne fu requis
Estriers, ainz sailli en la sele.
'Sire,' ce dist la damoisele,
'Por Dieu et por anor vos pri
1156 Que vos ne me lessiez ici,
Que ce seroit grant vilenie.
Se je fui fole et esbahie,
No me devez a mal torner;
1160 Que je n'osoie o vos aler,
Tel paor oi quant je vos vi
Si povrement d'armes garni,
Et cil ert armez si tres bien   *26b*
1164 Qu'il ne li failloit nule rien.'
'Bele,' fait il, 'ce est neiant.
Pou vos vaut vostre covrement;
Rien ne valt ceste coverture.
1168 Tel foi, tel amor, tel nature
Puet l'en sovent trover en feme:
Qui autre blef que il n'i same
Voudroit recoillir en sa terre
1172 Et cil qui en feme vialt querre
Fors sa nature n'est pas sage—
Toz jorz l'ont eü en usage
Puis que Dieus fist la premerainne.
1176 Qui de les servir plus se painne
Et plus lor fait bien et anor
Plus s'en repent au chief do tor;
Et qui plus les anore et sert
1180 Plus s'en corrouce et plus i pert.
La pitiez ne vos venoit mie
De garder m'anor et ma vie,
Ainz vos venoit tot d'autre chose.
1184 Li vilains dist: "A la parclose
Voit l'en con tote riens se prueve."
Cil qui fainte et fause la trueve
Et la cherist et ainme et garde,
1188 Ja puis Dieus ne l'ait en sa garde.
Or gardez vostre conpaignie.'
Atant l'a sole deguerpie,
Si qu'il ne sot qu'ele devint;   *26c*

1192 A son droit chemin s'en revint.
      De s'aventure a mout pensé.
        Tant a par la forest erré
      Q'au vespre vint en son païs.
1196 Grant joie en firent si ami:
      Lo quidierent avoir perdu.
      S'aventure si con el fu
      Lor a de chief en chief contee—
1200 Mout volentiers l'ont escoutee—
      A premiers bele et perillose,
      Et aprés laide et anuiose
      Por s'amie que il perdi,
1204 Et puis con il se conbati
      Por les levriers a grant meschief;
      Ensi fina tot a un chief.

LA MULE SANS FREIN

Li vilains dist en reprovier *26c*
Que la chose a puis grant mestier
Que ele est viez et ariez mise.
4 Por ce par sens et par devise
Doit chascuns lou suen chier tenir,
Qu'il en puet mout tost biens venir
A chose qui mestier avroit.
8 Mains sont prisiees orendroit
Les viez voies que les novelles
Por ce qu'en les tient a plus beles— *26d*
Et si sont miaudres par sanblant;
12 Mes il avient assez sovent
Que les viez en sont les plus chieres.
Por ce dist Paiens de Maisieres
Qu'en se doit tenir totes voies
16 Plus as viés q'as noveles voies.
    Ici conmence une aventure
De la damoisele a la mure
Q'a la cort au roi Artu vint.

20 Un jor de Pentecoste avint
Que li rois Artus cort tenoit
A Cardoil, si con il soloit.
Et si ot chevaliers assez
24 De totes terres amassez,
Qui a la cort venu estoient.
Avec la roïne restoient
Les dames et les damoiseles,
28 Don il i ot assez de beles,
Qui a la cort erent venues.
Tant ont les paroles tenues
Que li baron aprés mengier

32   Furent alé esbanoier
      Parmi la sale amont as estres.
      Si regardent par les fenestres
      Tot aval, tres parmi un pré.
36   Mes mout i orent pou esté
      Que il virent sor une mure
      Vers lo chastel, grant aleüre,
      Venir une seule pucele,
40   Qui mout ert avenanz et bele.   *27a*
      La damoisele issi venoit,
      Que en sa mule point n'avoit
      De frain, ne mes seul lo chevestre.
44   Li chevalier ce que pot estre
      Entr'aus durement s'en mervellent:
      Mout en parolent et consellent,
      Et dïent que bien lou savroit
48   La roïne, s'ele i estoit,
      Por quel besoing vient en la terre.
      'Keus,' fait Gauvains, 'alez la querre;
      Et au roi dites qu'il i viegne,
52   Que nul essoigne no detiegne
      Que a nos ne viegne orendroit.'
      Li seneschaus s'en va tot droit
      Ou la roïne et li rois sont.
56   'Sire,' fet Keus, 'venez amont
      Ou vostre chevalier vos mandent.'
      Et il maintenant li demandent:
      'Seneschal, que nos voillent il?'
60   'Venez en avec moi,' fet il,
      'Et je le vos ensaignerai;
      L'aventure vos montrerai
      Que nos avon trestuit veüe.'
64   Atant la pucele est venue
      Et devant la sale descent.
      Gauvains vet encontre courant,
      Et des autres mout en i corent
68   Et mout la servent et anorent.
      Mes bien paroit a son sanblant   *27b*
      Qu'el n'avoit de joër talant,
      Car mout avoit eü grant painne.

72 Li rois la mande et l'en li moinne.
Tantost con ele fu venue
Devant lou roi, si lo salue:
'Sire,' fet ele, 'bien veez
76 Qu'iriee et triste sui assez.
Et toz jorz mes ensi serai,
Ne ja mes jor joie n'avrai,
Tant que mes frains me soit renduz
80 Qui mauvaisement m'est toluz,
Don perdu ai tote ma joie.
Je sai bien que je lou ravroie
Se çaienz avoit chevalier
84 Qui de ce s'osast afichier
Qu'i[l] vousist ceste voie enprendre;
Et, se il lo me voloit rendre,
Que trestote soe seroie
88 Si tost con je mon frain ravroie
Sanz chalonge et sanz contredit.
Et je orendroit sanz respit
Por la soe amor tant feroie
92 Que ma mule li bailleroie,
Qui lou menra a un chastel
Mout bien seant et fort et bel.
Mes il ne l'avra mie en pes.'
96   A cest mot s'est Keus avant tres
Et dit qu'il ira lo frain querre,
Ja n'iert en si estrange terre.
Mes il vialt qu'ele lou besast   27c
100 Primes ançois qu'il i alast,
Et baisier la vost maintenant.
'Ha, sire,' fet el, 'jusq'a tant
Que lou freinc aiez, lo beisier
104 Ne vos voil je mie otroier;
Mes quant li frains sera renduz,
Lors vos iert li chastiaus renduz
Et li baisiers et l'autre chose.'
108 Keus plus angoissier ne l'en ose;
Cele li redit et conmande
Que la mule onques ne desfende,
Quele part qu'ele voille aler.

112 Keus n'a cure de demorer
    Iluec o aus plus longuement.
    A la mule s'en vet errant;
    Il i est montez par l'estrier.
116 Il n'ot cure do convoier.
    Quant il voient que il s'en va
    Toz seus, que conpaignon n'i a,
    Ne il n'i a arme portee
120 Fors que tant seulement s'espee,
    La pucele remest plorant,
    Por ce que bien voit, et creant,
    Que de son frainc ne ravra mie
124 A ceste foiz, que que il die,
    Qui a l'aler desor la mure
    Qui s'en vet courant l'anbleüre.
    Et la mule bien lo convoie,
128 Qui bien a aprise la voie.
        Et tant avoit Keus cheminé,   *27d*
    Estes lo vos enforesté
    En une forest haute et grant.
132 Mes n'ot gaires alé avant,
    Quant les bestes de laienz s'ont
    Trestotes amassees: sont
    Lïons et tigres et liepart.
136 Totes s'en vienent cele part
    Por Keu qui i devoit aler.
    Mes ainz qu'il i poïst passer,
    Se sont tant les beste[s] hastees,
140 Q'a l'encontre li sont alees.
    Et Keus en a eü paor
    Si [g]rant c'onques mes n'ot graignor;
    Et dist que, s'il n'eüst enprise
144 La voie, por nule devise
    Qu'en li seüst faire des mois
    N'entrast il ja mes en cest bois.
    Mes les bestes, par conoissance
148 De la dame et par enorance
    De la mule que eles voient,
    Les deus genouz a terre ploient:
    Ensi por l'anor de la dame

152 S'agenoilloient de la jame,
Et por ce a seür se tienent
Qu'en la forest gisent et vienent.
Ne la püent plus anorer.

156 Mes Keus n'i vost plus demorer,
Plus tost qu'il puet d'iluec s'en part.
Et li lïon et li liepart   *28a*
S'en vet chascuns a son abit.

160   Et Keus en un sentier petit
Ou la mule s'est enbatuz,
Qui n'estoit mie trop batuz.
La mule lou sentier bien sot,

164 Que maintes foiz alé i ot,
Qui fors de la forest lo mainne,
Ou mout avoit eü grant painne.
Estes lo vos desforeté.

168 Mes n'ot gaires avant alé,
Quant il vint en une valee
Qui mout estoit parfonde et lee;
Et si estoit mout perillouse,

172 Mout crüeus et mout tenebrose
Q'o siecle n'a home si fort
Qui n'i eüst paor de mort,
S'en la valee trespassast.

176 Tot adés covient qu'il i past;
Voille o non, entre[r] li estuet:
Il i entre, quant miaus ne puet.
A quelque poinne i est entrez,

180 Mes mout i est espoëntez,
Que il veoit el fons dedenz
Mout granz coluevres et sarpenz,
Escorpïons et autres bestes,

184 Qui feu gitoient par les testes,
De coi il ot mout grant paor.
Et pis li faisoit la puor;
Que des cele ore qu'il pot nestre,

188 Ne fu mes en si puant estre,   *28b*
Et bien se va qu'il n'est chaüz.
A po qu'il n'est do sen issuz,
Et dist qu'il vousist estre ançois

192 Avecques les lïons o bois,
Ou il avoit devant esté.
Ja ne fera si grant esté
Ne de chaut si tres grant ardure
196 Que laienz n'ait toz jorz froidure
Con o plus mestre cuer d'iver,
Tant la mauvestié de l'iver,
Qui, laienz adés est assise;
200 Et tot adés i vente bise
Qui la grant froidure i apent;
Si reventent li autre vent
Qui la dedenz sont ahurté.
204 Tant i a de maleürté,
Que n'en diroie la moitié.
Tant a tote voie esploitié
Qu'il est venuz jusqu'a l'issue.
208 Atant une plainne a veüe,
Si est auques aseürez.
Tant fet qu'il en est eschapez
De l'ardure, de la puor;
212 Ja ne quida veoir lo jor
Qu[e] il fust de ce leu issuz.
En une plainne est descenduz,
A sa mule a la sele ostee.
216 Lors voit il eve enmi la pree
Mout pres d'iluec: une fontaine,
Qui mout estoit et clere et sainne
Et qui mout bien i avenoit.
220 Avironee entor estoit
De flors, de pins et de genoivre.
Maintenant sa mule i aboivre,
Que ele en avoit grant mestier.
224 Il meïsmes por refroidier,
Por ce que bele li sanbloit,
De la fontainne autresi boit.
Puis a atornee sa mure,
228 Si se remet en l'anbleüre.
Car granz li sanble estre la voie,
Ja ne quide mes que il voie
Ce que il aloit porchaçant.

28c

232 Tant a alé Keus chevauchant
Q'a une grant eve est venuz;
Mes de ce fu mout esperduz
Que parfonde la vit et large,
236 Et si n'i trueve nef ne barge,
Ne nule planche, ne passage.
Tant a alé par lou rivage
Que par aventure a trovee
240 Une planche ne gaires lee;
Mes nequedant bien lo portast,
Se par desor aler osast,
Que ele estoit de fer trestote.
244 Auques lou passage redote,
Puis que issi noire la voit,
Si quide bien que nul esploit
Ne porroit faire de passer: 28d
248 Encor li vient miaus retorner
Que il soit iluec perilliez—
Ançois en iert miaus conselliez;
Et dit bien que dahez ait il
252 Se il se met en tel peril
Por tel noient, por tel oiseuse.
Trop li sanble estre perilleuse
La voie que venuz estoit,
256 Mes li passages li sanbloit
Estre plus perilleus assez.
      Atant s'en est Keus retornez
Si se remet en son traïn.
260 Bien a tenu lo droit chemin,
Ensi con il venuz estoit.
A la valee vint tot droit,
Ou trova la pute vermine.
264 De chevauchier onques ne fine
Tot droit parmi, tant qu'il fu fors,
Si fu il mout doillanz do cors,
Et debrisiez et debatuz.
268 En la forest s'est enbatuz
O les bestes sauvages sont.
Encontre venues li sont
Tantost con eles l'aparçurent;

272 Par tel aïr vers lui coururent
  Que je quit bien qu'il lo menjassent,
  Se por la mure nou laissassent
  A qui il portoient anor.   *29a*
276 Et Keus en a eü paor
  Si grande que por dis citez
  Ne vousist estre o bois entrez,
  Ne por tot l'avoir de Pavie.
280 Fors do bois en la praerie
  Est entrez devant lo chastel.
   Li rois Artuz, cui mout fu bel
  De ce que revenir lo voit,
284 As fenestres venuz estoit,
  Et Gauvains et Gueherïez,
  Et messire Yvains et Girflez,
  Et autres chevaliers assez
288 Que il i avoit apelez.
  Quant lo seneschal venu voient,
  Por la pucele querre envoient.
  'Damoisele,' font il, 'venez:
292 Vostre frainc orendroit avrez,
  Que Keus est ja bien aprochiez,
  Si a lou frainc, bien lo sachiez.'
  Mes il mentent, qu'il n'en a mie,
296 Et cele a haute voiz s'escrie:
  'Certes, s'il avoir lo deüst,
  Ja si tost revenuz ne fust.'
  Lors ront ses chevous et detire.
300 Qui lors veïst lo grant martire
  Qu'ele demoinnë et lo duel!
  'Morte seroie ja mon vuel,'
  Fet se ele, 'se Dieus m'aït.'
304 Et Gauvains en riant li dist:
  'Damoisele, un don me donez.'   *29b*
  'Sire, quel?'—'Que mes ne plorez,
  Ainz mengiez et si soiez liee:
308 Ja mar en seroiz deshaitiee,
  Que je vostre frain vos rendré
  Et de bon cuer vos aiderai.'
  'Sire,' dit ele, 'dites vos

312 Que mon frainc avrai a estros?'
'Oïl voir.'—'Et je mengerei
Et tote haitiee serai,
Mes q'en convenant le m'aiez.'

316 Lors s'en est Gauvains afichiez
Que se ja nus avoir lou doit,
Il lou ravra, ou que il soit.
Lors s'est la pucele esmeüe,

320 Au pié de la sale est venue
A sa mule. Et Keus est alez
A son ostel toz adolez,
Mout tristes et mout angoisseus.

324 Et li rois no tient mie a jeus
Quant dite li fu et retrete
La malvaistié que Keus ot fete,
Et por ce n'ose a cort venir.

328 La parole plus maintenir
Ne voil a lui a ceste foiz,
Mes de la damoisele orroiz
Conment ele est au roi venue.

332   Tant a la parole tenue:
Que Gauvains li a creanté
Que li frains sera aporté;
Et dist que il l'aportera,

336 Ja en si fort leu ne sera,
Son frainc, mes qu'il ait lo congié.
'Mout volentiers li otroi gié,'
Fet se li rois et la roïne,

340 Qui l'outroient. El lor encline
Et si fet mout Gauvain haster;
Mes Gauvains la vialt acoler
Primes ançois qu'il s'en alast:

344 Il fu bien droiz qu'il la besast.
Ele mout volentiers lo bese.
Or est la pucele mout aise,
Car ele set bien, tot sanz faille,

348 Qu'el lou ravra, conment qu'il aille.
N'i est donc plus ses plaiz tenuz.
Gauvains a la mule est venuz
Si sailli dedenz les arçons.

29c

352 Plus de trente beneïçons
Li a la damoisele oré,
Et tuit l'ont a Dieu conmandé.
Gauvains iluec plus ne sejorne,
356 Mes d'iluec maintenant s'en torne.
Mes s'espee n'i laissa mie.
   Entrez est en la praerie
Qui lo mainne vers la forest
360 O les bestes sont a recet,
Et li lïon et li liepart.
Maintenant s'en vet cele part.
La o Gauvains passer devoit,
364 A l'encontre li vont tot droit.
Tot maintenant que il revoient
La mul[e] que il conoissoient,
Les deus genouz a terre plïent;
368 Vers lou chevalier s'umelïent
Par amor et par conoissance.
Et ce est la senefiance:
Que a force lou frainc ravra,
372 Ja en si fort leu ne sera.
Mes quant Gauvains les bestes voit,
Si quide bien et aparçoit
Que peor ot, quant il passa,
376 Et Keus por ce s'en retorna.
Riant s'en est outre passez,
Ou petit sentier est entrez
Qui droit lou moinne a la valee
380 Qui si estoit envenimee;
Si s'en va sanz arestement,
Que il nes redote noient,
Tant que d'autre part est venuz.
384 Enmi la plainne est descenduz
Ou estoit la fontainne bele.
A sa mule a osté la sele,
Si la torche et si la ratorne.
388 Ilueques gaires ne sejorne,
Que trop li est grieve la voie.
   Gauvains chemine tote voie
Tant que il vint a l'eve noire,

29d

392 Qui estoit plus bruianz que Loire.
De li tant voil dire sanz plus   *30a*
C'onques si laide ne vit nus,
Si orrible, ne si crüel.
396 Ne sai que vos en deïsse el,
Et si vos di sanz nule fable
Que ce est li fluns au deable:
Par sanblant et par avison
400 N'i voit l'en se deables non.
Et n'i a mie de passage.
Tant est alez par lo rivage
Que il a la planche trovee,
404 Qui n'est mie plus d'un dor lee,
Mes ele estoit de fer trestote.
Auques lou passage redote,
Et par ce voit bien et entent
408 Que Keus n'osa aler avant
Et que d'iluec est retornez.
Gauvains s'est a Dieu conmandez,
Si fiert la mule; et ele saut
412 Sor la planche, qui pas ne faut,
Mes assez sovent avenoit
Que la moitiez do pié estoit
Fors la planche par dedesor.
416 N'est mervelle s'il a peor,
Mes plus grant paor li faisoit
Ce que la planche li pleioit.
Passez est outre a quelque painne,
420 Mes ice est chose certainne
Que, se la mule ne seüst
La voie, que cheoiz i fust;
A ceste foiz s'en est gardez.   *30b*
424   Maintenant s'est acheminez.
Qui Fortune otroie et promet
En un petit sentier se met,
Qui lou moinne vers un chastel
428 Mout bien seant et fort et bel.
Li chastiaus si tres forz estoit
Que nul asalt ne redotoit,
Que clos estoit a la reonde

432   D'une eve grant, lee et parfonde.
Et si estoit tot entor clos
De granz pieus, bien aguz et gros;
Et en chascun des pieus avoit,

436   Mes qu'en un seul ou il failloit,
Une teste de chevalier.
Gauvains ne vost mie laissier.
Ne huis ne porte n'i avoit.

440   Li chastiaus si fort tornoioit
Con muele de molin qui muet,
Et con la trompe que l'en suet
A la corgiee demener.

444   Tot adés li covient entrer,
Mes mout durement se mervelle,
A soi meïsmes se conselle
Que senefie et que puet estre.

448   Mout en voudroit bien savoir l'estre,
Mes nen est mie recreant.
Atant sor lou pont tornoiant
Est arestez devant la porte,

452   Et hardement mout li enorte
Que de bien fere ne recroie.
Li chastiaus tot adés tornoie,
Mes il dist que tant i sera

456   Qu'a quelque painne i entrera.
Ce li revient a grant anui
Que, qua[n]t la porte est devant lui,
Que ele l'a mout tost passé.

460   Mout a bien son point esgardé
Et dit que il i entrera
Quant la porte endroit lui sera,
Que que il li doie avenir.

464   Atant voit la porte venir,
Si point la mule de randon,
Et ele saut por l'esperron
Si s'est en la porte ferue;

468   Mes ele i est si conseüe
Par derriers, si que de la queue
Pres de la moitié li desneue.
    Ensi est entrez en la porte,

30c

472 Et la mule mout tost l'enporte
    Parmi les rues do chastel,
    Cele qui do veoir fu bel.
    Et de ce est auques dolanz
476 Que il nen a trové laienz
    Feme ne home ne enfant.
    Tot droit par desoz un auvant
    D'une maison s'en est venuz.
480 Mes ançois qu'il fust descenduz,
    S'en vint uns nains parmi la rue
    Toz abrivez, si lo salue,
    Si li dist: 'Gauvains, bien veignant!'   *30d*
484 Et Gauvains ne rest mie lant,
    Si li rent mout tost son salu
    Et li a dit: 'Nains, qui es tu?
    Qui est ta dame et qui tes sire?'
488 Mes onques ne li vost plus dire
    Li nains, ainz s'en reva tot droit.
    Gauvains mesconnut ce qu'il voit
    Et se mervelle qu'estre puet.
492 —Et li nains respondre ne vuet!
    Et s'il se daignast a li prendre,
    Il li convenist raison rendre!—
    Mes volentiers aler l'en lesse.
496   Maintenant vers terre s'eslesse.
    Parmi une arche a regardee
    Une cave parfonde et lee,
    Qui mout estoit basse soz terre.
500 Mais il dit qu'il voudra enquerre
    Toz les reduiz ainz qu'il s'en aille;
    Ne se prisoit une maaille
    Se trestot l'estre ne savoit.
504 Atant, ez vos que issir voit
    De la cave amont un degré
    Un vilain trestot herupé.
    Bien deïst qui l'eüst veü
508 Qu'il eüst son oirre perdu.
    Mout sanble estre li vilains fel:
    Plus estoit granz que saint Marcel,
    Et sor son col a aportee

512 Une jusarme grant et lee.
    Mes mout se mervelle Gauvain   *31a*
    De ce que il vit lo vilain:
    Mor resanble de Moretaigne,
516 Ou de ces vilains de Champaigne
    Que li solaus a toz tanez.
    Devant Gauvain s'est arestez
    Si l'a maintenant salüé.
520 Et Gauvains a mout regardé
    Sa contenance et sa figure:
    'Et tu aies bone aventure,'
    Fet Gauvains, 'se por bien lo diz!'
524 'Oïl certes, mes a hardi
    Te tieng quant çaiens iés venuz.
    Mout as or bien tes pas perduz,
    Qu'il ne puet estre en graingno[r] serre
528 Li frains que tu iés venuz querre,
    Que bones gardes a entor.
    Mout t'estuet rendre grant estor,
    Si m'aït Dieus, ainz que tu l'aies.'
532 'De noient,' fet Gauvains, 't'esmaies,
    Que certes assez en rendrai,
    Si m'aït Dieus; ainz i morrai
    Que je lo frainc n'aie tot quite.'
536 Et cil onques plus ne respite;
    Mes por ce qu'il voit aserir,
    Cil s'entremet de lui servir
    Et tot droit a l'ostel lo moinne;
540 De lui aseoir mout se painne.
    La mule ra bien ostelee.
    Une blanche toaille lee   *31b*
    A deus bacins prent li vilains
544 Si li done a laver ses mains,
    Que laienz n'a plus de maisniee.
    Ja estoit la table dreciee
    O Gauvains assist au mengier,
548 Si menja, qu'il en ot mestier.
    Et cil l'en done a grant plenté
    Si lo sert a sa volenté.
    Tot maintenant que mengié a,

552 Et li vilains la table osta
Et si li a l'eve aportee.
    Une grant coche haute et lee
Li a fete por lui cochier,
556 Car mout lo vialt bien [a]aisier,
Con a tel chevalier covient.
Maintenant delez lui revient.
'Gauvains,' fet il, 'enz en cest lit
560 Sanz chalonge et sanz contredit
Girras tu toz seus anuit mes.
Ice te demant tot en pes
Ançois que tu t'ailles cochier:
564 Por ce que t'ai oï prisier
Te partis orendroit [un] jeu
Et por ce que je voi mon leu.
Si pren tot a ta volenté.'
568 Et Gauvains li a creanté
Qu'il en prendra, loquel que soit.
'Di!' fet Gauvains, 'que orendroit,
Si m'aït Deus, l'un en prendré
572 Ne de mot ne te mentiré,
Que je te tieng a mon bon oste.'
'Anuit,' fait il, 'la teste m'oste
A ceste jusarme trenchant;
576 Si la m'oste par tel convant
Que la toe te trencherai
Lou matin, quant je revenrai.
Or pren,' fet il, 'sanz contredit!'
580 'Mout savré,' fait Gauvains, 'petit,
Se je ne sai louquel je preigne.
Je prendré, conment qu'il aviegne:
Anuit la toe trencherai
584 Et lou matin te renderai
La moie, se viaus que la rende.'
'Mal dahez ait qui miaus demande,'
Fet li vilains. 'Or en vien donc!'
588   Lors lou moinne. Desor un tronc
Li vilains lo col li estent.
Maintenant la jusarme prent
Gauvains si li coupe la teste

31c

592 A un cop, que plus n'i areste.
Li vilains resalt maintena[n]t
Sor ses piez, et sa teste prent;
Dedenz la cave en est entrez.
596 Et Gauvains s'en est retornez
Si s'est couchiez isnelement.
Jusqu'au jor dort seürement.
    L'endemain, des qu'il ajorna,
600 Gauvains se lieve et atorna.
Atant ez vos que li vilains   *31d*
Revint toz haitiez et toz sains,
Et sa jusarme sor son col.
604 Or se puet bien tenir por fol
Gauvains, quant il ot regardee
La teste que il ot coupee;
Mes ne lou redota noiant.
608 Et li vilains parrole atant,
Qui n'estoit de rien esperduz.
'Gauvains,' fet il, 'je sui venuz,
Et si te rapel de covent.'
612 'Je nel contredi de noient,
Que bien voi que fere l'estuet,
Ne conbatre pas ne se puet.'
Et si lou deüst il bien faire,
616 Mes desloiauté ne viaut fere.
Por ce que coven[t] li avoit,
Dist que volentiers li tendroit.
'Or [en] vien donc,' fet li vilains.
620 Fors de laienz s'en ist Gauvains,
Lou col li estent sor lo tronc.
Et li vilains li dist adonc:
'Lesse col venir a plenté.'
624 'Je n'en ai plus,' fet il, 'par Dé,
Mes fier i, se ferir i viaus.'
Ce seroit domachë et diaus,
Si m'aït Dieus, s'il i feroit!
628 Sa jusarme hauce tot droit,
Qui lo fet por lui esmaier,
Mes n'a talant de lui tochier,
Por ce que mout loiaus estoit,   *32a*

632 Et que bien tenu li avoit
    Ce qu'il li avoit creanté.
      Et Gauvains li a demandé
    Conment lou frainc porra avoir.
636 'Bien lou porras,' fait il, 'savoir;
    Mais ainz que midis soit passez
    Avras tu de bataille assez,
    Que de gaber ne te tendra,
640 Que conbatre te convendra
    A deus lïons enchacnez.
    N'est mie trop abandonez
    Li frains, ainz i a male garde.
644 Mau feus et male flame m'arde!
    S'il i avoit dis chevaliers,
    Tant sai les deus lïons a fiers
    Que ja nus n'en eschaperoit,
648 Qui conbatre les lesseroit—
    Mes que ge t'i avré mestier.
    Si t'estuet ainz un poi mengier
    Que tu voises a la bataille,
652 Por ce que li cuers ne te faille,
    Ne que ne soies plus pesanz.'
    'De mengier seroit il noianz,'
    Fet Gauvains, 'en nule maniere,
656 Mes porchacë une armeüre
    Dont je me puisse aparrellier.'
    'Çaienz a,' fet il, 'bon destrier,
    Que nus ne chevaucha des mois,
660 Si a assez autre harnois
    Que volentiers te presterai.
    Mes tot ançois te mostrerai
    Les bestes que tu armez soies,
664 Savoir se tu te recreroies
    De conbatre avec le[s] lïons.'
    'Si m'aït sainz Pantelïons,'
    Fait Gauvains, 'ja ne les verrai
668 Jusquë a aus me conbatrai;
    Mes armez moi delivrement.'
    Et cil l'arme tot erranment
    D'armes bones de chief en chief,

32b

672 Qui bien en sot venir a chief,
Et si li amainne un destrier.
Gauvains i monta par l'estrier,
Que il n'est de rien esperduz.

676 Si li aporte set escuz,
Qui li avront mout grant mestier.
Et li vilains vet deslïer
Un des lïons si l'i amoinne.

680 Et li lïons tel orgoil mainne,
Si grant forsen et si grant rage,
Que o ses piez la terre arrache
Et sa chaenne runge as denz.

684 Quant il par fu fors de laienz
Et il choisi lo chevalier,
Lors se conmence a hericier
Et de sa queue se debat.

688 Certes, qui o lui se conbat,
D'escremir li convient savoir,
Ne ne li convient mie avoir
Cuer de chievre, ne de limace.

692 Devant, en une onie place,
Lou lesse li vilains aler.
Gauvains nou daigne refuser,
Ainz li passe, trete s'espee;

696 Et cil a sa hure levee
Si lou fiert, et cil refiert lui:
Bien s'entrefierent amedui.
Au premier cop l'a si feru

700 Que il li a l'escu tolu,
Li lïons, et a lui sachié.
Cil li a autre aparellié,
Li vilains, et Gauvains lou prent.

704 Lou lïon fiert par mautalent
Parmi l'eschine de l'espee,
Mes la piaus est dure et serree,
Si dure que ne puet trenchier.

708 O lïon n'a que correcier,
Si li revient conme tenpeste,
Si lou refiert parmi la teste
De sa coe, et li a tolu

32c

712 Lou secont et lo tierz escu,
　　Si que do quart nen a il mes.
　　'Or puez tu trop atendre mes,
　　Par ma barbe!' fait li vilains.
716 Lors lou fiert messire Gauvains
　　A estrous, que tote s'espee
　　Li enbat jusqu'en la coree,
　　Que lou lïon estuet morir.
720 'Or me laissiez l'autre venir,'
　　Fait il. Et li vilains lo lesse.　　　　*32d*
　　Mout fet grant duel et si s'engresse
　　De son conpaignon que mort voit.
724 Vers lou chevalier vient tot droit
　　Si lou requiert de tel vertu
　　Q'au premier cop li a tolu;
　　Et li vilains autre aparelle
728 Et de quanqu'il puet le conselle.
　　Et li lïons li vient corant,
　　Qui mout l'enchauce par devant;
　　As ongles jusq'a la ventaille
732 Li deronpi tote la maille,
　　Et si li retout son escu.
　　Et cil li a autre rendu.
　　Mes or set bien et aparçoit
736 Gauvains que, se il li toloit
　　Cestui, que ce seroit moleste.
　　Parmi la greve de la teste
　　Lo fiert de l'espee trenchant,
740 Que jusqu'es denz tot lo porfant,
　　Et li lïons chiet a la terre.
　　　'De cestui est finé la guerre,'
　　Fet Gauvains, 'et fete la pes.
744 Or me rent,' fet il, 'desormés
　　Lou frainc, foi que tu doiz ton pere.'
　　'N'ira mie issi, par saint Pere,'
　　Fait cil, 'n'i avra mestier ganche.
748 Je verré ainz tote ta manche
　　De ton hauberc de sanc vermel.　　　*33a*
　　Se tu viaus croire mon consel,
　　Desarme toi et si menjue

752 Tant que force te soit venue.'
   Mes il ne vialt por nule peine.
    Et li vilains tot droit lo mainne
   Parmi chanbres et parmi huis,
756 Que bien savoit toz les reduis,
   Tant qu'en la chanbre vient tout droit
   Ou li chevaliers se gisoit
   Qui parmi lou cors ert feruz.
760 'Gauvains, bien soiez tu venuz,'
   Fait il, tantost con veü l'a;
   'Fortune t'a envoié ça!
   Por ce que je sui ja gariz,
764 Et si es tu assez hardiz,
   Mes conbatrë o moi t'estuet.'
   Des qu'autrement estre ne puet,
   Ja, ce dit, no contredira.
768 Et cil maintenant se leva
   Qui s'arme tot a son voloir.
   Mes trespassé vos dui avoir
   Ce que ne doi pas trespasser,
772 Ainz fait mout bien a reconter,
   Por ce que navrez se levoit.
   Une costume tele avoit:
   Quant un chevalier d'autre terre
776 Por la pucele venoit querre
   Lo frainc qui la dedenz estoit,
   A lui conbatre se devoit;
   Et s'il estoit par lui vaincuz,
780 Ja eschanges n'en fust renduz,
   Se de la teste non trenchier
   Et puis en un des piez fichier
   De coi li chastiaus clos estoit.
784 Et se autrement avenoit
   Que cil refust par lui vaincuz,
   Uns autres pieus seroit feruz,
   Tant q'autres chevaliers venist
788 Que cil par bataille vainquist.
    Ensi sont cil andui armé,
   Et li vilains a amené
   A chascun d'aus un bon destrier;

33b

792 Et il i saillent sanz estrier
Et les escuz pendent as cous.
Desormés en orroiz les cous.
Maintenant qu'il furent monté,
796 Lors a li vilains apresté
Deus lances groses, si lor baille
Por conmencier cele bataille.
Lors s'esloingnent li un de l'autre,
800 Puis s'entrevienent tot sanz faudre;
Par vertu tieus cous s'entredonent,
A pou qu'il ne se desarçonent.
Les lances brisent et esloissent,
804 Et li arçon derriere froissent,
Et deronpirent li estrier;
N'i remest corroie a trenchier,
Que ne püent lou fes soffrir.   *33c*
808 A terre les estuet venir.
Tout maintenant em piez revienent
Et les escuz enbraciez tienent.
Durement a ferir s'essaient;
812 Sor les escuz tieus cous se paient
Que les estanceles en volent,
As espees les escuz dolent
Si que les pieces en abatent.
816 Deus liuees s'entreconbatent,
Que seulement plain pié de terre
Ne puet l'uns sor l'autre conquerre.
Si a mout Gauvain anuié
820 De ce qu'il a tant detrïé;
Si lou requiert de tel vertu
Que trestot li a porfendu
L'iaumë, et lo cercle coupé.
824 Et si l'a lors si estoné
Que il est enbrunchiez vers terre;
Et, lo vassal, a lui lou serre:
Gauvains lou sache par grant ire
828 Et fait sanblant de lui ocirre.
Et cil maintenant li escrie:
'Gauvains, ne m'ocirre tu mie!
Fous fui quant a toi me prenoie,

832 Mes encor hui matin quidoie
Que soz ciel n'eüst chevalier
Qui contre moi s'osast drecier,
Et tu m'as a force conquis,
836 Et si te monte or a grant pris.   *33d*
Et je te quidoie trenchier
La teste et en ce pel fichier
Ou il n'en a nules fichiees.
840 Si ai totes celes trenchiees
Qui tot entor ce paliz sont
A chevaliers qui çaiens ont
Venu por autretel afere.
844 Ausi quidoie je toi faire,
Mes soz ciel tel chevalier n'a.'
Gauvains lo let, et il s'en va;
En la chanbre s'est desarmez.
848   'Vilains,' fet Gauvains, 'or pensez
Conment porrai lo frainc avoir.'
'Gauvains,' fait il, 'viaus tu savoir
Que tu as a fere premiers?
852 A deus serpens, felons et fiers,
Qui sanc gietent de leus en leus,
Et par la boche lor salt feus,
Conbatre te convient ançois!
856 Mes bien saches que cil harnois
Ne t'avra ja vers aus mestier.
Un autre vé t'aparellier,
Qui plus ert forz et plus tenanz.
860 Il a bien çaiens quatre cenz
Haubers tresliz, forz et entiers,
Qui furent a ces chevaliers
Dont tu vois les testes coupees.'
864 Armes li a tost aportees
Li vilains de plusors manieres.   *34a*
Unes armes fors et entieres
Li baille por soi atorner.
868 Lors dist Gauvains: 'Va amener
Les dïables que tu disoies.'

. . . .

Fet cil, 'mes ainz que soit passez

872 Midis, avras a fere assez.
     Il n'a soz ciel home si fier
     Fors moi qui les ost aprimier
     Ne qui les ost neïs veoir.'
876 Gauvains li dist: 'Ne te chaloir.'
     Lors va deslïer les sarpanz,
     Qui mout par sont et fiers et granz,
     Li vilains, et amainne amont,
880 Qui mout sauvages bestes sont,
     Si que partot de leu en leu
     Est ses escuz enpris de feu.
     Par vertu Gauvains lou requiert;
884 Tel cop de l'espee lo fiert,
     Si con l'escriture tesmoingne,
     Si que la teste li reoingne;
     Si l'a tué isnelement.
888 Ne sai que j'alasse acontant,
     Mes ainz que midis fust passez
     Les a andeus si conrëez
     Que tuit sont mort et detrenchié.
892 Auques a lo vis entochié
     Do sanc et de la porreture.
     Li vilains reprent l'armeüre
     De coi il conbatuz estoit.   *34b*
896   Mes ançoiz qu'il desarmez soit,
     Li nains petiz li vint devant
     Qui primes par desoz l'auvant
     Vint a lui si lou salua
900 Ne plus dire ne li daigna,
     Ainz s'en ala si fierement.
     'Gauvains,' fet il, 'je vos present
     De par ma dame lo servise,
904 Mes que il soit par tel devise
     Que avecques li mengeras,
     Et a ton voloir en feras
     Tot sanz contredit et sanz guerre
908 Do frain que tu iés venuz querre.'
     Lors dist Gauvains qu'il i eroit,
     Se li vilains lo conduisoit,
     Car mout bien se fioit en lui;

912 Main a main s'en vont amedui.
Mout l'a bien li vilains mené;
Tant ont de chanbre en chanbre alé
Qu'en la chanbre vienent tot droit
916 O la dame en un lit gisoit
Qui avoit envoié lo nain
Por querre monsaignor Gauvain.
Maintenant que venu lo vit,
920 Contre lui va, si li a dit:
'Gauvains, bien soiez vos venu,
Si m'est il par vos avenu
Mout granz anuiz et granz domages,
924 Que totes mes bestes sauvages
Avez mortes en ceste voie.
Si vos covient il tote voie
Avec moi orendroit mengier.
928 Onques, voir, mellor chevalier
Ne plus preu de vos ne conui.'
El lit s'asïent amedui,
Mes ne fu mie, ce me sanble,
932 Li liz ne de sauz ne de tranble
O la dame et Gauvains seoient,
Que li quatre pecol estoient
Tuit de fin argent sororé.
936 Sus avoit un paile roé,
Qui toz iert a pierres ovrez,
Et autres richeces assez.
Se descrire les vos voloie,
940 Trestot mon tens i süeroie,
Mes de ce n'estuet aparler.
L'eve demande por laver;
Li vilains maintenant lor baille
944 Les bacins d'or, et la toaille
Lor aporte por essuier.
Atant asïent au mengier
La dame et messire Gauvains.
948 Li nains les sert et li vilains,
Que laienz n'a plus de mesnie.
Mout par est la dame haitie
Et bele chiere fait son oste.

34c

952 Trestot delez li, coste a coste,
    Lo fet seoir la damoisele
    Et mengier a une escüele,   *34d*
    Qui mout lo loe et mout lo prise.
956 Des mes ne faz autre devise
    Ne plus ore ne vos en cont.
    Mes maintenant que mengié ont
    Et la table lor fu ostee,
960 L'eve a la dame demandee;
    Li vilains maintenant li baille.
    Gauvain est tart que il s'en aille,
    Que mout quide avoir demoré.
964 Lors a la dame demandé
    Lo frainc, que bien lo doit avoir.
    'Sire,' fet ele, 'mon pooir
    Et moi met en vostre servise,
968 Que mout avez grant chose enprise
    Por ma seror en ceste voie.
    Je sui sa suer et ele est moie,
    Si vos en doi mout anorer.
972 S'il vos plaisoit a demorer
    Çaienz, a saignor vos prendroie
    Et tot cest chastel vos rendroie,
    Dont j'é encore trente et huit.'
976 'Dame,' fet il, 'ne vos anuit,
    Tart m'est, ce vos di par ma foi,
    Que je soie a la cort lo roi,
    Que ensi l'ai mis en covent.
980 Mes donez moi delivrement
    Lo frainc que je sui venuz querre.
    Trop ai esté en ceste terre.
    Or est ensi: plus n'i serai,   *35a*
984 Et neporquant bon gre vos sai
    Do bien que vos me presentez.'
    'Gauvains,' fait el, 'lo frainc prenez,
    Vez lou la a ce clo d'argent.'
988 Et il tot maintenant lou prent
    Et mout tres grant joie en demoine.
        Et li vilains la mule amoinne,
    Gauvains met lo frainc et la sele,

992 Congié prent a la damoisele.
Et ele conmande au vilain
Qu'il face monsaignor Gauvain
Tot sanz enconbrier fors issir,
996 Et lou chastel feïst tenir
Tot qoi, tant c'outre fust passez.
Messire Gauvains est montez,
Qui de la voie fu mout bel.
1000 Li vilains conmande au chastel
Qu'il fust toz coiz, et il s'esta.
Gauvains seürement passa,
Et quant il a lou pont passé,
1004 Vers lou chastel a regardé,
Et si a lors parmi les rues
Si granz conpaignies veües
De gent qui laienz queroloient
1008 Et si grant joie demenoient
Que, se Dieus l'eüst conmandé,
N'i eüst il pas plus joé;
Li uns a l'autre se deporte.
1012 Encor estoit desor la porte
Li vilains qui l'ot fors mené,
Et Gauvains li a demandé
Quieus senefïance c'estoit
1016 Que la dedenz veü n'avoit
A l'entrer ne petit ne grant,
Et or i voi[t] joie si grant
Que trestuit de joie tençoient.
1020 'Sire,' fet cil, 'repost estoient
Es crotes por les cruautez
Des bestes c'ocises avez,
Qui si grant effrois demenoient,
1024 Que, quant par aventure issoient
Les genz fors por aucune ovraingne,
Ne remansist q'a quelque painne
Ne les covenist deslïer,
1028 Ses aloient toz depecier
Par lor orgoil et par lor rage.
Et or dïent en lor langage:
Dieus les a par vos delivrez,

35b

1032 Et de toz biens enluminez
      La gent qui en tenebre estoient.
      Si grant joie ont de ce qu'il voient
      Qu'il ne püent graingnor avoir.'
1036 Ice, sachiez tres bien de voir,
      A Gauvain mout bien atalente.
        Maintenant se mist en la sente
      Qui vers l'eve lo moinne droit
1040 O la planche de fer estoit;
      Outre passe seürement.
      Tant ala aprés chevauchant
      Qu'il est venuz en la valee   *35c*
1044 Qui de vermine est aornee.
      Outre est seürement passez,
      Dedenz la forest est entrez
      O les bestes sauvages sont.
1048 Maintenant q'aparceü l'ont,
      Contre li vont si lou convoient.
      Les deus genoz a terre ploient
      Et de lui aprochier s'aessent;
1052 Les piez et les janbes li baisent
      Et font a la mule autresi.
      Gauvains de la forest issi,
      Qui de l'aler ne tarda mie.
1056 Entrez est en la praerie
      Qui do chastel estoit voisine.
        Li rois Artus et la roïne
      Furent alé esbanoier,
1060 Et avecques maint chevalier
      Qui de lor conpaignie sont,
      De la sale es loges amont.
      Et Gauvains tot adés venoit.
1064 La roïne primes lo voit,
      Si l'a as chevaliers mostré.
      A l'encontre li sont alé
      Et chevalier et damoiseles.
1068 Mout fu liee de ces noveles
      La damoisele quant el ot
      Que messire Gauvains veno[i]t—
      Cele cui estre doit li frains.

1072   Venuz est messire Gauvains,
        Et la pucele va encontre.   *35d*
        'Sire,' fait ele, 'bon encontre
        Vos doint Dieus, et tot lo deduit
1076   Qu'on puet avoir et jor et nuit.'
        'Et vos aiez bone aventure,'
        Fait cil qui descent de la mure
        A terre par l'estrier d'argent.
1080   La pucele en ses braz lo prent
        Si lou baise plus de cent foiz.
        'Sire,' fait ele, 'il est bien droiz
        Que je mete tot a devise
1084   Lo mien cors en vostre servise,
        Que bien sai que ja ne l'eüsse
        Par nul home que je seüsse
        Dedenz lo chastel envoier.
1088   Car mort en sont maint chevalier
        Qui les testes coupees ont,
        Qui de l'avoir nul pooir n'ont.'
        Lors li a Gauvains recontees
1092   Les aventures qu'ot trovees:
        De la grant valee et do bois,
        Et de la fontainne a espois,
        Et de l'eve qui noire estoit,
1096   Et do chastel qui tornoioit,
        Et des lïons que il ocist,
        Et do chevalier qu'il conquist,
        Et del vilain lo covenent,
1100   Et la bataille do sarpent,
        Et del nain qui lo salua
        Et plus dire ne li daigna,
        Et coment aprés li revint,   *36a*
1104   Et conment mengier lo covint
        En la chanbre a la damoisele
        Qui suer estoit a la pucele,
        Et coment li frains fu renduz,
1108   Et quant do chastel fu issuz
        Conment il i avoit veües
        Les queroles parmi les rues,
        Et conment issuz s'en estoit

1112 Sanz enconbrier et sanz destroit.
       Quant Gauvains a ce raconté,
       Et la pucele a demandé
       Congié as barons de la cort,
1116 La roïne Guenievre i cort,
       Et li rois et li chevalier
       I sont alé por li proier
       Qu'avec aus laienz demorast,
1120 Et des chevaliers un amast
       Qui sont de la Table Reonde.
       'Sire, Damedieus me confonde,'
       Fet ele, 'se j'onques osasse,
1124 Se volentiers ne demorasse,
       Mes je ne puis por nule painne.'
       Sa mule demande, on li mainne,
       Si est montee par l'estrier.
1128 Et li rois la vet convoier,
       Mes ele dit que nul conduit
       Ne vialt avoir, ne lor anuit,
       Et si estoit il auques tart.
1132 Congié prent et si s'en depart,
       Si se remist en l'anbleüre.   *36b*

       De la damoisele a la mure,
       Qui s'en est tote seule alee,
1136 Est ci l'aventure finee.

REJECTED READINGS OF THE MANUSCRIPT

We use a capital letter to show that the word in question is the first in its line. To this list must be added those words printed in our text with letters added enclosed within square brackets.

LE CHEVALIER À L'ÉPÉE

69 Si que] Ƶ que—157 Salüé l'ont mout d.] Saluez les a d.—158 lor s. lor r.] sō s. li r.—172 Qu'il] Q̄ il—185 quil] q̄l—276 la b.] li b.—277 Li oste] Tantost —294 ist] est—321 el] ele—442 ont] a—472 lo p.] la p.—606 tot perdu] espdu —636 Se el] Se il—808 vespree] uespee—853–4 Between these lines the scribe has repeated line 852—901 et puis lui] lui Ƶ puis—996 dor] dō—1197 Lo] Co

LA MULE SANS FREIN

178 q.m.] q. il m.—185 ot] ist; paor] puor—198 Tant] Tot—468 ele i est] ele sest—518 arestez] apͥstez—528 iés] iest—559 enz en] enz enz—565 orendroit un jeu] or endroit ·ieu—629 Qui lo] Qⁱ l lo—671 chief en chief] chies ē chies— 713 quart] .iiii.—815 pieces] piecēt—930 El lit] Es liz—985 presentez] prēsentez —1109 Conment il i a. v.] Ƶ conment il a. v.—1126 on li mainne] on li amainne

NOTES

Unless otherwise stated, references to the romances of Chrétien de Troyes are to those editions specified in the Bibliography on p. 29. References to modern scholars, except where amplified, are also as indicated in the Bibliography.

LE CHEVALIER À L'ÉPÉE

In the MS the *Chevalier à l'épée* follows the *Voie d'Enfer*, the respective *explicit* and *incipit* being: *Ci fenist la voie d'anfer et conmance do chevalier a l'espee.*

1–3 These lines strongly suggest an oral presentation of the romance.

8 *monsaignor* G. Honorific title usually applied to Gauvain in the early texts, less commonly to other knights, e.g. Yvain, Kay (see L. Foulet's articles on 'Sire, Messire' in *Romania* LXXI and LXXII, 1950–1).

9–11 The *tant par* of l. 9 also modifies the *prisiez* of l. 10, and in l. 11 *reconter* is used absolutely, the sense being: Gauvain was so very well bred and so esteemed for deeds of arms that no one could adequately tell of it.

15–17 For *Se* Armstrong erroneously reads *Si*. The lines mean: 'If I cannot list them all, that is no reason why nevertheless I should desist from having my say.'

18 A later (early sixteenth-century?) hand has written *chrestien de troyes* in the margin.

18–28 In l. 19 the scribe when writing *blasmer* was correcting his first attempt, the letters *bla-* being written over what might have been *ore-* or *ote-*.

Lines 18 and 19 as they stand make excellent sense: 'Chrétien de Troyes, methinks, must not incur rightful blame . . .', implying that Chrétien de Troyes, the author of stories about Arthur and his other knights (ll. 20–21), might rightly be blamed if he failed to narrate an adventure concerning Gauvain (l. 24).[1] The poet realises that Gauvain is too valiant to be overlooked (l. 25) and says that he is pleased now to be the first to tell a story with Gauvain as the protagonist (ll. 26–7). This only makes sense if the *Crestïen de Troies* of line 18 and the *je* elsewhere in lines 1–28 are one and the same person, exactly as occurs in the introductions to *Erec et Enide*, *Cligés*, *Lancelot* and *Perceval*.

For Armstrong, as for Gaston Paris, who did not reckon with the

---

[1] See Introduction, p. 8.

possible identity of *je* with *Crestïen de Troies*, lines 18–19 made no sense if *ne* were taken as a negative. Armstrong saw in *ne* a dialectal variant of *en*, while Gaston Paris considered *ne* a scribal error which he proposed correcting to *en*. For them the (anonymous) author of *Ch* was saying that Chrétien de Troyes *was* to be blamed for not devoting a story to Gauvain.

We accept that this passage asserts that the author of the *Chevalier à l'épée* is Chrétien de Troyes. For the truth of the assertion, see the discussion in the Introduction, pp. 7–9.

22 Grammatically *qui* refers to *mesniee*, the nearest noun, and therefore *fu* is the singular, but as is normal in Old French the sense reference could equally well be to both *cort* and *mesniee*.

25 We take the subject of *ert* to be Gauvain, who 'was too worthy a man to be forgotten'.

26 = Chrétien, *Yvain*, l. 33.

27 *premier*. As frequently happens at this date, the two functions, adjectival and adverbial, of *premier* are not clearly distinguishable. See Foulet in Roach under **premerain**.

30 *Cardoil*: Carlisle. Often mentioned as one of King Arthur's courts (cf. *M*, ll. 21–2).

32 *Yvain*. Great friend of Gauvain in Chrétien's romance.

34 *tot jorz* is kept here in spite of the more common *toz jorz*, ll. 67, 68 etc. If the meaning 'always, usually' (even if limited to the period of this summer in Carlisle) is not considered satisfactory, it may well be thought that the text is corrupt and that the unusual form *tot jorz* has crept in in place of a phrase meaning, e.g., 'one day' which might make better sense.

42 *blanches* inserted above the line.

48 ff. Cf. the young Perceval's delight at the birdsong in the forest (*Conte du Graal*, ll. 85–90).

52 ff. For the ironic undertones in the situation of the 'Pensif Chevalier' who 's'oublie' (cf. l. 94) see P. Ménard, *Le Rire et le sourire dans le roman courtois en France au moyen âge* (Genève, 1969), pp. 243–6, 465–6.

69 MS *Et que*. If this line depends on what has gone before, the correction *Si* for *Et* proposed by Gaston Paris is necessary. The scribe seems to have repeated *Et* from the previous line.

78 ff. At this point begins the main action of the romance which, in its general outline, shows noteworthy similarities with Gauvain's encounter in the *Conte du Graal* with the King of Escavalon and his sister, the old king's daughter (ll. 5713 ff.). The points of resemblance are as follows: When Gauvain is travelling late in the day, he comes across a knight who offers him a lodging, but who does not personally escort him to his splendid castle. There the host's sister (daughter) is to keep him company; and she is instructed to offer him her affection and deny him nothing. The two are left alone together while the host is out in his woods. Gauvain pledges the girl his service, and each delights in the other's presence. Their intimacy,

however, provokes an attack on the hero which puts his life at risk. From this he escapes unscathed and later leaves the castle.

Since we know that the author of *Ch* is familiar with Chrétien's writings, to which he refers and which he demonstrably uses at other points, it seems to us that, despite the absence of significant verbal parallels, he has patterned this part of his work on the episode in the *Conte du Graal*. Into this scheme he worked important elements from Chrétien's *Lancelot* to produce the characteristic seduction test (see notes to ll. 454 ff., 588–9, 598–603).

83–5 Gauvain's greeting might be thought over-elaborate, though typical of his *courtoisie*.

89–95, 110–111 Gauvain's frankness and honesty are stressed here, as in ll. 716 ff., 1198–1206. Cf. *M*, ll. 1091–1112.

105 *Sou* = *Se le* 'and . . . it'.

120 'Then the knight woke up.' In this context with the knight going on to speak, *esveller* as a neuter verb (with *lo chevalier* obl. for nom. as its subject) is preferable to taking it as an active verb 'he woke up the knight'.

125 For the word omitted by the scribe we have supplied the adverb *tost*, which in the context (see ll. 121–2) seems more appropriate than Armstrong's *bel*.

127–8 It is surprising to find Gauvain with shield, lance and sword, since he had left court 'en desduit' (l. 91), and they were not mentioned among his preparations described in ll. 36–46. But cf. ll. 225, 857, 915–16, etc.

152 *se mist o pas petit*. It is unlikely that *o* is a reduction of the diphthong *au* (= *a+le*) which is a much later sound-change. We therefore assume that, as at l. 515, *o* = *ou* (= *en+le*) although we have found no other example of *Se metre en un pas*.

154 ff. With the shepherds' well-intentioned advice compare the similarly unheeded warnings given to the heroes of *Erec* (ll. 5448 ff.) and *Yvain* (ll. 5106 ff.).

157–8 MS *Saluez les a doucement | El non Dieu son salu li rent*. Here the verb *rent* is incorrect and the substitution of *rendent* impossible. Therefore Gaston Paris rewrote the lines to make the shepherds speak first, and we have followed him in this but not in linking the phrase *el non Dieu* with the preceding line.

160–3 Cf. *Erec*, ll. 5666–71:

> . . . 'Mar i fus,
> biax chevaliers, genz et adroiz.
> Certes ne seroit mie droiz
> que ta vie si tost fenist,
> ne que nus enuiz t'avenist
> don bleciez fusses ne leidiz.'

172 MS *Que il*. This could be kept, if the rest of the line read *dïent la verité* or *li dïent la verté*.

180 *nus* is the direct object of *avons veü* and should, if the declension system is being observed, be *nul*. The same thing, *nus* for *nul*, occurs in l. 213.

184 *dist*. This form appears to be preterite, though the sense requires a present indicative. There is evidence of the muting of *s* before -*t* in the rhyme *vit*: *revenist* (189-90), in the spelling *ocist* (195) for the pres. indic. of *ocire* rhyming with *dit* (196), and in the back-spelling *list*<*legit* (803). We therefore confidently accept *dist* as a mere orthographical variant for *dit*, present indicative 3rd person.

185 MS *quel* has been corrected by us to *quil = qui le*.

189-90 'For nobody ever saw anyone who came back from there.'

199 This line as given in the MS makes some sense: 'To abandon the traversing of his territory'. Gaston Paris, however, thought that the scribe had again given way to his weakness for copying from adjacent lines and that *son païs* was an error of this kind. He proposed *l'oirre que j'ai empris*.

200-2 For Gauvain's concern about his reputation 'en son païs', see also ll. 581-9, 624-36.

203-4 'He journeyed on at the ambling pace of his horse. . . .' For this pace see Foulet in Roach p. 11 **ambleüre**

205 *cil* i.e. the knight, who has indicated the valley at l. 149.

219 *Ainz*. The adversative use of *ainz* requires a preceding negative clause, which in this instance is understood. Something like 'He did not linger by the lists . . .' would fit the case.

226 *lou Gringalet*. Originally the name of Gauvain's horse (it occurs in a Welsh triad as Kein Caled: see Rachel Bromwich, *Trioedd Ynys Prydein*, Cardiff, 1961, pp. ciii-cvi), it later appears also as a common noun.

254-7 As it stands the MS reads 'I could not ever pass over (see l. 257) the beauty . . . nor do I wish to do so'. This is acceptable grammatically but one might suspect that *porroie* needs an infinitive of its own, such as *dire* or *retrere*, or that l. 254 once read *Je ne vos diroie en un jor* or *Dire ne porroie en un jor*, but in this case one would expect *Mes* and not *Ne* in l. 257.

266 We keep the MS reading *qu'il* with causal sense (rather than correcting to *qu* or *quant*), though there is a suspicion that the scribe has let himself be influenced by l. 268.

275 *la salua*. Gaston Paris corrects this to *le salua* and one can see that the parallelism of construction: *Gauvains s'esbahi et neporquant sailli sus* and *la damoisele s'esbaï et neporcant le salua* might argue in favour of altering the text. Nevertheless the MS makes sense and it may be natural for Gauvain to greet the lady first.

276-7 MS *Tantost par la main li bailla* / *Tantost a mon saignor Gauvain*. This is plainly faulty and Armstrong made the obvious correction, which we follow.

278-91 Cf. the King of Escavalon's instructions to his sister in the *Conte du Graal*, ll. 5728-47, 5792-802.

304 'Neither too much nor too little was said to her.' Might it not however be preferable to replace the impersonal *l'en* by *il* (=Gauvain)?

311 Taking *plaisir* as an infinitive we could translate 'If he found favour in her eyes'. Taking *plaisir* as a noun the meaning could be 'If it were pleasing to her'.

318–19 'But on no account would she consent to reveal her feelings to him.'

331 Gaston Paris refused to accept the reduced form *cranté* as belonging to the poet's language. Arguing that the scribe had used it to get rid of an embarrassing *s'os* for *se vos*, he corrected the line to: *Que s'os avoie creanté*, restoring the feminine *e* which, it is true, is found in every other use of the verb in this text.

338 This line is anacoluthonic: 'And no matter what my father tells you'.

350–2 Cf. the laying of the table in *Sir Gawain and the Green Knight*, ll. 884–6, including the use of protective over-cloths (*sanap*):
> Sone watz telded vp a tabil on trestez ful fayre,
> Clad wyth a clene cloþe þat cler quyt schewed,
> Sanap, and salure, and syluerin sponez.

355–6 Cf. *M* 956–7.

373–5 The lord's instructions to the damsel to entertain the hero while he is away in his woods reflect the situation in the *Conte du Graal* (see note to ll. 78 ff.). The poet of *Sir Gawain and the Green Knight* seems to have been prompted by l. 373 to introduce his extended and vivid hunting scenes (see Part II of this edition).

391–2 'for of this one (= adventure) he (the host), who has shut him (Gauvain) up within his walls, is assured.' Armstrong altered *ceste* to *cest* (= this man, i.e. Gauvain) and resolved the beginning of l. 392 as *Qu'il a* (where *Qu'* = Gauvain and *il* the host). We read: *Qui l'a*, where *Qui* goes with *il*, making the Old French for *celui qui*, referring to the host; *l'* now refers to Gauvain.

403 *nule* refers presumably to *volenté*; her father was never willing to say what he had in mind.

405 *S'il* = *Si+il* 'And he', or *Se+il* 'If he'.

416 =*M*, l. 1: 'The proverb had it that', 'there was a proverbial saying that'.

418–20 Proverb. Cf. Morawski, No. 216: 'Au vespre loe on le jor, au matin son oste.' The sense of the proverb expressed here is repeated in a different form in ll. 1184–5.

442 MS *Il a*. This we take to be an error induced by l. 441.

454 ff. In the following episode we find an apparently original combination of elements from two widespread motifs: the perilous bed, and the seduction test. In Chrétien's *Lancelot* these motifs are found in separate episodes (see especially ll. 459–534 and 1195–1280), from which the poet of *Ch* seems to borrow (see below, notes to ll. 588–9, 598–601). *Ch* and *Lancelot* have the following features in common: the hero is apprehensive at being obliged to sleep with a *damoisele*; the bed is of unusual richness; no

intercourse takes place; the hero receives a flesh-wound from a weapon that flies at him; he is much concerned for his honour; his worth is subsequently recognised. These elements are worked into the basic scheme derived from the *Conte du Graal* (see note to ll. 78 ff.).

461 'that she is a good match for him.'

469 *s'il contredit*. Probably 'if he gainsays him' (see Introduction, p. 23).

472 MS *la prist*. The error *la* for *lo* may well have been caused by the scribe's looking at *la main*.

476 We keep MS *est*, but this is so suspiciously close to the *est* of the previous line that *ert*, in keeping with the rest of the imperfect tenses, seems a tempting correction.

500-3 The sense of these lines does not run absolutely smoothly. The basic idea concerns the privacy obtained by shutting the doors and this would be better brought out by correcting *son conmandement* to *mon conmandement*. As it is, the injunction to do the knight's bidding is a little intrusive.

503 *mestier*. This word appears in full in *M* 649 and 747 and we have so expanded both *mest*[7] (*M* 7, 223, 548 and 857) and *mestĕr* (here and in *M* 2). In this last abbreviation it would be possible to expand the superscript *i* to *ri* and read *mestrier* as Armstrong does.

517 I.e. 'without her having to be asked to do so'.

520 MS *Ml't = la bese = *. The scribe has indicated that he wants something deleted, but instead of attaching his erasure signs to *ml't*, which he has repeated from the previous line, he has put them in the wrong place.

545-6 The rhyme *porte : estorde* could easily be rectified by a correction to *estorte*. Similarly at ll. 561-2 *maintenant : brant* would be justified if one were absolutely certain that the incorrect forms came from the scribe and not from the poet, who frequently uses oblique forms for his subjects.

547 *biaus sanblant* for *bel sanblant* seems a startling mixture of forms, but we do not feel compelled to make a correction as Armstrong did.

552-3 'He immediately wreaks justice on him, if he can catch him out in any error.'

553 MS *Si lentreprent*. In this text *si* is never used for 'if' and Gaston Paris's correction is essential. See also ll. 469, 1102.

572-4 The King of Escavalon's sister likewise fears that Gauvain will be killed for her sake (*Conte du Graal*, ll. 5875-7).

582-3 If *il* is neuter (i.e. the equivalent of *ceste chose* in l. 626) and *celez* an analogical neuter nom. for *celé* agreeing with it, the meaning would be 'that it could not be hidden, so that it was known everywhere . . .' (i.e. it could not be prevented from becoming common knowledge); and *en* would have its loose meaning 'in this matter', 'as regards this'. However, if *celer* could in this context have the extended meaning of 'shield', the *il* and *celez* could be masc. and the meaning be 'that he could not be shielded from everyone knowing . . .', with *en* anticipating the following clause.

586 We might expect the same tense, *avroit*, here as in l. 584, but the looseness of construction is not excessive.

588–9 Cf. *Lancelot*, ll. 1112–5:

> 'Ne ja Dex n'ait de moi merci,
>
> . . . .
>
> ... s'asez mialz morir ne vuel
> a enor que a honte vivre.'

Conte du Graal, ll. 6179–82:

> 'N'ai pas de ma mort tel paor
> Que je miex ne weille a honor
> La mort soffrir et endurer
> Que vivre a honte et parjurer.'

Wace, *Le Roman de Brut* (ed. I. Arnold, SATF, 1938–40), ll. 8929–30:

> 'Mult valt mielz murir a enur
> Que lunges vivre a desonur.'

See also Tony Hunt in *Forum for Modern Language Studies* VI (1970), p. 22, n. 73.

593 I.e. 'You cannot get out of it.'

598–603 Cf. *Lancelot*, ll. 522–7:

> El covertor est li feus pris
> et es dras et el lit a masse.
> Et li fers de la lance passe
> au chevalier lez le costé
> si qu'il li a del cuir osté
> un po, mes n'est mie bleciez.

606 MS *talant esperdu*. The past participle seems so obviously repeated in error from the previous line that we accept Gaston Paris's correction to *tot perdu*.

620–1 '[Even] a wise man can easily undertake something that turns out to his disadvantage.'

629–30 Cf. *M* 39–40.

632–4 'nor did she oppose him with anything more than the threat of a sword wielded by nobody.'

650 'No one could have found anything to criticise in her.'

685 *en la chanbre*. As the following lines make clear, the host does not enter the room at this point.

690 *lui* = Gauvain.

694 ff. The poet's resumption of the honorific *messire*, which he had not used since l. 514, corresponds to Gauvain's recovery of his dignity and his release from a humiliating situation.

698 The host expected and hoped to find Gauvain dead, hence his grief at getting a loud and clear reply from him.

705–7 In the *Conte du Graal* the King of Escavalon vows to protect the hero from harm, since he is his guest (ll. 6078–80).

746 *bien lo sai*. This probably refers to what follows because the host cannot know that his guest's name was Gauvain or his previous questions would have been unnecessary. He does however know of his superlative qualities, because the sword-test had demonstrated just that, and he could well have known of Gauvain's qualities by repute.

746 ff. Gauvain figures here as the hero predestined to rid a castle of some baneful and mysterious custom. He plays a similar role in *M*, as in the *Conte du Graal* (Château des Merveilles); and cf. *Erec* (Joie de la Cort), *Lancelot* (Land of Gorre), *Yvain* (Château de Pesme Aventure). On the other hand, Gauvain's acceptance of the girl and apparent marriage to her (l. 818) is surprising in view of his traditional character as the 'gay bachelor'. He is more likely to reject an offer of marriage, as in *M*.

752–8 'Do you know how I have tested all the knights in the world who go in search of adventures? Could they have lain in this bed, yet would they all have had to die one after the other until it happened that the very best should come.'

He had not in fact tested all the knights, but he had made his test open to them all, and, once the best has been found, all the others have automatically been proved inferior. With this interpretation there is no need to postulate a lacuna after l. 754 as Gaston Paris did.

762 'and how he [the best one] has rightly stood the test, for it [the sword] has chosen you as the best.'

818 Throughout the Middle Ages, marriage could be contracted by mutual declaration of consent (*per verba de praesenti*), and even the presence of a priest was not strictly necessary. This is apparently what happens here, although later in the story we find the girl referred to as *pucele*, *damoisele* just as before and also as Gauvain's *drue* (ll. 847, 957) and *amie* (l. 1203). Moreover, contrary to the ethic of even unconsecrated marriage, the hero is willing to surrender her if she is won from him in fair combat (ll. 934 ff.); and in the end he completely abandons her (ll. 1190–1). On medieval marriage see M. Schumacher, *Die Auffassung der Ehe in den Dichtungen Wolframs von Eschenbach* (Heidelberg, 1967), especially pp. 32 ff.

825–7 'If he returned successfully to the assault on the gracious damsel, I am delighted and she was in no way sorry.'

835 Instead of supplying *lo*, which is Armstrong's correction for a hypometric line, one could assume a hiatus *ostë ala*.

844 *li*. Armstrong printed *l'i* meaning 'take her thither, to my country'; we take *li* to be a tonic accusative pronoun.

853 After this line the scribe has repeated line 852.

861 ff. The source of the 'maiden and the dogs' episode is unknown. Arm-

strong (pp. 63–7) cites parallels in *La Vengeance Raguidel*, the Prose *Tristan*, and Heinrich von dem Türlin's *Diu Krône*; but these seem derivative from *Ch*. Armstrong also considers it likely that the tenth novel in the second day of the *Decameron* is based on *Ch*; and he suggests a prototype in the eastern *History of the Forty Vezirs*.

Although the inclusion of the episode can be criticised on psychological grounds, the girl's sudden faithlessness being particularly unexpected (cf. A. Micha in R. S. Loomis, ed., *Arthurian Literature in the Middle Ages*, Oxford, 1959, pp. 363–5), it is consistent with the general ironical and burlesque tone of the romance.

889 *il*. This cannot of course refer to Gauvain and the girl (except by a gross oversight on the poet's part); it must stand for Gauvain and his host who had indeed both traversed the forest.

901 MS *Saluer lui et puis enquerre*. In this position *lui* would be a second pronoun object for *lou quida salüer* and we prefer to make it the object of *enquerre*, assuming a blunder on the scribe's part.

918 *E[r]t*. Correction proposed by Gaston Paris.

919 'So he [Gauvain] had, compared with him, the worst of the bargain.'

952–3 'If you make me a present of what is [already] my own, you are indeed a powerful fellow.' Rather heavy irony. The knight has already won the girl and is not proposing to wait until Gauvain gives his assent.

956 It is interesting to find a *jeu parti* figuring in both *Ch* and *M*. The choice here is, of course, made by the girl, not Gauvain. See Paul Remy, 'Jeu parti et roman breton', *Mélanges . . . Delbouille*, II (Gembloux, 1964), pp. 545–61.

968 *li* = *le li*; 'Gauvain willingly grants him this.'

974 Lit. 'now there is nothing more', i.e. 'the moment of decision has come'.

988–97 This assertion of the feminine attitude to love savours more of the fabliaux than of *amour courtois* as usually presented in the romances. It surely carries a humorous hint of Gauvain's insufficiency in the girl's eyes.

991 MS *drue et moillier*. We keep the MS reading in spite of Gaston Paris's correction *ou* for *et*; after all, did not Enide claim to be both the *fame* and the *amie* of Erec (*Erec*, ll. 4650–1)? For the particular situation here and the girl's position as Gauvain's wife and *drue* see note to l. 818.

994 *par lui*. We keep the MS reading *par* and understand by it: 'She would never have such love from him, if he were useless in bed, as would enable her to feel the slightest esteem for him'. Armstrong's correction *por* seems to us to introduce an inconsistency between the senses of lines 994 and 996.

995 We keep the MS *que s'il* even though it makes the second *que* (l. 966) redundant—a grammatical infelicity which is by no means rare.

996 MS *don de sel*. The commonest form derived from Gaulish **durnos* 'fist' is *dor*, which we have substituted for *don*. There are other forms, however, among them *dou*, which might possibly have stood in our scribe's exemplar.

1043 *Choisir* is here ambiguous. It could mean 'for us to see which one . . .' or 'for her to choose which one . . .'.

1053–4 'that he would take them [by force] without more ado just as he would do now', i.e. as he would have to do now if he did not accept the *jeu parti*.

1073 '. . . for you will not take a single one of them away'. *Mie* is here used with substantival force; for *mener* 'take away' see l. 1034.

1099–1100 Gauvain's application of the proverbial opinion about dogs is odd. By his reasoning the dogs should have gone to the girl who had reared them, not to Gauvain who had merely seen them in her father's house.

1101 MS *Feme*, with *me* added above the line.

1102 See note to l. 553.

1108–9 For this anti-feminist sentiment cf., e.g. *La Folie Tristan d'Oxford* (ed. E. Hoepffner, Strasbourg, 2nd edn., 1943), ll. 937–8:

> 'Mult par at en chen grant franchise
> E at en femme grant feintise.'

See also P. Ménard, *Le Rire et le sourire* . . . , p. 233.

1110 *il* = the strange knight.

1116 *l'uns* = the strange knight, who is also the subject of *feri* in l. 1118.

1120 *li* = *le li*.

1129 At first sight this line appears to mean 'between the horse's legs'; but this would be the only instance in either *Ch* or *M* of the oblique case used as genitive (apart from the stock phrase *la cort lo roi M* 978), and in any case this kind of genitive is only used of human beings. The phrase therefore means 'his horse between his legs', i.e. with the knight still in the saddle (cf. l. 1126).

1140–2 This does not seem to accord with the highest ideals of chivalry (though the knight, it is true, had not asked for mercy). Contrast, e.g., Gornemant de Goort's instructions to the young Perceval never to slay a defeated knight (*Conte du Graal*, ll. 1639–47).

1144–5 Gauvain is not fighting for profit and does not take the spoils to which he is entitled.

1152–3 The leap into the saddle without the use of stirrups is commonly found, especially in epic literature, as an indication of the knight's vigour or violent mood. Cf. *M*, ll. 351, 792. On this feature see Otto Springer, 'The "Âne Stegreif" Motif in Medieval Literature', *Germanic Review* XXV (1950), pp. 163–77. Springer found one probable example in Chrétien (*Erec*, ll. 718–20).

1168–88 With this misogynistic tirade and that of ll. 1096–1109 compare *Le Conte du Graal*, ll. 5855–65, which probably suggested the feature to the poet of *Ch.*:

> 'Se feme doit faire nul bien,
> En cele n'a de feme rien
> Qui het le mal et le bien aime;

> Tort a qui puis feme le claime,
> Que la en pert ele le non.
> Mais tu iez feme, bien le voi,
> Que cil la qui siet dalez toi
> Ocist ton pere, et tu le baises!
> Quant feme puet avoir ses aises,
> Del soreplus petit li chaut.'

Though less common in the romances than in the fabliaux (cf. note to ll. 988–97), such outbursts are by no means rare (cf., e.g., *Conte du Graal*, ll. 3863–76). The originality of the *Ch*-poet is to place them in the mouth of the amorist Gauvain.

1181–3 'This consideration of yours for me did not arise from any concern for my honour and my life, but it sprang from quite other motives.'

1184–5 Proverb. Cf. Morawski, No. 44: 'A la bone fin veit tout.'

1196 MS *si ami* is a correct nom. pl. but it does not rhyme. If the poet in fact wrote *si amis*, the mixed forms would be no stranger than, for example, *li plait* at l. 1110.

1197 MS *Co*. Armstrong made what seems the obvious correction to *Lo*. Gaston Paris argued that *co = cou = quel = quil* just as *sou = sel = sil* in l. 105. The meaning would be: 'for they thought they had lost him'.

LA MULE SANS FREIN

This text in MS Berne 354 immediately follows the *Chevalier à l'épée* with *explicit* and *incipit* as follows: *Ci fenist dou chevalier a l'espee et conmance la mule sanz frain.*

1–16 Based on Chrétien's *Erec*, ll. 1–14:

> Li vilains dit an son respit
> que tel chose a l'an an despit
> qui molt valt mialz que l'an ne cuide;
> por ce fet bien qui son estuide
> atorne a bien quel que il l'ait;
> car qui son estuide antrelait,
> tost i puet tel chose teisir
> qui molt vandroit puis a pleisir.
> Por ce dist Crestïens de Troies
> que reisons est que totevoies
> doit chascuns panser et antandre
> a bien dire et a bien aprandre;
> et tret d'un conte d'avanture
> une molt bele conjointure ...

In our text 'Paien' elaborates the lesson found in some proverbs, e.g.

'Meauz valent les vieilles voies que les noveles' (Morawski, No. 1237; cf. Hill, p. 53, and Smith, p. 130).

1-2 Line 1, which is a stock phrase, occurs in *Ch*, l. 416, as does the rhyme *reprovier* : *mestier*.

6-7 These two lines have given editors some difficulty.

Orłowski, Jenkins and Smith suspected corruption in the text. Orłowski changed *biens* (substantive) to *bien* (adverb), glossing *venir a* as 'devenir' and *mestier* as 'valeur'. His text would then presumably mean: 'for it can speedily become something valuable.' Jenkins changed *A* in l. 7 to *E*, taking both *biens* and *chose* as subjects of *puet venir*, with *il* as a neuter pronoun subject anticipating the two nouns. This would mean: 'for out of it there can speedily come some good thing and something which would be useful'. Smith changed *A* to *E* on the grounds that this is a common scribal error and indeed occurs again, in his view, in *M* 543. He does not translate his version.

Hill kept the MS reading unchanged, but did not say what he thought the lines mean.

We too print what we find in the MS. We take *il* as a neuter impersonal pronoun anticipating the subject, and *en venir a* to mean 'come to, accrue to', and translate the lines as follows: 'for value may very soon accrue to a thing which proved (i.e. turned out to be) useful'. Alternatively, if as Foulet in Roach asserts (s.v. **a**) '*avec*, *a* et *o* peuvent avoir le même sens', one might translate 'good may come with something that turned out useful'.

14 Though we see *Paiens* as the humorously adopted antonym of *Crestiens*, *Maisieres* is no doubt a real place. Orłowski found 48 communes so named, three of them in southern Champagne (pp. 14-15). A later hand has copied the name in the margin here and below col. 26c.

18 = l. 1134. This is apparently the author's title for his poem.

18 *mure*. This dialectal form occurring always at the rhyme belongs to the language of the author (as it does to that of Chrétien de Troyes). Internally *mule* is used, except at l. 274, which the scribe wrote on two lines with *mure* at the end of the first. At l. 336 there is an incorrect *mul*.

20-2 For Arthur holding court in Carlisle at Whitsuntide cf. *Yvain*, ll. 1-7.

23 The scribe wrote *assez* twice and struck out the first.

39 *une seule pucele* 'a solitary maiden'.

59 *voillent*. The subj. is used here, we assume, as an elegant alternative for the ind. pr. or condit.

67-8 Cf. *Erec*, ll. 6297-8:

> et trestuit li autre i acorent,
> si les salüent et enorent . . .

72 *li* = *la li* or read *l'i moinne*.

75 ff. The maiden whose bridle has been wrongfully taken from her (apparently by her sister, in whose keeping it now is—see l. 970) may be compared

with the younger daughter of the Sire de la Noire Espine, also dispossessed by her sister, in *Yvain*. But this feature of *M* remains obscure, and one cannot be sure of a relationship with its analogue in Chrétien's romance.

87 With *que* in this line is to be understood a repetition of *je sai bien* from l. 82. The damsel makes two assertions: that she would get her bridle back if one of Arthur's knights were willing to undertake the adventure and that when she came into undisputed possession of the bridle she would give herself to the knight who had given it back to her. (Her promise is verbally fulfilled in ll. 1082–4.)

95 'But he will not get it [the bridle] peaceably', i.e. without a great deal of fighting. A forward reference to the fights with lions, serpents and the defending knight in the castle.

98 'Be it in never so strange a land' 'However strange the land in which it may be'. For this construction see also *M* 336, 372.

115 A mule is normally no mount for a knight, but this is plainly a supernatural beast. Note that Kay mounts by the stirrups, whereas Gauvain often leaps, more heroically, into the saddle (l. 351; cf. l. 792 and note to *Ch*, ll. 1152–3). This motif of the leap into the saddle without the use of stirrups helps to add an epic flavour to the narrative (cf. note to ll. 748–9).

117–26 'When they see him departing alone, for there is no companion with him and no arms are being carried save only his sword, the damsel remained in tears because she sees plainly, and I agree, that she will certainly not get her bridle back on this occasion, no matter what he, who is riding on the mule which departs at a spanking pace, may say.'

There is just a possibility that the scribe has, in error, written *il voient* instead of *ele voit* in l. 117. The damsel is gifted with foreknowledge, because though Gauvain sets out no more formidably armed (ll. 357,656 ff.), she knows that he, unlike Keu, will succeed. See ll. 346–8.

We have not found the phrase *avoir l'aler* ('to have the going' = 'to go', l. 125) attested elsewhere.

133 *s'ont* thus resolved from MS *sōt* to avoid identical rhyme with l. 134. For aux. *avoir* with reflexive verb, see K. Nyrop, *Grammaire historique de la langue française*, Vol. VI (Copenhagen, 1930), p. 214.

147–59 It is not clear why the beasts should do obeisance to the mule in honour of the *dame*, since its owner is the *damoisele*. If we knew the source of this part of the tale, the mystery might be resolved. In fact general analogies with the Yvain story have been recognised (see, e.g., R. S. Loomis, *Arthurian Tradition and Chrétien de Troyes*, Columbia U.P., 1949, pp. 283–7; R. L. Thomson in his edn. of *Owein*, Dublin, 1968, pp. xcii–xciii); and the presence of the beasts in the forest traversed by the hero figures among the parallels. It may be significant that their nature and behaviour correspond more closely to the description in *Owein* (which may be considered as close to Chrétien's source) than to that in *Yvain*, ll. 276 ff. In the Welsh version the hero encounters a monstrous herdsman who struck with his club a stag

> till it gave out a mighty belling, and in answer to its belling wild animals came till they were as numerous as the stars in the firmament, so that there was scant room for me to stand in the clearing with them and all those serpents and lions and vipers and all kinds of animals. And he looked on them and bade them go graze. And then they bowed down their heads and did him obeisance, even as humble subjects would do to their lord. (*The Mabinogion*, tr. G. Jones and T. Jones, London, 1949, p. 159)

The apparent familiarity of the author of *M* with the source of *Yvain* might be adduced in favour of the identification of 'Paien de Maisières' with Chrétien de Troyes.

151–5 'Thus they knelt in honour of the lady, and by doing so they ensure that they can have their lair and come and go in the forest. They cannot do her greater honour.'

160 ff. In *Owein* (but not in *Yvain*) the knight passes from the forest into a valley (Jones and Jones, p. 159). The Irish *Tochmarc Emire* (*The Wooing of Emer*), which shows other parallels to *Owein/Yvain* and *M*, also presents a valley infested with monsters (see Thomson, op. cit., p. xcii).

The description of the valley in *M* offers typical infernal characteristics: darkness, fire-breathing reptiles, stench, cold and wind (see D. D. R. Owen, *The Vision of Hell*, Scottish Academic Press, 1971, pp. 205–6).

177 'whether he will or no', 'willy nilly'.

185 We accept the emendation *paor* for *puor* at the end of this line, proposed by Antoine Thomas and followed by Orłowski, as giving better sense as well as avoiding the same word at the rhyme.

187 *pot nestre* = pret. 3 of *nestre* i.e. *nasquié* 'was born'.

194–205 'There will never be so great a summer heat nor so great a scorching heat, but that therein there is forever cold as in the very heart of winter, so much, methinks, the bitterness of winter perpetually reigns there; and perpetually there blows the north wind to which pertains the great coldness there; and the other winds which—clashing together in it—likewise blow. There is such misery there that I could never tell half of it.'

Line 198, with its identical rhyme and *Tot*, hard to justify as either adj. or adv., may well be scribally corrupt; we amend to *Tant*.

For *qui* intercalated = *ço quit* cf. Béroul, *Tristran* (ed. A. Ewert, Oxford, 1939), l. 1854.

211 *ardure*. Heat is not one of the characteristics of the valley of icy cold as previously described. Perhaps the poet is referring to the flames from the beasts mentioned in l. 180.

214 ff. Cf. the meadows and fountain of the Earthly Paradise commonly visited in vision literature after the places of punishment (see Owen, loc.

cit.). But again the Owein/Yvain story provides an analogy:

> 'And from there thou shalt see a vale like a great waterway; and in the middle of the vale thou shalt see a great tree with the tips of its branches greener than the greenest fir trees. And under that tree is a fountain. . . .' (*Owein*, in Jones and Jones, op. cit., p. 159)

216 *eve*. The only water in this spot is the fountain, and our punctuation takes account of this fact. But cf. the reference to a 'waterway' in the quotation from *Owein* above.

221 The scribe has written *de p¹ns*, with *i* added above the line and attention called to the addition by the mark that serves him as a caret mark. Orłowski printed *d'epins* (i.e. *espins* with reduction of preconsonantal *s*); Méon read the words as *d'epus*, which Godefroy, III, 324, lists but does not gloss. See note to l. 1094.

229–31 'Because the road seems so long to him, he never thinks that he will see what he was seeking.' For *car* 'because' beginning a sentence see also *Cligés*, l. 2980.

238 ff. Cf. the infernal Bridge of Dread (see Owen, loc. cit.). The similarity is strengthened by the later reference to devils (ll. 398–400). There is a similar structure, however, in *Tochmarc Emire* (see Thomson, ed. *Owein*, p. xcii), which suggests that the poet may have found it in some form in his main source. See also note to ll. 391–400.

245 *la* refers to *eve*, previously mentioned at l. 233.

258 ff. For Kay's lack of success in his undertakings and consequent humiliation cf. his encounters with Erec and Perceval (*Erec*, ll. 3937 ff.; *Conte du Graal*, ll. 4274 ff.) and his unsuccessful defence of Guenevere in *Lancelot* (ll. 82 ff.). The abortive expedition by a subsidiary character as a prelude to the hero's adventures is also a feature of *Owein/Yvain*. The name of the unsuccessful knight in *Yvain* is Calogrenant, which R. S. Loomis resolved as Cai-lo-grenant, 'Kay the Grumbler' (*Arthurian Tradition* . . . , p. 275), so again it is possible that *M* preserves a feature from some pre-*Yvain* version of the story.

337 With our punctuation *son frainc* is oblique in apposition to *l'* in l. 335; without the comma in l. 336 it would be oblique used as subject of *sera*.

342–5 There is an amusing contrast between the damsel's attitude to Gauvain here and to Kay in ll. 99–107. In the romances the ladies are usually as prompt to return Gauvain's affection as he is to offer it.

351 See note to l. 115.

357 Cf. note to ll. 117–26.

358–64 'He went into the meadow which leads to the forest where the beasts, the lions and the leopards, lurk. Immediately he goes thither. They (the beasts) go straight to meet Gauvain at the spot where he would have to pass.

With our punctuation and sequence of events, *vet* in l. 362 offers no difficulty and there is no need (i) to alter to *vont*, as Jenkins did because he took the subject to be the beasts, nor (ii) to argue that though the subject is the beasts, a singular verb can correctly be used with it, as Hill did (*Romanic Review* IV, 1913, pp. 394–5). We agree with Mario Roques's justification of the singular verb, but disagree with him when he makes the mule and not its rider the subject.

368–72 The beasts do obeisance to Gauvain himself (cf. ll. 1048–53) in contrast to their behaviour in their encounter with the less worthy Kay, where it was stressed that they were honouring the lady and the mule (ll. 147–55).

375–6 The position of the subject *Keus* is somewhat odd but the sense is clear: 'that Kay was afraid when he passed that way, and went back for that reason'.

391–400 Cf. *Lancelot*, ll. 3009–14; *Conte du Graal*, ll. 1312–16. The parallel with *Lancelot* can be extended, since there the river is also spanned by a 'male planche' (l. 3021, i.e. the sword bridge), and a vision of lions is associated with it as a vision of devils is here.

399–400 'to all appearances one only sees there a vision of devils'.

415 'over the edge of the plank'.

425–6 'He whom fortune favours and smiles on enters on a small path'.

433–7 Cf. *Erec*, ll. 5730–5:

> ... devant ax sor pex aguz
> avoit hiaumes luisanz et clers,
> et voit de desoz les cerclers
> paroir testes desoz chascun;
> mes au chief des pex an voit un
> ou il n'avoit neant ancor ...

For other instances of the impaled heads motif in French and Celtic literature see R. S. Loomis, *Arthurian Tradition* . . . , p. 176.

438 The line appears to mean 'Gauvain would not give up', but this absolute use of *laissier* is not widely attested and Jenkins thought that the line was corrupt, though his suggested emendation *Gauvains ne voit mie d'huissier* is a desperate remedy.

439–59 There is apparent confusion in the poet's mind regarding the gate. First he says there is none (l. 439: Smith suggests a possible emendation of *avoit* to *veoit*); then Gauvain is said to stop in front of it (l. 451), although it passes him at great speed (ll. 440–3, 458–9).

440 ff. For analogues to the spinning castle in other literature see Orłowski, pp. 73–89, and G. Huet in *Romania* XL (1911), pp. 235–42. For a likely prototype in the Irish *Fled Bricrend* (*Bricriu's Feast*) see Loomis, *Arthurian Tradition* . . . , pp. 207–8, 283–6.

442–3 Cf. *Cligés*, ll. 3760–1:

> S'est plus tornanz que n'est la tronpe
> Que l'escorgiee mainne et chace.

448 'He would greatly like to know its nature (i.e. all about it).'

450 *pont tornoiant*. No other example of this phrase is known to us. It is clear from the context that the bridge is separate from the castle and does not spin with it or on its own axis. We therefore take it to be a synonym of *pont torneïz* 'drawbridge'.

458-9 There are several instances in this text of the popular or careless repetition of *que*, one of the two being superfluous.

460 Either: 'He weighed up very carefully the situation in which he found himself', or 'He kept a sharp look-out for his opportunity'.

465-70 Compare the entry of Owein/Yvain into the lady's castle. There, however, the mount was cut in two (*Mabinogion*, tr. Jones and Jones, p. 164; *Yvain*, ll. 942-53). If one equates the helpful mule in *M* with the helpful lion in *Yvain*, it may be noted that there (ll. 3378-83) part of the lion's tail is cut off.

468 MS *sest conseu*. Having found no other instance of a reflexive use of *consivre* to support the MS reading, we correct *sest* to *i est*. The error would be yet another case of the scribe's eye straying to a neighbouring line.

469 This *si* is redundant.

474 This is the reading of the MS. It is a difficult line; *cele* for us refers, and is grammatically related, to the mule (l. 472), glad to find itself in the castle: '(she) who rejoiced to see it (the castle)'. For Mario Roques *cele* was in the oblique case functioning as genitive and he understood the sense to be: 'the castle of that lady who was delighted to see him [Gauvain]', but no mistress of the castle has yet been mentioned. Mario Roques's reference to ll. 921 and 950 does little to make the idea more attractive. Hill kept *cele*, but did not explain. Orłowski replaced *cele* by *celui*, presumably referring to *l'* [Gauvain] in l. 472.

483 It is surprising that the dwarf and the churl (l. 559) should know Gauvain's name, even if (ll. 525 ff.) the churl knows or guesses his errand. Orłowski corrected *Gauvains* to *soiez*.

492 Hill kept the MS reading *Et li nains* in his edition, but, when reviewing Orłowski's text, praised the change to *Que* which the latter had made. It seems to us possible to follow the manuscript. It is necessary to assume that the dwarf had not departed but, in l. 489, had just turned about preliminary to doing so; we infer from l. 495 that Gauvain could still have stopped him. The sequence of Gauvain's reactions is as follows: (1) He fails to understand what he sees and (2) wonders what this can be; (3) he reflects on the dwarf's failure to reply; (4) he thinks that if he could so demean himself he would force an explanation from the dwarf, but (5) concludes by letting him depart and dismounting from his horse.

504 ff. For the probable prototype of the *vilain* in the giant Curoi of *Fled Bricrend* and the source of the beheading test in 'The Champion's Covenant' found in the same Irish text, see especially G. L. Kittredge, *A Study of Gawain and the Green Knight* (Cambridge, Mass., 1916), pp. 10-76, and Loomis, *Arthurian Tradition* . . . , pp. 208, 282-4. In *M* Gauvain plays the

role of the Irish hero Cuchulainn. Kittredge fully discusses the French cognate versions in the *Livre de Caradoc*, *Perlesvaus* and *Hunbaut*.

508 'that had made his journey in vain'; i.e. the churl's appearance was so daunting as to destroy for anyone who saw him all hope of further progress, cf. l. 526.

510 *Saint Marcel*. There are two saints of this name: the pope, martyred in A.D. 309 and patron of grooms and horses, and the fifth-century Bishop of Paris who was reputed to have delivered that city from a dragon. Neither seems to have been regarded as of unusual stature.

513–6 Whereas Mario Roques emended *lo vilain* to *li vilains*, we think that the MS reading can be retained. We take the sense of l. 514 to be 'at the sight of the churl'. The transitive verb *resanble* has two direct objects, *mor* and *de ces vilains* = '(some of) those peasants', where *de* has a partitive sense (cf. *Yvain*, l. 153, and *Venj. Rag.*, l. 3728, quoted in Tobler-Lommatzsch II, 1208).

518 MS *aprestez*. This is almost certainly a scribal error, though Tobler-Lommatzsch quote *uns sains angles fu deseur vous aprestés* from *Aiol* and are prepared to allow the meaning 'appear'. This seems dubious, and J. Orr adversely criticised it in *Medium Ævum* V (1939), p. 78. Mario Roques corrected to *apressez* and Jenkins to *arestez*. We select *arestez* as going better with *devant Gauvain*.

523–4 *diz* : *hardi* do not rhyme.

541 This use of *re-* in *ra ostelee* is neat and economical. Having lodged Gauvain, the churl then turned to the mule and put it in its turn into comfortable quarters.

544 *li* = *les li*.

552 For this use of *et* introducing the main clause after a temporal clause see Foulet, *Petite syntaxe*, §421.

555 *por lui cochier*. Here *lui* is almost certainly a tonic reflexive pronoun in accordance with common O. Fr. usage. Nevertheless, the active use of *cochier* 'put to bed' cannot be entirely excluded, and in that case *lui* would not be reflexive.

556 If one wanted to keep the MS *aisier* as a trisyllabic *aïsier*, this might be supported as a variant of *aaisier* by the form *ahisier* listed in Godefroy, I, 8. We have preferred to correct to the normal form.

565 *partis*. For *partir* conjugated as an inchoative verb see M. K. Pope, §882 and Fouché, *Verbe*, pp. 23 ff.

[*un*]. The scribe has started to write the indefinite article in the form ·*i*·, but after writing the first point and the *i* he has continued with this letter as the initial of *ieu*.

570 *Di!* We take this to be the 2nd pers. sg. impve. meaning 'Speak out! Say on! [for I shall choose . . .]'. Grammatically it could also be the 1st pers. sg. ind. pr. meaning 'I say [that I shall choose . . .]'.

574–9 Though the churl's offer and Gauvain's acceptance of it seem to imply a choice of two alternatives (ll. 565, 567, 569, 571, 581), only one is set out here. It does not, however, seem necessary to postulate a lacuna in the text, in which the churl would have spelled out in full the other alternative, presumably to have the first stroke and Gauvain the second (see Mario Roques, pp. 146–7). Cf. Hunbaut's similar explanation to Gauvain of the *vilain*'s challenge (*Hunbaut*, ed. J. Stürzinger and H. Breuer, Dresden, 1914, ll. 1484–99):

> '. . . .i. ju parti
> Vos part, que bien vos sai aprendre,
> Mais il est mout sauvage au prendre.
> En l'un et en l'autre a meschief:
> Vos li poés trencier le cief
> De cele hace tot avant,
> Ja nus ne vos serra garant.
> Son col vos abandonne et livre
> Par covent que tot a delivre
> Le vostre li tendés aprés.
> Et il de vos se tenra pres.
> Et si tenra le hace as mains,
> Ne vos fera ne plus ne mains
> Que seulement ·i· cop sans plus.
> Li gius est partis, n'i a plus.
> Le quel que vos plaira, prendés . . .'

Paul Remy (in *Mélanges . . . Delbouille* II, 1964, pp. 557–60) considers that both *M* and *Hunbaut* present 'un faux jeu parti', and cites in support a similar instance in *Perlesvaus* (ed. W. A. Nitze & T. A. Jenkins, ll. 2883–90).

580 'I shall indeed be a fool'.

584 *renderai*. This is a northern dialectal form (see M. K. Pope, §972) with which contrast *rendrai* l. 533, *rendroie* l. 974, and *prendré* l. 571. If one wanted to eliminate it an extra syllable could easily be found, e.g. *Et lou matin je te rendrai*.

611 'I remind you of our agreement'. For the construction cf. *apeler de covant* in Tobler-Lommatzsch, I, 436.

615–6 We take *faire* to be a *verbum vicarium* for *contredire*, l. 612, or *conbatre*, l. 614, and translate: 'And indeed he ought to have gainsaid (or opposed) it, but he does not wish to perform a disloyal action'.

618 *li* = *le li*. 'He said that he would willingly keep his promise to him'.

621–4 The stretching of the neck seems to be a primitive feature (see Kittredge, op. cit., pp. 14, 72–3).

623 'Stretch out plenty of neck'.

629 *Qui*. The scribe has written a final, unpronounced -*l*. The sense is that the churl, 'who is doing it to frighten him', raises his axe on high.

637–8 Cf. ll. 871–2 and *Yvain*, ll. 4295–6:

'car einz que midis soit passez
avrai aillors a feire assez . . .'

649 There is a violent anacoluthon here; one must understand: '[and the same
fate would befall you] were it not for the fact that I shall be of service
to you!'

650 This is the first of a series of attempts by the churl to get Gauvain to eat
something. See note to l. 714.

652–5 ' " . . . so that your courage may not fail and so that you may no longer
be downhearted." "Eating would be utterly useless," said Gauvain. . . .'

655–6 *maniere* does not rhyme with *armeüre*. It looks as though the MS is
corrupt at this point and Hill corrects to *maniere nule*, which gives an
imperfect rhyme of the kind that our poet does not disdain. Cf. 681–2.

666 Jenkins suggested that the author may be punning on the name of the
saint, which he broke down into *pante* = 'fire-breathing monster' + *lion*.
St Pantaleon, martyred by decapitation in A.D. 305, was patron of medicine.
It is interesting to find his name connected with Troyes: a synagogue,
converted into a church not later than 1216, was dedicated to him; and
Pope Urban IV, born at Troyes ca. 1200, was baptised Pantaleon.

676 Cf. the shields taken by Gauvain when he left Arthur's court in *Le Conte
du Graal*. Four MSS mention seven shields, the others two (see A. Hilka's
variants to l. 4805).

678–741 Cf. Gauvain's fight with the lion released by a *vilain* in *Le Conte du
Graal*, ll. 7851–70. There too his shield is torn from his grasp by the beast.
Important analogies with Gauvain's various combats in this section of *M*
are to be found in Renaut de Beaujeu's *Le Bel Inconnu* (ed. G. P. Williams,
C.f.m.â., 1929) and in the Prose *Lancelot* (ed. H. O. Sommer, *The Vulgate
Version of the Arthurian Romances*, Vols. IV and V, Washington, 1911–12).
Le Bel Inconnu tells how Guinglain, at the Cité Gaste (Senaudon), fights
a knight and confronts a fire-breathing serpent. In the Prose *Lancelot* (Vol.
IV, pp. 345–6) Gauvain encounters a serpent in the Grail Castle and fights
with a knight; and later (Vol. V, pp. 298–300) Bohort fights a knight,
kills a lion, and confronts a serpent. It has been proposed that Chrétien's
main source for the *Conte du Graal* was a form of the Fair Unknown
legend (see D. D. R. Owen, *The Evolution of the Grail Legend*, Edinburgh
& London, 1968), and the author of *M* seems to show knowledge of both
(cf. his likely knowledge of *Yvain* as well as its source). For the relationship
of the Prose *Lancelot* to these texts see Owen, ibid., pp. 175–7.

699–703 The word order in these lines is remarkable. Had the subject of the
first sentence, *li lions*, appeared in the line immediately following *a si feru*,
this would have been a typical example of this author's use of bold
enjambement. However, with the intercalation of the relative clause in
l. 700, *li lions* appears to take on a grammatical relationship with *il* and
become the subject of *a tolu*, which *il* then anticipates. This construction
would then be identical with that of ll. 702–3, where *cil* anticipates *li*

vilains, the real subject of *a aparellié*. For a similar construction involving noun and pronoun see l. 826. Jenkins rejected such a use of *cil* (l. 702), which he replaced by *si*, thus producing a normal sentence with bold enjambement.

711 *coe*. Traditionally, since Aristotle, the lion was believed to have a claw hidden in the tuft of hair at the end of its tail, which would then be a formidable weapon. We therefore keep the MS reading, which Jenkins rejected in favour of an emendation to *poe*, 'paw'.

713 In the MS the line has one syllable too many. We adopt Mario Roques's suggested emendation *quart*, for *quatre*, and translate: 'so that there is nothing left of the fourth'.

714 *mes*. We take this to come from MISSUM; the rhyme with *mes*<MAGIS, correct in 12th-c. Francien (Pope §575), might be approximate here. We translate: 'Now you may wait too long for food', 'You may put off eating too long' (and become enfeebled, cf. l. 752, or even be killed by the lion and so never eat). The churl has already proposed a meal, which Gauvain has refused (ll. 650-5). He returns to the theme in l. 751, and again Gauvain refuses to eat. Only when all the tasks are accomplished does the hero sit down to his meal (ll. 905, 946-57).

Chrétien also sometimes shows a preoccupation with eating, e.g. in the Gauvain section of the *Conte du Graal*, ll. 8212-55 (13 references!). In the same text, shortly after his fight with the lion (see note to ll. 678-741), Gauvain refuses to eat on being invited by Clarissant (ll. 8049-59):

> . . . 'Sire, quant vos plera,
> Ma dame veoir vos venra.
> Mais li mengiers est atornez,
> Si mengerez, se vos volez,
> Ou cha aval ou la amont.'
> Et mesire Gavains respont:
> 'Bele, je n'ai de mengier cure
> Li miens cors ait male aventure,
> Quant je mengerai n'avrai joie
> Devant que teus noveles oie
> Dont je me puisse resjoïr . . .'

On being reassured, however, Gauvain consents to eat with the *dame* of the castle (ll. 8201 ff.).

726 *li* = *le li* and *le* stands for 'shield'.

736-7 Gauvain fears the loss of this shield because it is the seventh and last of those mentioned in l. 676. The first is disposed of at l. 700; the second, third and fourth at l. 712; the fifth at l. 726; the sixth at l. 733.

737 The unnecessary repetition of *que* is a stylistic blemish which is not unusual in Old French.

744 The scribe wrote *fet fet il* and barred out the first *fet*.

747 There are other trials to come and the churl says that Gauvain can escape none of them.

748-9 For the epic flavour of these lines cf. *La Chanson de Roland*. Roland will strike stout blows with Durendal:

> 'Sanglant en ert li branz entresqu'a l'or.'
>
> 'Tut en verrez le brant ensanglentet.'
>
> 'De Durendal verrez l'acer sanglent.'

> (Ed. J. Bédier, ll. 1056, 1067, 1079)

And later, Oliver acknowledges:

> 'Ja avez vos ambsdous les braz sanglanz!'

> (l. 1711)

758-9 This mysterious knight who lies wounded through the body is reminiscent of the Fisher King in *Le Conte du Graal*. But cf. also the knight who attacks Guinglain, Gauvain, and Bohort (see note to ll. 678-741). The use of the def. art. *li* (unless an error for *uns*) suggests a well-known figure, since this knight has not been mentioned before in the romance.

760-5 Again we are reminded of Perceval's visit to the Fisher King at the Grail Castle, with its element of predestiny (cf. l. 762 and the knight's knowledge of Gauvain's identity) and the hint that the hero's presence is connected with the knight's healing.

765-7 Cf. *Erec*, ll. 5429-31:

> '. . . bien voi qu'aler vos i estuet.
>
> Des qu'autrement estre ne puet,
>
> alons . . .'

Compare too Gauvain's rather grudging agreement to take the *vilain's* blow (*M*, ll. 612-14).

770-1 'I almost passed over what I must not omit' i.e. I nearly omitted a vital point in my narrative.

776 *por la pucele* i.e. on behalf of the damsel who was at Arthur's court.

780-1 'he would get no compensation (nothing in exchange) for it (sc. his journey) save having his head cut off'.

781 On this construction see A. Tobler, *Vermischte Beiträge I* (Paris, 1905), p. 19.

786 The facts of the situation are not immediately obvious. If the defending knight is defeated (i.e. the situation envisaged in ll. 784-5), the challenger's head would not go on a stake and there would be no need to put in a new stake. After a successful defence the empty stake would be crowned with the challenger's head (i.e. the situation envisaged in ll. 779-83), and then a new stake would have to be put in to await the next challenge. Logic would be maintained if, in the event of the defender's being defeated, his head were placed on the empty stake, and the successful challenger con-

tinued the custom by becoming the new defender. This, however, does not transpire in this text. A similar situation is fully and clearly explained in *Erec*, ll. 5730–64. See also note to ll. 433–7.

792 See note to l. 115.

794 = *Erec*, l. 862.

800 *faudre*. This does not rhyme with *autre* and both Jenkins and Orłowski correct to *fautre*, 'lance-rest'. A phrase commonly used in the description of fighting with lances is '*lance sor fautre*'; there exists also the adverbial phrase *sor fautre* 'swiftly, impetuously'. But there are other approximate rhymes in this text.

800 ff. Cf. Chrétien's account of the duel between Cligés and Gauvain:

> Si s'antrevienent d'un eslais
>
> .   .   .   .
>
> Les lances es escuz flatissent,
> Et li cop donent tel esfrois
> Que totes desques es camois
> Esclicent, et fandent, et froissent,
> Et li arçon derriers esloissent,
> Et ronpent ceingles et peitral;
> A terre vienent par igal,
> S'ont treites les espees nues . . .
>
> (*Cligés*, ll. 4875, 4878–85)

For ll. 800–802 cf. also *Lancelot*, ll. 2682–5:

> si s'antrevienent de randon,
> et des lances tex cos se donent
> que eles ploient et arçonent . . .

814 = *Lancelot*, l. 2686.

817–18 Cf. *Erec*, ll. 959–60.

823 As it stands the MS reading requires a hiatus *l'iaumë et*. The poet may well have used the form *le hiaume*, in which case there would have been no hiatus with final feminine *-e* of a polysyllable.

826 Jenkins would completely recast the words *Et lo vassal* into *Par lo nasal*. Orłowski corrected to *li vassal* and took these mixed forms as the subject of *serre*. We think some sense can be made of *lo vassal* as an accusative. The meaning of ll. 824–6 is so involved that we translate (replacing most of the pronouns by nouns) as follows: 'And Gauvain then dealt the knight such a stunning blow that the knight is bowed towards the ground; and Gauvain clutches him (this knight) to him'. For similar syntax see note to ll. 699–703.

836 'and now this redounds greatly to your credit', '. . . is a fine feather in your cap'.

839 The plural is curious and perhaps it does no more than provide a rhyme for the eye, but the poet is not always so concerned with this.

846–7 We take *il* to be the wounded knight and the subject of *s'est desarmez* to be Gauvain.

852 ff. For the fight with the serpents see note to ll. 678–741.

858 *vé*. For *vai*, first pers. sg. ind. pr. of *aler* see Fouché, *Verbe*, p. 425. Just as *ai* (Ch 327) and *avrai* (M 649) become *é* and *avré* in this scribe's spelling, so does *vai* become *vé*.

870 There is no line rhyming with l. 869 and the scribe has left a blank. On the assumption that the churl's reply to Gauvain began in l. 870 we print *Fet cil*, and not *Fet cil:* in l. 871.

871–2 See note to ll. 637–8.

885 The scribe wrote *escriṣture*, with the second *s* expuncted. Our reading *escriture* is therefore the MS reading.

   The line is a conventional reference to a real or supposed source (cf., e.g., *Conte du Graal*, l. 709).

895 If the *coi* = *armeüre* = defensive armour, the use of the preposition *de* is curious. The auxiliary *estre* can be considered correct, though there is only one example in Tobler-Lommatzsch, II, 584 (*Comment il sont as paiens conbatu*, from *Aymeri de Narbonne*), and this is classified under the reflexive verb and perhaps may be intended for *s'ont conbatu*. If the line as it stands is too suspect, one might conjecture that the scribe has miscopied an original *de coi il conrëez (covertuz?) estoit* 'with which he was equipped', 'which he was wearing'.

909 *eroit*. This is a dissimilated form of *iroit* due to the preceding *i* (cf. W. Roach, *The Continuations of the Old French 'Perceval'*, II, p. 602, quoted by Smith).

930 There is a general resemblance between the situation of Gauvain sitting on the bed with the lady of the castle after his trials are over and his being in the presence of the queens in the Château des Merveilles and sitting on the bed with Clarissant (*Conte du Graal*, ll. 8093 ff.). For other analogues see Owen, *The Evolution of the Grail Legend*, pp. 147–8.

931–8 Cf. the richness of the Lit de la Merveille in *Le Conte du Graal* (ll. 7692–7716), e.g.:

> Enmi le palais fu uns lis
> Ou n'avoit nule rien de fust,
> Qu'il n'i ot rien qui d'or ne fust
> Fors que les cordes solement
> Qui totes estoient d'argent.
>
> .   .   .   .   .
>
> Desor le lit ot estendue
> Une grant coute de samit;
> En chascun des pecols del lit
> Ot un escarbocle fermé . . .

(ll. 7692–6, 7700–3)

946–9 Compare the situation in *Le Bel Inconnu* where the Gaste Cité had been depopulated by the magicians, and after the spell was broken by Guinglain, he was attended in the castle with Blonde Esmeree by his squire, a dwarf and two other companions.

953 MS *fiet*, with *i* expuncted.

956–7 Cf. *Ch*, ll. 355–6.

959 Tables were commonly set up on trestles and removed after the meal (cf. *Conte du Graal*, ll. 3260–76).

961 *li* = *la li*.

962 ff. Gauvain's eagerness to depart, despite the offer of the castle and against the lady's wishes, is comparable with his situation in *Le Conte du Graal*, where he is reluctant to stay in the Château des Merveilles, of which he has earned the lordship, though the queens wish to detain him (see, e.g., ll. 8330–9).

964–5 'Then he asked the lady for the bridle.'

968–71 The lady, despite the implications of ll. 75–81, here seems to be on good terms with her sister. Analogies with the Château des Merveilles episode in the *Conte du Graal* and with the Fair Unknown stories suggest that in the original version of this part of *M* the lady may not have been a free agent.

999 'who was delighted to be on his way'.

1002 ff. With the release of the townsfolk and their joy at their liberation we may compare the people's joyful return to the Gaste Cité in *Le Bel Inconnu* (ll. 3456 ff.). Cf. also the rejoicing of the delivered captives in *Lancelot* (ll. 3902 ff.) and in *Yvain* (ll. 5774 ff.), and the townsfolk's reaction to Erec's 'Joie de la Cort' victory (*Erec*, ll. 6310 ff.).

1010 'there would not have been more merrymaking there'.

1018 *voi*[*t*]. We emend the MS to read *voit*, 3rd p. s.; it would be possible to keep *voi*, 1st p. s., only if this line were held to be direct speech, as R. T. Hill interpreted it.

1020–9 'They were hidden in the cellars on account of the ravages of the beasts you have slain, which made such a great noise when the inhabitants happened to come forth for some purpose or other that there was nothing for it but (at whatever cost) to unleash them, and they would go and tear them all to pieces in their fierce arrogance and frenzy.'

1030–3 Cf. *Luke* I.79: Christ's coming will 'illuminare his, qui in tenebris, et in umbra mortis sedent'; also *Isaiah* IX.2: 'Populus, qui ambulabat in tenebris, vidit lucem magnam.' For the apparently deliberate equation of Gauvain's feat with the Harrowing of Hell see D. D. R. Owen in *Forum for Modern Language Studies* VI (1970), p. 46, and in *The Vision of Hell*, p. 206.

1058–67 Cf. Erec's arrival with Enide at Caradigan (*Erec*, ll. 1501 ff.).

1069–70 The MS form, *venot*, of the imperfect will not do for an -*ir* verb, and the correction *venoit* must be made. However, as the text contains a number of approximate rhymes, it is not necessary to alter *ot* (<AUDIT) to *oit*, even though this is a well attested form, to produce a perfect rhyme.

1085 *l'* i.e. the bridle.

1088 MS *mor*ᶜ, with *t* added above line and with caret mark.

1094 *a espois*. Godefroy, III, p. 543, glosses a singular form *espoit*, with this example in support, as 'jaillissement'. Tobler-Lommatzsch, III, i, 1204, using Méon's (unreliable) version, conjecture *espois* (?) instead of Méon's *espus* at line 221 and *a[s] espois* here with the meaning 'spear', and assume this to be the name of the fountain, *La Fontaine as espois*. We reject these explanations since all the other references are accurate and precise ones to incidents earlier in the romance. In this case the reference is to l. 221, the *fontaine . . . avironnee entor . . . de flors, de pins et de genoivre*. We conjecture that *espois* means 'thicket' 'clump of trees', i.e. the pines and the juniper. Only one dictionary that we have consulted (R. Grandsaignes d'Hauterive, *Dictionnaire d'ancien français*, p. 259) appears to know this word and our suggestion is that it is a cognate of the common *espoisse*, related to it as *pré* is to *pree*, and meaning a smaller thicket than one denoted by *espoisse*. For us, the *fontaine a espois* is 'the fountain in its thicket', the use of the preposition *a* being similar to that in *a recet*, l. 360, where the wild beasts are 'in their lairs'.

1100 'vers faux, lisez: *et de la bataille au sarpent*' states Mario Roques categorically. But where is the line faulty? The meaning is unequivocal, and the construction as far as the incriminated *la b.* is concerned is the same as for *lo covenant* in the preceding line. We think that *do sarpent* is as good Old French as *au s.* or *ou s.* and that the MS reading can be retained.

1109 We assume the scribe, with his eye on an adjoining line, has introduced a superfluous *Et*. We adopt Orłowski's emendation.

1123 The dependence of *se . . . osasse* on *se demandasse* would be more easily apparent if lines 1123 and 1124 were interverted.

1126 The scribe wrote *sa mule demande on li amainne*, with one syllable too many. Orłowski corrected *demande* to *mande*; but this word can only be used of persons. Mario Roques corrected to *sa mule quiert*, an emendation involving more alteration of the text than we have made, basing ourselves on l. 72.

1127 *Si* or *S'i*? Because of the occurrence of *i monter* elsewhere, e.g. in lines 115 and 674, the latter deserves consideration. If accepted, it would provide the only instance in *M* of *se* for *si* 'and'. See Introduction, p. 22.

GLOSSARY

References are not exhaustive. Cross-references are not normally given for the simpler variations such as *en* : *an*. Most verbal forms are listed under the infinitive, and if this form actually occurs in one or both of the texts it is immediately followed by a line-reference; isolated forms, which might not be automatically looked up under their infinitive stem, are glossed just as they occur. Substantives are normally glossed under their oblique singular form, adjectives under their oblique singular masculine form, but again isolated forms are sometimes glossed and parsed separately. First and third person personal pronouns and paradigms of *cil*, *cist* and *qui* have been collected under the nominative forms; ample cross-references have been provided. An asterisk indicates an explanation or comment, or a translation of the phrase in which a word occurs, in the Notes. The Glossary is selective; words easily recognisable from Modern French have been omitted, but this principle has been applied with the maximum concern for beginners in Old French.

The following abbreviations are used:

a. active
acc. accusative
adj. adjective
adv. adverb
art. article
aux. auxiliary
comp. comparative
condit. conditional
conj. conjunction
dat. dative
def. definite
dem. demonstrative
exclam. exclamation
f. feminine
fut. future
gen. genitive
impers. impersonal
impf. imperfect
impve. imperative
ind., indic. indicative

indec. indeclinable
indef. indefinite
inf. infinitive
interj. interjection
interr. interrogative
l. line
m. masculine
n., neut. neuter
neg. negative, negation
nom. nominative
num. numeral
obj. object
obl. oblique
ord. ordinal
p., part. participle; particle
pers. person, personal
pl. plural
poss. possessive
pr., pres. present
prep. preposition

pret. preterite
pron. pronoun
q.v. *quod vide* (which see)
refl. reflexive
rel. relative
s., subst. substantive
sf. substantive feminine
sg. singular

sm. substantive masculine
subj. subjunctive
superl. superlative
s.v., sub voce (under the word)
v. verb, *verbum*
v. *vide* (see)
voc. vocative

a, *prep.* (possession) *Ch* 214, 1061; (instrument) *M* 443, 575, 683; (dative of advantage) *Ch* 1090, *M* 19; (indicating purpose, function) *Ch* 281; =**avec** *M* 7*, 543, 1011; *main a main* hand in hand *Ch* 428, *M* 912; *coste a coste* side by side *M* 952; *a or* (made) of gold *Ch* 38; *a toz jorz* for ever *Ch* 202; *ne a nul jor* never *Ch* 254; *a briés moz* briefly *Ch* 258, 275

aage, *sm.* life *Ch* 212

[a]aisier *M* 556; *ind. pr.* 6 **aessent** *M* 1051; *v.a.* make comfortable *M* 556; *v. refl.* be happy *M* 1051

abandoner, *v.a.* exert, apply *Ch* 1136; leave alone, unattended *M* 642

abatre, *v.a.* strike off *M* 815

abit, *sm.* den, lair *M* 159

aboivre; *ind. pr.* 3 of **abevrer,** *v.a.* water (give water to an animal) *M* 222

abrivé, *p.p. adj.; venir abrivez* come up at full speed *Ch* 1033, *M* 482

acheminer, *v. refl.* set out, to be on one's journey *Ch* 887 (v. also **re-**), *M* 424

achoison, *sf.* situation, eventuality *Ch* 611; reason, cause *Ch* 706 pretext *Ch* 718

acointier, *v.a.* inform *Ch* 343

acoler *M* 342, *v.a.* embrace *Ch* 520

aconplir *Ch* 1090, *v.a.* accomplish, do *Ch* 1090, 1094

aconter *Ch* 356, *v.a.* detail, specify *Ch* 356, 793; tell, relate *M* 888

acreanter, *v.a.* agree to *Ch* 977

adés, *adv.* always *M* 199; *tot a.* always, unceasingly *M* 200, 454; at once, immediately *M* 176, 1063

adeser, *v.a.* touch *Ch* 634*

adolé, *p.p. adj.* dejected, miserable *M* 322

adonc, *adv.* thereupon *Ch* 1016, *M* 622

adroit, *adj.* fine, elegant *Ch* 161

aessent; v. **[a]aisier**

afaitement, *sm.* social graces *Ch* 273

afere, *s.* fortune, rank, dignity *Ch* 739; errand *M* 843

afichier *M* 84, *v. refl.; s'a. de* pledge oneself, undertake *M* 84, 316

afubler, *v.a.* don, throw round the shoulders *Ch* 45

agu, *adj.* sharp, pointed *M* 434

ahi, *exclam. Ch* 160

ahurter, *v.n.* clash together *M* 203

aidier *Ch* 985; *subj. pr. 3* **aït** *Ch* 1079, *M* 303: *v.a.* help *Ch* 1079, *M* 303;
v. refl. acquit oneself (sexually), make love *Ch* 985; *se Dieus m'aït M* 303,
si m'aït Dieus (sainz Pantelions) so help me God (St P.) *M* 531, 534, 571, 627,
(St. P.) 666

ainz, *conj.* (adversative) but *Ch* 219*, 687, 1183, *M* 307, 695; rather *M* 772;
sooner, rather *M* 534; *adv.* before, before that *Ch* 432, *M* 748; (by confusion with **ainc**) never *Ch* 870; *qui a. a.* vying with each other to be first
Ch 787; *a l'a. que il pot* as swiftly as he could *Ch* 1132; **ainz** (. . .) **que,**
conj. before *M* 138, 501, 650; rather *M* 534

aïr, *sm.* violence *Ch* 1118; ferocity *M* 272

aire, *sf.* room *Ch* 456

aise, *adj.* pleased, satisfied *M* 346

ajornement, *sm.* day-break *Ch* 118

ajorner, *v. impers.* become day, dawn *Ch* 684, *M* 599

aler *Ch* 35, *M* 111; *ind. pr. 1* **vé** *M* 858*, *3* **va** *Ch* 153, *M* 54, **vait** *Ch* 782, **vet**
Ch 1150, *M* 66; *condit. 3* **eroit** *M* 909*; *subj. pr. 2* **ailles** *M* 563, **voises** *M*
651, *3* **aut** *Ch* 378, **aille** *Ch* 961, *M* 348, *5* **ailliez** *Ch* 1032; *v.n.* go;
conment qu'il aille come what may *M* 348; **s'en aler,** *v. refl.* go away *Ch*
153; *bien se va que . . . ne* is lucky not to, very nearly *M* 189; **aler** *inf. subst.*
going *M* 125*, 1055; *l'a. arriere* return *Ch* 841

aleüre, *sf.* pace, speed *Ch* 153, *M* 38

amasser, *v.* assemble *M* 24, 134

amedui; v. andeus

amener *M* 868; *pres. ind. 1* **amain** *Ch* 278, *3* **amainne** *M* 673, **amoinne** *M*
679: *v.a.* bring *Ch* 278, *M* 673

amer; *ind. pr. 1* **ain** *Ch* 1069, *3* **ainme** *Ch* 1: *v.a.* love, like, esteem *Ch* 1, 310,
M 1120; *a. par amor(s) Ch* 286, 316

ami, *sm.* lover *Ch* 592; **amie,** *sf.* beloved, mistress *Ch* 365, 924; **amis,** *sm. voc.*
(term of address) *Ch* 182

amont, *adv.* above *M* 33, 1062; up *M* 56, 879; over *Ch* 229; *prep.* up *M* 505

amor, *sf.* love *M* 91; *v.* also **amer**

anbleüre, *sf.* amble *Ch* 203*, *M* 126, 228

ançois, *adv.* rather, on the contrary *Ch* 290, *M* 191, 250; first, before that *M*
855; **ançois que, ançoiz que,** *conj.* before *M* 100, 343, 662, 896

andeus, *pron. pl.* both; *m. nom.* **andui** *M* 789, **amedui** *Ch* 464, *M* 698, 912,
930; *obl.* **andeus** *Ch* 692, *M* 890

angoissier *M* 108, *v.a.* importune, pester

angoissos, angoisseus, *adj.* anguished, in anguish *Ch* 678; distressed, forlorn
M 323

anor, *s.* honour *Ch* 5, 287, *M* 151, 275; *a a.* honourably, in honour *Ch* 588;
porter a. revere, honour *M* 275

anorer *M* 155, *v.a.* honour, do honour to *M* 68, 971

anui, *sm.* chagrin *Ch* 669; harm, vexation *Ch* 707, *M* 923; trouble, vexation *M*
457; *fere a. a* worry, vex *Ch* 637

anuier; *subj. pr. 3* **anuit** Ch 279, M 976: *v.a.* displease Ch 279, M 819

anuit, *adv.* this night M 574, 583; *a. mes* for the rest of this night Ch 672, M 561

anuitier, *v. impers.* grow dark, become night Ch 68

aorner, *v.a.* fill, infest M 1044

aparler M 941, *v.n.* speak

aparrellier M 657, *v.a.* supply M 702, 727; procure M 858; *v. refl.* get ready Ch 37; *s'a.* (*d'une armeüre*) arm, equip oneself M 657

apendre, *v.n.* pertain, belong M 201

aprester Ch 36, *v.a.* make ready M 796; *p.p.* made ready, prepared Ch 346; in readiness (summoned?) Ch 368

aprimier M 874, *v.n.* approach, draw near Ch 596, M 874

aprochié, *p.p.* of **aprochier,** near, close at hand M 293

araisoner; *pret. 3* **araisona** Ch 133: *v.a.* address Ch 133, 1064

arche, *sf.* archway M 497

ardoir, *v.n.* burn Ch 477; *v.a.* burn M 644

ardure, *sf.* heat, burning M 195★

aresner, *v.a.* attach by reins Ch 79

arestement, *sm.* stopping M 381

arester, *v.n.* stop, tarry M 592; *v. refl.*; *p.p.* **aresté** Ch 1020, **aresteü** Ch 1023 stop, halt

ariez; *v.* **arriere**

arme, *sf.* weapon M 119; *pl.* arms Ch 225★; armour Ch 942, M 671; deeds, feats of arms Ch 10; **unes armes** suit of armour Ch 940, M 866

armeüre, *sf.* suit of armour M 656

arriere Ch 65, **arrier(s)** Ch 604, 941, **ariez** M 3, *adv.* back; *metre a.* put aside M 3

as = a + les Ch 218, M 284

asalt, *sm.* attack Ch 656, M 430

asanbler, *v.* assemble Ch 262

aseoir M 540; *ind. pr. 6* **asïent** M 930, 946; *pret. 3* **assist** M 547, *6* **asistrent** Ch 349: *v.a.* settle in make comfortable M 540; place Ch 643; *v.n.* and *refl.* sit down Ch 349, 394, M 547, 930, 946; be situated M 199★

aserir M 537, *v. impers.* become evening, grow dusk

aseürez, *p.p. adj.* reassured M 209

assez, *adv.* fully Ch 114; very M 12; a great deal Ch 115, 440, M 257; many M 23

ataindre, *v.a.* catch up with Ch 1151

atalenter, *v.n.* please, suit M 1037

atant, *adv.* thereupon, straightway Ch 972, M 64

atenprer, *v.a.* tune Ch 799

atillier Ch 490, *v.a.* adorn

atorner Ch 139, *v.a.* attire Ch 46; adorn, deck out Ch 480, 843; get ready Ch 139; prepare Ch 241, 791; harness Ch 853, M 227; *v. refl.* dress, arm oneself M 600, 867

au =a+le *Ch* 4, 216

aubrisel, *sm.* small tree *Ch* 105

aucun *Ch* 76, *pron.* and *adj.* any *Ch* 76, *M* 1025

auques, *adv.* rather, quite, somewhat *Ch* 899, *M* 209, 244

aus; v. il

ausi, *adv.* thus, in the same way *M* 844

autre, *ord. num.* second *Ch* 226, 656.

autresi, *adv.* also, likewise *Ch* 679, *M* 226

autretel, *adj.* similar, same *M* 843

auvant, *sm. M* 478, 898 porch

aval, *adv.* down *Ch* 71, *M* 35

avant, *adv.* forward *Ch.* 2, *M* 96; onwards *Ch* 67, *M* 168

ave(c)ques, *prep.* with *Ch* 137, *M* 192; *adv.* with (them) *M* 1060

avenant, *adj.* fair, attractive, graceful *Ch* 630, 646, *M* 40

avenir *M* 463; *p.p.* **avenu** *Ch* 56; *ind. pr. 3* **avient** *M* 12; *pret. 3* **avint** *Ch 3*, *M* 20; *subj. pr. 3* **aviegne** *M* 582: *v.n.* befall, happen *Ch* 3, *M* 12, 413; be fitting, appropriate *M* 219; *comment qu'il aviegne* come what may *M* 582

aventure, *sf.* adventure, tale of adventure *Ch* 3, 27, 390, *M* 17; strange event *M* 62; *par a.* by chance *M* 239, 1024; *et tu aies (vos aiez) bone a.!* may it go well with you! *M* 522, 1077

avesprer *Ch* 62, *v. impers.* grow dark, late *Ch* 434; *il prenoit a a.* dusk was beginning to fall *Ch* 62

avironer, *v.n.* surround *M* 220

avison, *s.* vision *M* 399

avoier, *v.a.* direct, guide *Ch* 76

avoir *Ch* 784, *M* 317; *p.p.* **eü** *Ch* 1174; *ind. pr. 1* **ai** *Ch* 837, **é** *Ch* 327; *4* **avon** *Ch* 175, **avons** *Ch* 181; *pret. 1* **oi** *Ch* 1161, *3* **ot** *Ch* 41, *M* 23, *6* **orent** *Ch* 115; *fut. 1* **avré** *M* 649, *3* **avra** *Ch* 499, *5* **avrez** *Ch* 124, **avroi z** *Ch* 769; *subj. pr. 1* **aie** *Ch* 844, *5* **aiez** *M* 315; *subj. impf. 3* **eüst** *Ch* 201: *v.a.* and *aux.*; *v. impers.* (+*acc.*) there is, are etc. *Ch* 252, 285, 747, (with *i*) *Ch* 122, 492, *M* 23, (with *il* and *i*) *M* 119; *inf. subst.* riches, wealth *M* 279

bacin, *sm.* basin, bowl *M* 543, 944

baille, *sm.* bailey, court enclosed between two lines of fortifications *Ch* 210, 220

baillier, *v.a.* present *Ch* 276; give, hand over *Ch* 883, *M* 92

barbe, *sf.* beard; (in oath) *par ma b. M* 715

barge, *sf.* boat *M* 236

baron, *sm.* man of rank, noble (not necessarily a baron—*li baron* includes all the knights at the court) *M* 31, 1115

bataille, *sf.* fighting, fight *M* 638, 651

batre, *v.a.*; (*sentier*) *batu* beaten, well trodden *M* 162

bel *Ch* 207, **biau** *Ch* 230; *neut. Ch* 677, *M* 282; *sg. nom.* **biaus** *Ch* 194; *f.* **bele** *Ch* 283; *adj.* fair, beautiful *Ch* 194, 207, *M* 94; all right, well *Ch* 677;

estre bel a rejoice, be pleasing *M* 282, 474*, 999; *adv.* courteously, elegantly *Ch* 306; charmingly *Ch* 397; beautifully, splendidly *Ch* 480; aptly, fittingly *Ch* 719

belement, *adv.* gently, at your own pace *Ch* 146

beneïçon, *s.* blessing *M* 352

besoing, *sm.* urgent, pressing business *Ch* 876, *M* 49

biaus; v. **bel**

bien fere; v. **fere**

blecier, *v.a.* wound *Ch* 163, 601

bloi, *adj.* fair (of hair) *Ch* 303, 641

boche, *sf.* mouth *M* 854

bocle, *sf.* boss (of a shield) *Ch* 1119

boivre *Ch* 361, *v.a.* drink *Ch* 361, *M* 226

bon *Ch* 740, **buen** *Ch* 1102, *sm.* will, desire; *faire vos bons* carry out your wishes, do all you wish *Ch* 740; *(a)conplir ses bons* gratify her desires *Ch* 1094, 1102

bonement, *adv.* courteously *Ch* 292; cordially *Ch* 366

boscheron, *sm.* woodman, woodcutter *Ch* 77

boter, *v.a.* thrust *Ch* 1141

bozon, *sm.* quarrel, arrow (of cross-bow) *Ch* 1122 v. *giet*

braies, *sf. pl.* breeches *Ch* 41

branc; *nom.* **branz** *Ch* 730: *sm.* sword *Ch* 533, 562

brief, *adj.* short *Ch* 258, 275

brief, *sm.*; *en b.* in writing *Ch* 13

c' = **qu'** *conj.* that *Ch* 185

ça, *adv.* here *Ch* 134, 148, *M* 762; *entendez ça* give heed to me *Ch* 722

çaienz, çaiens, *adv.* in here *Ch* 543, *M* 83, 525

car, *conj.* for *Ch* 75, *M* 71; because *M* 229, (introducing *impve.*) *Ch* 87, 446

cave, *sf.* cellar *M* 498, 505, 595

ce; *nom.* **ce** *Ch* 19; *obl.* **ce** *Ch* 144, *M* 84, **cen** *Ch* 463, **ice** *M* 420, 562: *dem. pron. neut.* that, it; *por ce* for this reason, on that account *Ch* 16, *M* 4; therefore, and so *Ch* 26, *M* 10; *ce que* the fact that *M* 418

cel; v. **cil**

celer, *v.a.* hide, conceal *Ch* 582, 626

cen; v. **ce**

cercle, *sm.* circlet (part of helmet) *M* 823

cest, cestui; v. **cist**

chaenne, *sf.* chain *M* 683

chalemeler, *v.n.* play the reed-pipe *Ch* 800

chaloir *M* 876, *v. impers.*; *ne te c.* (*inf.* as *neg. impve.* 2) do not worry *M* 876

chalonge, *sf.*; *sanz c. et sanz contredit* without my (your) right being challenged or gainsaid *M* 89, 560

chalongier *Ch* 922, *v.a.* claim the possession of, contend for *Ch* 922

chanbre, *sf.* (private) apartment *Ch* 250 *M* 757

chanceler, *v.n.* slip, be deflected *Ch* 659

change, *sm.* exchange *Ch* 1103

char, *sf.* meat *Ch* 357, flesh *Ch* 649

charriere, *sf.* road, cart-track *Ch* 66, 1127

charroier *Ch* 551, *v.n.* steer a course

chastel; *nom.* **chastiaus** *M* 106; *sm.* castle, fortified town *Ch* 207, 772, *M* 38, 93; *rendre le c.* (metaphorical) *M* 106

chastoier *Ch* 504; *ind. pr. 1* **chasti** *Ch* 335: *v.a.* advise, instruct, warn

chauces, *sf. pl.* hose *Ch* 39

chaucier; *p.p. fem.* **chauciees** *Ch* 41; *pret. 3* **chauça** *Ch* 38: *v.a.* put on *Ch* 38

chaut, *sm.* heat *M* 195

cheoir, chair; *p.p.* **cheoit** *M* 422, **chaü** *M* 189; *ind. pr. 3* **chiet** *M* 741; *pret. 3* **chaï** *Ch* 1128: *v.n.* fall

chevalerie, *sf.* knightly deed, feat of arms *Ch* 934

chevestre, *sm.* halter *M* 43

chevous, *sm. pl.* hair *M* 299

chief, *sm.* head *Ch* 303, 641; end *Ch* 221; *a un c.* finally *Ch* 1206; *de c en c.* from beginning to end *Ch* 90, 1199; from head to foot *M* 671; *venir a c.* finish, complete *Ch* 14; perform a task thoroughly *M* 672; *traire a (bon) c.* achieve success, come through successfully *Ch* 323, 333, 667, 726; *au c. do tor* finally, in the end *Ch* 1178

chier, *adj.* valuable *M* 13; *avoir c. Ch* 193, 880, *tenir c. M* 5 value, appreciate

chiere, *sf.* face; *fere bele c.* make good cheer, eat well *Ch* 446, *M* 951; (*+ dat.*) act hospitably, make welcome *M* 951

chiés, *prep.* at the house of *Ch* 1061

chievre, *sf.* goat *M* 691

choisir *Ch* 765, *v.a.* see *Ch* 1043★, *M* 685; distinguish, choose *Ch* 763, 765

chose, *sf.* thing (referring to human being) *Ch* 1015

ci, *adv.* here *Ch* 121, 537, 591, *M* 1136

ciel, *sm.* sky, heaven; *soz c.* in the whole world, anywhere in the world *M* 833, 845, 873

cil, *dem. pron. and adj.;* *m. sg. nom.* **cil** *Ch* 1, 83, 800, *M* 536, 702★; *obl.* **cel** *Ch* 63, 178; **celui** (as *gen.*) *Ch* 1000; *pl. nom.* **cil** *Ch* 797, *M* 789; *f. sg. nom.* **cele** *Ch* 308, 515, 910, *M* 109; *obl.* **cele** *Ch* 74, *M* 136; *pl.* **celes** *M* 840

cist, *dem. pron. and adj.;* *m. sg. nom.* **cist** *Ch* 457, 803, **cest** *Ch* 715; *obl.* **cest** *Ch* 184, *M* 96, **ce** *Ch* 177, 779, *M* 213, 838; **cestui** (as *acc.*) *M* 737, 742; *pl. obl.* **ces** *M* 862; *f. sg. nom.* **ceste** *Ch* 102, 391★; *obl.* **ceste** *Ch* 498, *M* 85; *pl.* **ces** *M* 1068

cité, *sf.* city, town *Ch* 30, *M* 277. More or less synonymous with **ville** *Ch* 47. Both words are applied to the same town, Carlisle. See Foulet in Roach, pp. 43, 44

clamer, *v.n. ind. pr. 3* **clainme** *Ch* 1038: lay claim *Ch* 1038

clo, *sm.* nail, hook *M* 987

clos, *p.p.* of **clore** *v.a.* enclose *M* 431, 783

coart, *adj.* cowardly, craven *Ch* 7

coche, *sf.* couch, bed *M* 554

cochier *Ch* 467, **couchier,** *v.n.* and *refl.* go to bed *Ch* 471, 467, *M* 563, 597; *por lui c.* on which he may go to rest *M* 555*

coe, queue, *sf.* tail *M* 469, 711

coi; *v.* **qui** and **qoi**

col, *sm.* neck *Ch* 657, *M* 589, 623; shoulder *M* 511, 603

coluevre, *s.* snake, serpent *M* 182

con=**comme** *Ch* 421, 1054, *M* 22, 197; =**comment** *Ch* 1095, 1185

con-=**com-**

conbatre *M* 614, *v.n.* and *refl.* fight *Ch* 1204, *M* 855, 895*; oppose *M* 614; *c. a M* 640, 668, *c. avec M* 665, *c. o M* 688 fight with

conduit, *sm.* escort *M* 1129

confondre, *v.a.* confound (in oath) *M* 1122

congié, *sm.* permission, leave (to depart) *Ch* 841, 949, *M* 337; *querre c., demander c.* ask leave to depart *Ch* 835, *M* 1114; *doner c.* grant leave to depart *Ch* 849; *prendre c.* obtain permission *Ch* 949; take leave *M* 992, 1132

conmander; *ind. pr. 1* **conmant** *Ch* 197, 290: *v.a.* and *refl.* commend *Ch* 197, *M* 354, 410; bid, order *Ch* 290, 1031, *M* 109, 993

conment que, *conj.* however; *c. qu'il aille M* 348, *c. qu'il aviegne M* 582 come what may

conoissance, *sf.* recognition *M* 147, 369

conoistre; *pret. 1* **conui** *M* 929: *v.a. M* 366 know

conpaignie, *sf.* company *M* 1006, 1061; *porter c.* keep company *Ch* 100, 283

conpler, *v.a.* accomplish, do *Ch* 1102

conquerre *Ch* 935, 945, *v.a.* win, gain *Ch* 935, *M* 818; vanquish, overcome *M* 835, 1098

conrëer, *v.a.* deal with, put into a sorry state *M* 890

consel, *sm.* advice *M* 750

consellier, *v.a.* help *M* 728; *v.n.* discuss, debate *M* 46; advise *M* 250; *v. refl.* reflect *M* 446

conseü, *p.p.* of **consivre,** *v.a.* catch, strike *M* 468

contenance, *sf.* appearance, visage *M* 521

contenir, *v. refl.* behave, act *Ch* 623

conter *Ch* 20; *p.p.* **conté** *Ch* 89; *ind. pr. 1* **cont** *Ch* 8, *3* **conte** *Ch* 23; *pret. 1* **conté** *Ch* 613; *impve. 5* **contez** *Ch* 714: *v.n.* tell *Ch* 8, *M* 957

contre, *prep.* against *M* 834; *venir c.* come towards *Ch* 891; *aler c.* go towards *M* 920, 1049

contredire *Ch* 239, *v.* oppose, gainsay, (+ *acc.*) *Ch* 185, 239, 469*, *M* 612, 767, (+ *dat.*) *Ch* 404

contredit, *sm.* objection, opposition *Ch* 1013, *M* 579; *sanz c.* without dispute *Ch* 1010, *M* 907; *v.* also **chalonge**

convant, covent, *sm.* condition, agreement M 576, 611*, 617; *metre en c.* promise, agree M 979; *avoir c.* (+*dat.*) have an agreement with M 617

convenant, covenent, *sm.* bargain, compact M 1099; *avoir en c.* pledge, solemnly promise M 315

convenir, covenir, *v. impers.* be necessary M 176, 1027*, (with *acc.* of person +*inf.*) Ch 551, 756, (with *dat.* of person+*inf.*) M 444; befit M 557

convoier M 1128, *v.a.* take along M 127; accompany, escort M 1049, 1128; *inf. subst.* escort, company M 116

cop, *sm.* blow Ch 1134, M 592, 699; *au premerain c.* immediately, instantly, Ch 616

cope, *sf.* cup, goblet Ch 354

corage, *sm.* feelings Ch 307

coree, *sf.* entrails, vitals M 718

corgiee, *sf.* whip M 443

correcier, *v. refl.* be miserable, distressed Ch 1180; *inf. subst.* rage M 708

corroie, *sf.* leather strap M 806

cors, *sm.* body Ch 84, 511, M 266, 759; person, self Ch 193, 260, M 1084

cort, *sf.* court Ch 21, M 19; *tenir c.* hold court M 21

cortois, *adj.* courtly Ch 136, 382; *estre c.* act in a courtly fashion Ch 938

cortoisement, *adv.* in courtly fashion Ch 37, 300

cortoisie, *sf.* courtliness, pleasing manners Ch 261; courtly action Ch 933

coste, *sf.*; *c. a c.* side by side M 952

coster, *v. impers.* pain, grieve Ch 449

costume, *sf.* custom Ch 135, M 774

cous; v. **cop**

coute, *sf.* bedspread Ch 481, 662

coutel, *m.pl.* **coutiaus,** knife Ch 352

covenent; v. **convenant**

covenir; v. **convenir**

covent; v. **convant**

covertor, *sm.* coverlet Ch 602

coverture, *sf.* deceit, covering up Ch 1167

covrement, *sm.* deceit, covering up Ch 1166

covrir Ch 719, *v. refl.* shield Ch 719

creant, *sm.* permission, consent Ch 1070

creanter, Ch 318; *p.p.* **creanté** Ch 102 **cranté** Ch 331*; *ind. pr. 1* **creant** Ch 767, M 122; *subj. impf. 3* **creantast** Ch 318: *v.a.* grant Ch 102, 767; consent Ch 318; promise, pledge M 333, 568, 633

criembre; *ind. pr. 3* **crient** Ch 467; *subj. impf. 3* **cremist** Ch 431: *v.a.* fear Ch 431

croire Ch 191, M 750; *ind. impf. 3* **creoit** Ch 969: *v.n.* believe Ch 191; *v.a.* believe in, trust Ch 969, M 750

crote, *sf.* cellars, undercrofts M 1021

crüel, *nom.* **crüeus,** *adj.* daunting, grim M 172, 395

cuer, *sm.* heart, *Ch* 325; courage *M* 652; (metaphorical) *c. d'iver M* 197; *de bon c.* willingly *M* 310

cui; v. **qui**

cuir, *sm.* skin *Ch* 600

cure, *sf.*; *n'avoir c. de* have no desire for *Ch* 779, *M* 116; have no desire to *M* 112

dahez, *sm.* (lit.) God's hatred; *(mal) dahez ait* a curse on, God damn *M* 251, 586

dame, *sf.* lady (of noble birth) *Ch* 789, *M* 148 (see Foulet in Roach); mistress *M* 487

damoisele, *sf.* damsel, girl (of noble birth *Ch* 253*, 270, *M* 18, 27; lady *M* 953

de, *prep.* concerning *Ch* 8, *M* 185; as regards *M* 654; for, in the matter of *Ch* 10; (after comparative) than *M* 352, 929

deable, *sm.* devil *M* 398, 400; **diable,** monster (from hell, referring to the dragons) *M* 869

debatre, *v. refl.* lash *M* 687; **debatu,** *p.p. adj.* fatigued, tired out *M* 267

debonaire, *adj.* honourable, worthy *Ch* 938

debrisié, *p.p.* worn out, exhausted *M* 267

deci, desci, desi; d. a *Ch* 80, 204, 682; **d. q'a** *Ch* 218, *prep.* up to, as far as; **des ici en avant,** *adv.* henceforth *Ch* 410; **de si que,** *conj.* (+*subj.*) until *Ch* 413, 1026

declin; v. **torner**

decoupé, *p.p. adj.* cut-away *Ch* 39. (See M. G. Houston, *Medieval Costume in England and France*, London, 1939, p. 55.)

dedenz, *prep.* and *adv.* in, inside *Ch* 392, *M* 181; into *Ch* 473, *M* 595; *d. les arçons* into the saddle *M* 351

dedesor, *adv.*; *par d.* over, on top of *M* 415*

deduire *Ch* 281, **desduire** *Ch* 35; *impve.* 5 **deduisiez** *Ch* 244: *v.n.* and *refl.* enjoy oneself, seek pleasure

deduit, *sm.* pleasure *Ch* 1, 280, *M* 1075; rejoicing *Ch* 788, 809; *en d.* for pleasure, recreation *Ch* 91; *par d.* for your pleasure *Ch* 437

degré, *sm.* stairs, staircase *M* 505

deguerpir, *v.a.* leave, abandon *Ch* 1190

delez, *prep.* beside *Ch* 107, *M* 558, 952; *trestot d.* close beside *M* 952

delivre, *adj.* hale, in good health *Ch* 702

delivrement, *adv.* instantly, without more ado *Ch* 715, 813, *M* 669, 980

demaintenant, *adv.* immediately, straightway *Ch* 82, 302, 815

demander, *v.n. Ch* 441

demanois, *adv.* immediately *Ch* 381, 473

demener, *M* 443; *ind. pr.* 3 **demoin(n)e** *M* 301, 989: *v.a.* give vent to, manifest *M* 301, 989, 1023*; *d. a la corgiee* whip *M* 443

demoree, *sf.*; *fere d.* delay longer *Ch* 348

demorer *Ch* 215, *M* 112, *v.n.* and *refl.* stay, linger, tarry *Ch* 57, 99, 215, *M* 112, 156

departir, *v. refl.* depart M 1132

depecier M 1028, *v.a.* tear to pieces

deport, *sm.* delay, (enforced) renunciation Ch 669

deporter Ch 35, *v.n.* and *refl.* amuse oneself, spend time enjoyably Ch 35, 281, M 1011

derechief, *adv.* again Ch 170

deronpre, *v.a.* and *n.* break, shatter M 732, 805

derriere, *adv.* behind M 804; *par derriers* from behind M 469

des, *prep.* from, since M 187; **des que,** *conj.* as soon as M 599; since, seeing that M 766

descovert, *adj.*; **a d.** *adv.* plainly, clearly Ch 711

descovrir Ch 317, *v.a.* (used absolutely) disclose, reveal one's feelings Ch 317

desdire; *subj. pr. 3* **desdie** Ch 291: *v.a.* oppose Ch 291; contradict Ch 1107; **se desdire de,** *v. refl.* go back on (one's word) Ch 1075

desduire; v. **deduire**

desduit; v. **deduit**

desfendre, *v.a.* oppose, gainsay M 110

desforeter, *v.n.* get out of, come out of the forest M 167

deshaitié, *p.p. adj.* distressed M 308

desi, desci, des ici; v. **deci**

desneue, *ind. pr. 3* of desnouer, *v.a.* break off M 470

desor, *prep.* on M 125, 588; above M 1012; **par d.,** *adv.* over M 242

desoz, par desoz, *prep.* beneath, under Ch 939, M 478, 898

destre, *adj.* right Ch 264

destroit, *sm.*; *sanz d.* without difficulty, easily M 1112

desus, *prep.* on Ch 351

desvoier; *pret. 3* **desvoia** Ch 58: *v. refl.* go astray Ch 58

desvoloir, *v.a.* not to wish, dissent from Ch 284

detiegne, *subj. pr. 3* of **detenir,** *v.a.* keep back, detain M 52

detirer, *v.a.* pull, tug M 299

detrenchier Ch 468, *v.a.* cut to pieces M 891

detrïer, *v.n.* hold back, delay M 820

deus, *num. adj.* two Ch 122, M 150

devant, *adv.* (time) before Ch 816, M 193; (place) in front, ahead M 692; *aler au d.* go to meet Ch 874; *venir d.* (+ *dat.*) come up to M 897

deviner, *v.a.* make a conjecture, surmise Ch 536

devise, *sf.* agreement M 904; persuasion M 144; *a d.* freely, as one wills M 1083; *par d.* designedly, deliberately M 4; *par d. que* on the understanding that M 904; *faire d.* make mention, tell M 956

deviser Ch 216, *v.a.* describe Ch 216, 927; *v.n.* discuss Ch 395

devoir; *ind. pr. 1* **doi** Ch 16; *pret 1* **dui** M 770★; *subj. impf. 3* **deüst** M 297: *modal v.* must, have to Ch 16, M 771; may be likely to, be the one to M 297, 317; almost, all but do something M 770★; signify, mean Ch 863

di, *sm.*; *toz dis* always Ch 573

diaus; v. **duel**

dire *Ch* 188; *ind. pr. 1* **di** *Ch* 336, *M* 397, *2* **diz** *M* 523, *3* **dit** *Ch* 151, *M* 97, dist *Ch* 184★, *M* 304, *6* **dïent** *Ch* 417, *M* 47; *pret. 3* **dist** *Ch* 113; *condit. 1* **diroie** *Ch* 822, *M* 205; *impve. 2* **di** *M* 570★; *subj. pr. 1* **die** *Ch* 17, *3* **die** *Ch* 338, *M* 124, *6* **dïent** *Ch* 172; *subj. impf. 1* **deïsse** *Ch* 609, *M* 396, *3* **deïst** *M* 507; *v.a.* say, tell *Ch* 87; tell of *M* 869; (used absolutely) speak out, have one's say *Ch* 17

dis, *num. adj.* ten *M* 277, 645

disner *Ch* 296, *v.n.* dine

disner, *sm.* meal, principal meal of the day *Ch* 241

do *Ch* 221, 565, *M* 474★, **dou** *Ch* 20 = **de**+**le**

doblier, *sm.* tablecloth *Ch* 351

dogié *Ch* 642, **dougié** *Ch* 42, *adj.* fine, delicate *Ch* 42, 642

doie, *s.pl.* fingers' breadths *Ch* 661

dolant, **doillant**, *adj.* grieved, sad, afflicted *Ch* 668, 698★, *M* 266; anxious, troubled *M* 475

doler, *v.a.* hack at *M* 814

dom; v. **don**

domache; v. **domage**

domage, **domache**, *sm.* loss, wrong *Ch* 195, 572, *M* 923; pity *M* 626

don, *sm.* gift *M* 305; *vos fais un d.* I give you this assurance, I grant you *Ch* 288

don, *adv.* whence *Ch* 87

don, **dont**, **dom**, *pron. rel.* of, with which *Ch* 256, *M* 975; of whom *M* 28, 863; from which *Ch* 323, 1106; with which *Ch* 719, *M* 657; on account of which, wherefore *Ch* 1083, *M* 81; *adv.* whence *Ch* 544, 715

doner; *ind. pr. 1* **doin** *Ch* 672, **doins** *Ch* 770, *3* **done** *Ch* 566, *M* 544; *impve. 5* **donez** *M* 305; *subj. pr. 3* **doint** *Ch* 85, *M* 1075: *v.a.* give *Ch* 85; strike *Ch* 566

dongier, *sm.*; *sanz d.* without restraint, without restriction, without hindrance *Ch* 819; without hesitation *Ch* 1083

dor, *sm.* (small linear measure) palm's breadth *M* 404; small quantity *d. de sel* pinch of salt *Ch* 996★

doter *Ch* 414, *v.a.* fear *Ch* 299, 412; suspect *Ch* 578

dras, *sm. pl.* sheets *Ch* 481, 603; *d. de soie* silken hangings *Ch* 484

drecier *M* 834, *v.a.* put up, erect *M* 546; *v. refl.* stand up *M* 834

droit, *sm.* right *Ch* 162, *M* 344, 1082; *a d.* rightly *Ch* 762; *par d.* rightly, fittingly *Ch* 439; *prendre lo d.* wreak justice *Ch* 552★

droit, *adj.* right, correct *M* 260

droit, **droitement**, *adv.* straight, directly *Ch* 1058, *M* 262, 915

droiture, *sf.*; *a d.* on the direct route *Ch* 154; as was right, fitting *Ch* 780

drue, *sf.* lady-love, beloved *Ch* 847, 957; mistress *Ch* 991

duel; *nom.* **diaus** *M* 626: *sm.* grief *M* 301, 722

durement, *adv.* much, greatly *Ch* 539, *M* 45; loudly *Ch* 687; sharply *Ch* 905; vigorously, hard *Ch* 1125

efforcier; *pret. 3* **efforça** *Ch* 360; *subj. impf. 3* **efforçast** *Ch* 363; *v.a.* urge *Ch* 360

effrois, *sm.* noise, tumult *M* 1023*

el, *pers. pron. f.* = **ele** *Ch* 284, 286, *M* 70

el, *pron. neut.* something else *Ch* 425; anything else *Ch* 593*; else, other *M* 396; *de ce et d'e.* of this and that *Ch* 425

el = **en** + **le** *Ch* 158

en, em *M* 809, *prep.*; *en un este* one summer *Ch* 29; *pron.* (referring to a previous clause) as a result *Ch* 95; in this matter *Ch* 288

en = **on** *Ch* 18, *M* 10

enbatre, *v.a.* thrust *M* 718; *v. refl.* plunge *M* 161, 268

enbracié, *p.p.* of **enbracier,** on the arm (with the arm thrust through the straps of the shield) *M* 810

enbrunchier, *v.a.* bow down, strike down *M* 825

enchaener, *v.a.* chain up *M* 641

enchaucier, *v.a.* press hard on *M* 730

encliner, *v.n.* bow *M* 340

enclore; *p.p.* **enclos:** *v.a.* shut up *Ch* 392

enconbrier, *sm.* hindrance *M* 995, 1112

encontre, *prep.*; with verb of motion, *acourir, aler, saillir, venir,* run etc. to meet, to welcome *Ch* 222, 427, *M* 270; *adv.* to meet her/him *M* 66, 1073

encontre, *sm.*; *a l'e.* (with verb of motion) to meet *M* 140, 364, 1066; (in formula of greeting or welcome) *bon e.* good fortune *M* 1074

encortiner, *v.a.* hang, adorn with tapestries *Ch* 476

endemain, *sm.* next day *M* 599

endementres, *adv.* at the same time *Ch* 376

endroit, *prep.* as for *Ch* 288; for, as regards *Ch* 677; opposite, in front of *M* 462

enesloupas, *adv.* immediately, forthwith *Ch* 294, 1065

enforesté, *p.p. adj.* in a forest *M* 130

engin, *sm.* device, ruse *Ch* 402

engresser, *v. refl.* become enraged *M* 722

enluminer, *v.a.* give light to, illumine *M* 1032

enmi, *prep.* in the middle of *Ch* 1042, *M* 216, 384

enorance, *sf.* respect, honour, *M* 148

enorter, *v.a.* urge, exhort *M* 452

enploier, *v.a.* match *Ch* 461*

enprendre *M* 85, *v.a.* undertake *Ch* 620, *M* 143, 968; *enpris de feu* set on fire *M* 882

enquerre *Ch* 901; *p.p.* **enquis** *Ch* 108: *v.a.* ask, enquire *Ch* 108; examine *M* 500

ensaignier, *v.a.* point out, show *Ch* 205, *M* 61; **ensaignié** *p.p. adj.* well-bred, polished *Ch* 9

ensement, *adv.* likewise *Ch* 851

ensi, *adv.* thus *Ch* 1075, *M* 77; **e. con** *conj.* just as, exactly as *M* 261

entendre *Ch* 319, *v.a.* and *v.n.* pay heed (to), listen (to) *Ch* 2, 52, 134; understand *Ch* 309, *M* 407

entier, *adj.* entire, complete, perfect *M* 861, 866

entochier, *v.a.* befoul, poison *M* 892

entor, *prep.* about, around *Ch* 262, 478; *adv.* around *Ch* 232, *M* 220

entre, *prep.* between *Ch* 907; amongst *M* 45; *entre ... et* both ... and *Ch* 498, 781

entreconbatre, *v. refl.* fight *M* 816

entrecor, *sm.* swordknot *Ch* 534

entredoner, *v. refl.* exchange *M* 801

entreferir, *v. refl.* smite each other *M* 698

entremetre, *v. refl.* busy oneself *M* 538

entreprendre, *v.a.* surprise, catch out *Ch* 553*, 555; **entrepris** *p.p. adj.* worried *Ch* 298

entrer, *inf. subst.* entering, going in *M* 1017

entrevenir, *v. refl.* come together, rush at each other *M* 800

envenimé, *p.p. adj.* poisoned; *valee ... envenimee* valley infested with poisonous reptiles *M* 380

enviz.; a e., *adv.* unwillingly, regretfully *Ch* 867

envoisier, *v. refl.* make merry, enjoy oneself *Ch* 450

enz, intensifying *en*, *enz o chief de* on the very edge of *Ch* 1021, *enz en cest lit* here in this very bed *M* 559

erranment, *adv.* immediately, at once *Ch* 385, 688, *M* 670

errant, *adv.* swiftly, apace *Ch* 898; straightway *M* 114

errer *Ch* 386; *p.p.* **erré** *Ch* 109; *pret. 3* **erra** *Ch* 204: *v.n.* travel, journey *Ch* 109, 130, 204, leave, depart *Ch* 386

es=**en**+**les** *Ch* 84, *M* 740, 1021

esbahir; esbaïr, *v. refl.* be overwhelmed, dumbstruck *Ch* 268, 272; **esbahi** *p.p. adj.* amazed, taken aback, dumbfounded *Ch* 164, 607; stupid *Ch* 1158

esbanoier *M* 32, 1059, *v.n.* amuse oneself, pass time in relaxation

eschange, *sm.* exchange compensation *M* 780*

eschés, *sm. pl.* chess *Ch* 805

eschif, *adj.* ill-natured *Ch* 699

eschine, *sf.* back, spine *M* 705

esciënt; a e. *adv.* of a surety *Ch* 970

escondire *Ch* 313, *v.a.* refuse, reject; *inf. subst.* rejection *Ch* 324

escremir, *inf. subst.* fighting, sword-play *M* 689

escriture, *sf.* writing, written source *M* 885

escüele, *sf.* dish, platter *M* 954

esgarder *Ch* 70, *v.a.* gaze on *Ch* 266; look at, examine *Ch* 978; consider, look out for *M* 460; *v.n.* look *Ch* 526; look intently *Ch* 70

esgarer, *v.n.* get lost *Ch* 92

esgart, *sm.* decision, device *Ch* 962

eslessier, *v. refl.* rush, charge *Ch* 1116; *vers terre s'e.* dismount rapidly *M* 496

eslire *Ch* 759, *v.a.* choose

esloissier, *v.n.* shatter *M* 803

esmaier *M* 629, *v.a.* frighten, terrify *M* 629; *v. refl.* be afraid *M* 532

esmeü, *p.p.* of **esmovoir,** *v. refl.* move (away) *M* 319

esperdu, *p.p. adj.* dismayed, troubled *Ch* 605, *M* 234, 609, 675

esperir, *v. refl.* wake up *Ch* 118

esploit, *sm.; faire e. de* succeed in, find a way to *M* 246

esploitier, *v.n.* make an effort *M* 206

espoënté, *p.p. adj.* terrified *M* 180

espois, *sm.* thicket, clump of trees *M* 1094★

esposer, *v.a.* unite, (?) marry *Ch* 818★

essaier, *v. refl.* strive *M* 811

essoigne, *s.* hindrance, pretext *M* 52

essuier *M* 945, *v.n.* wipe, dry oneself

estancele, *sf.* spark *M* 813

esté, *s.* summer, summer heat *M* 194★

ester *Ch* 406; *impf. 3* **estoit** *Ch* 30; *pret. 3* **esta** *M* 1001; *impve. 5* **estez** *Ch* 1030: *v.n.* and *refl.* be, stay *Ch* 30, 406; stay, stop *Ch* 1030, *M* 1001

estes vos, *interj.* behold! *Ch* 344, *M* 130, 167

estoner, *v.a.* stun *Ch* 1135, *M* 824

estor, *sm.* fight, combat *Ch* 1050; *rendre e.* fight, engage in combat *M* 530

estordre, *v.n.* escape *Ch* 546★, 558

estovoir; ** *ind. pr. 3* **estuet *Ch* 383, *M* 177; *pret. 3* **estut** *Ch* 517; *fut. 3* **estouvra** *Ch* 740; *v.n.* and *impers.* be necessary

estraier *Ch* 1150, *v.n.* stray

estrange, *sm.* stranger *Ch* 1100; *adj.* strange *M* 98

estre *Ch* 384; *ind. pr. 1* **sui** *Ch* 453, *2* **iés** *M* 525, **es** *M* 486, *5* **estes** *Ch* 877, **iestes** *Ch* 194; *impf. 3* **ert** *Ch* 9, **estoit** *Ch* 56, *5* **estïez** *Ch* 574, *6* **estoient** *Ch* 478, **erent** *M* 29; *pret. 1* **fui** *Ch* 1158, *2* **fus** *Ch* 160, *3* **fu** *Ch* 10; *fut. 1* **iere** *Ch* 289, **serai** *Ch* 1025, **seré** *Ch* 1107, *3* **iert** *Ch* 195, *5* **seroiz** *M* 308; *condit. 1* **seroie** *Ch* 506, *5* **serïez** *Ch* 341; *impve. 2* **soiez** *M* 760, *5* **soiez** *Ch* 245; *subj. pr. 1* **soie** *Ch* 839, *2* **soies** *M* 653 *3* **soit** *Ch* 180, *5* **soiez** *Ch* 343; *subj. impf. 3* **fust** *Ch* 101, *5* **fussiez** *Ch* 163: *v.n.* and *aux.*

estre, *sm.* place, situation *M* 188; nature *M* 448★, 503

estres, *sm. pl.* upper rooms (rooms on an upper floor; see Foulet in Roach) *M* 33

estroitement, *adv.* roughly, harshly *Ch* 925

estros, estrous; *a e.* certainly, without fail *M* 312; with a will *M* 717

estuet, estut; v. **estovoir**

esvellier, *v.n.* wake up *Ch* 120

et, *conj.* (emphatic) yet, still *Ch* 756; well then! *M* 313

eve, *sf.* water *Ch* 347, *M* 216; river *M* 233, 391; piece of water (moat) *M* 432

ez vos, *interj.* behold! *M* 504, 601

fable, *sf.* fiction, fable *Ch* 803; lie *M* 397

faé, *p.p. adj.* enchanted *Ch* 568

faille, *sf.*; *sanz f.* for certain *M* 347

faillir; *ind. pr. 3* **faut** *M* 412; *impf. 3* **failloit** *Ch* 894; *fut. 1* **faudrai** *Ch* 1079: *v.n.* be lacking *Ch* 894, 1164, *M* 436; fail, let down *Ch* 1079, *M* 652; give way *M* 412

fain, *sm.* hay *Ch* 237

faint, *p.p. adj.* deceitful *Ch* 1186

faudre=**faillir, falloir;** *sanz f.* irrevocably *M* 800

fauser, *v.n.* act perfidiously *Ch* 112

felon; *nom. sg.* **fel** *Ch* 699; *sm.* and *adj.* wicked *Ch* 699, 1048; grim, terrible *M* 509, 852

fere *Ch* 139, **faire** *Ch* 319; *p.p.* **fet** *M* 326; *ind. pr. 1* **faz** *M* 956, **fais** *Ch* 288, *3* **fait** *Ch* 86, **fet** *Ch* 83, *6* **font** *Ch* 693; *pret. 3* **fist** *Ch* 36, *5* **feïstes** *Ch* 1041, *6* **firent** *Ch* 1196; *fut. 5* **ferez** *Ch* 933; *condit. 1* **feroie** *Ch* 856, *3* **feroit** *Ch* 1054; *subj. pr. 3* **face** *Ch* 468; *subj. impf. 3* **feïst** *Ch* 321, *5* **feïssiez** *Ch* 706; *impve. 5* **fetes** *Ch* 446, **faites** *Ch* 773; *v.a.* make, do, say *Ch* 83, *M* 50; *v. refl.* say *M* 303, 339; *modal v.* (+*inf.*) cause (to do or to be done) *Ch* 36, *M* 341; *v. vicarium Ch* 420, 1054, 1109, *M* 615*, 844; *faire que vilainne* act in an uncourtly fashion *Ch* 321; *le f. a* make love to *Ch* 561; *ne f. mie a* (+*inf.*) not to be necessary to *Ch* 914; *bien f.* act bravely, valiantly *M* 453; *que il font* how they are *Ch* 693

ferir *M* 625; *p.p.* **feru** *Ch* 1123; *ind. pr. 3* **fiert** *Ch* 562; *pret. 3* **feri** *Ch* 1118; *impve. 2* **fier** *M* 625: *v.a.* strike *Ch* 562, 599, *M* 411, 625; drive in *M* 786; *v. refl.* dart, shoot *Ch* 604, *M* 467

fermer, *v.a.* fortify *Ch* 208

ferrant, *adj.* iron-grey *Ch* 178

ferré, *p.p. adj.* surfaced with stone, metalled *Ch* 129

fes, *sm.* weight, strain *M* 807

fet; *pl.* **fez** *Ch* 23, *sm.* deed

fichier *M* 782, *v.a.* put, place, fix *M* 782, 838, 839; *v. refl.* thrust itself *Ch* 664

fier, *adj.* brave, spirited *M* 873; ferocious *M* 646, 852, 878

fierement, *adv.* haughtily *M* 901

figure, *sf.* form, aspect *M* 521

finer, *v.a.* and *n.* finish, come to an end *Ch* 1206, *M* 264, 742, 1136

flaüster, *v.n.* play the flute *Ch* 800

flun, *sm.* river *M* 398

foiz, *sf.* time *Ch* 785, *M* 164; *a ceste f.* on this occasion *M* 329, 423

fons, *sm.* depths, bottom *M* 181

force, *sf.* strength *M* 752; *a f.* by force *M* 371, 835

forfet, *sm.* misdeed, wrongdoing *Ch* 548, 955

forment, *adv.* greatly *Ch* 166, 243

fors, *adv.* out, outside *Ch* 512, 565, *M* 265; *prep.* except *Ch* 633*, *M* 874; outside *M* 415*; *f. de* out of *M* 165, 280; *f. que* save, except for *M* 120

forsen, *sm.* mad rage M 681

fort; *nom. sg.* **forz** M 859, **fors** M 866; *obl.* **fort** M 94; *adj.* strong, mighty M 94, 859, 866; secure, well fortified M 336, 372

fort, *adv.* swiftly M 440

frain Ch 908, M 43, **frainc** Ch 853, M 292, **freinc** M 103, *sm.* bridle

fraindre, *v.a.* break, Ch 1120

froidure, *sf.* cold M 196, 201

frois, *adj.* fresh Ch 474

froissier, *v.n.* break M 804

fuerre, *sm.* straw (stuffing of mattress) Ch 603

fuerre, *sm.* scabbard, sheath Ch 565, 598

fustoie, *sf.* clump of trees; *une clere f.* part of forest with widely spaced trees Ch 72

gaber M 639, *v.a.* jest about, make light of

gaires; *ne (. . .) g. adv.* hardly, scarcely Ch 990, M 132, 240

ganche, *sf.* evasion, way out M 747

garantir Ch 579, *v. refl.* protect

garde, *sf.* protection, watch Ch 525, 1000, M 643; fear Ch 769; guardian M 529

garder Ch 396; *subj. pr. 3* **gart** Ch 86: *v.a.* protect Ch 86; *v. refl.* protect oneself Ch 396, 1113; take care not to Ch 404, 618; *se g. de* be protected from M 423; *v.n.* refrain Ch 550

garir, *v.a.* cure, heal M 763

garnement, *sm.* clothes, adornments Ch 493

garnir, *v.a.* forewarn Ch 570; equip Ch 1162

gascort, *adj.* quite short Ch 43

ge; v. **je**

genoivre, *s.* juniper M 221

gent, jent Ch 502, 738, *sf.* (collective noun+ pl. verb) people M 1007, 1033; **genz,** *s. pl.* people M 1025

gent, jent Ch 651, *adj.* fair, handsome Ch 161, 511

gerre, guerre, *sf.* fighting, contest Ch 936, M 742, 907

gesir Ch 692, **jesir;** *p.p.* **geü** Ch 584, **jeü** Ch 628; *ind. pr. 6* **gisent** M 154; *impf. 3* **gisoit** M 758; *pret. 3* **jut** Ch 518, *6* **jurent** Ch 816; *f ut. 1* **jerré** Ch 456, *2* **girras** M 561, *3* **jerra** Ch 459, *5* **girois** Ch 499, **giroiz** Ch 509; *impve. 5* **gisiez** Ch 617: *v.n.* and *refl.* lie, lie down Ch 456, 607, M 154, 758

gié; v. **je**

giet, *sm.; g. de bozon* bowshot Ch 1122

giter, gitier, *v.a.* give, give forth Ch 479, M 184, 853; utter Ch 597

graer Ch 313, *v.a.* accept

grai(n)gnor, *adj. (comp. of* **grant***)* greater Ch 510, M 142, 1035

granment, *adv.* much, greatly Ch 130, 601

greve, *sf.* top of head (where scalp can be seen in parting of hair) *M* 738
grever, *v.a.* harm, wound *Ch* 1139
grief, *adj.* hard, difficult *Ch* 324, *M* 389
gris, *sm.* squirrel-fur *Ch* 487
guenchir, *v.n.* turn *Ch* 1131
guerpir, gerpir, *v.a.* abandon, throw over *Ch* 1004, 1101, 1105
guerre, *sf.* fighting *M* 742, 907

haïr; *ind. pr. 3* **het** *Ch* 1137: *v.a.* hate
haitié *Ch* 453; *f. sg.* **haitiee** *M* 314, **haitie** *M* 950: *p.p. adj.* joyful, in good spirits *Ch* 453, 462, *M* 314
hardement, *sm.* bold action, deed *Ch* 926; audacity, boldness *M* 452
harnois, *sm.* armour, equipment *M* 660, 856
hasart, *sm.* dice-game *Ch* 806
hauberc, *sm.* hauberk, coat of mail *Ch* 1144, *M* 749, 861
haucier, *v.a.* lift, raise *M* 628
hautement, *adv.* loudly, clearly *Ch* 697
herbergier *Ch* 387, *v.a.* lodge, put up *Ch* 387
herberjage, *sm.* outbuilding(s) *Ch* 211, 216
hericier *M* 686, *v. refl.* bristle up
herupé, *p.p. adj.* shaggy, shock-headed *M* 506
het; *v.* **haïr**
heu, *sm.* hilt, swordguard *Ch* 535
home; *nom. sg.* **hom** *Ch* 190; *obl. sg.* **(h)ome** *Ch* 7, 185, *M* 173; *sm.* man, person
honir, *v.a.* shame, disgrace *Ch* 635
honte, *sf.*; *a h.* shamefully, in shame *Ch* 589
hui, *adv.* today; *hui matin* this morning *M* 832
huis; *v.* **uis**
hure, *sf.* face, head *M* 696

i, *adv.* there *Ch* 57; *v.* also **il**
iaume, *sm.* helmet *M* 823
iauz = ieus (*pl.* of **ueil**) eyes *Ch* 643
ice = ce *M* 420, 1036
il, *pers. pron.*; *m. sg. nom.* **il** *Ch* 14, *M* 86, (used disjunctively) *M* 224; *acc.* **le** *Ch* 336, *M* 61, **lo** *Ch* 167, *M* 74, **lou** *Ch* 97, *M* 82, **l'** *Ch* 292, *M* 354, (after infinitive) **le** *Ch* 564; *dat.* **li** *Ch* 56, *M* 58, **l'** *Ch* 383(?), *M* 549, **i** *Ch* 52; *tonic form* **lui** *Ch* 24, *M* 462, **li** *Ch* 99, *M* 493, (used after *prep.*) *Ch* 222, *M* 329, (as *acc.*) *Ch* 319, *M* 538, 697, 1049, (as *dat.*) *Ch* 901; *f. sg. nom.* **ele** *Ch* 256, *M* 3, **el** *Ch* 284, *M* 70; *acc.* **la** *Ch* 257, *M* 68, **l'** *Ch* 264, (after infinitive) **la** *Ch* 981; *dat.* **li** *Ch* 290, *M* 304; *tonic form* **li** *Ch* 262, *M* 393, (used after *prep.*) *Ch* 267, *M* 393, 905, (as *acc.*) *Ch* 844, *M* 1118; *m. pl. nom.*

il *Ch* 115, *M* 58; *acc.* **les** *Ch* 692, *M* 648; *dat.* **lor** *Ch* 171, *M* 943; *tonic form* **eus** *Ch* 891, **aus** *Ch* 108, 169, *M* 45, (used after *prep.*) *Ch* 169, *M* 113; *neut. impers. nom.* **il** *Ch* 200, *M* 12; *acc.* **le** *Ch* 336, *M* 61, **lo** *Ch* 561, 723, *M* 294, **l'** *M* 979; (with *acc. pron.* implied) **li**=**le li** *Ch* 968★, *M* 618,=**la li** *M* 72★,=**les li** *M* 544, **lor**=**les lor** *M* 797; enclitic forms are entered separately

iluec, ilueques, *adv.* there *M* 113, 388; *d'iluec en avant* from that time on, afterwards *Ch* 944

ire, *sf.* anger *M* 827

irié, *p.p. adj.* angry *Ch* 506, *M* 76

isnel *Ch* 897; *m. obl. pl.* **isniaus** *Ch* 870; *adj.* swift

isnelement, *adv.* without delay, straightway *M* 597, 887

issi, *adv.* thus *Ch* 524, 636, *M* 41, 746; so *M* 245; *issi con* as, in the same way as *Ch* 1096

issifait, *adj.* such; *mener i. vie* spend one's time thus *Ch* 807

issir *M* 504; *p.p.* **issu** *Ch* 47; *ind. pr. 3* **ist** *Ch* 294: *v.n.* and *refl.* go out, come out *Ch* 47, *M* 504, 620; *v.* also **sen**

itant; *v.* **tant**

itel=**tel** *Ch* 502

ja *adv.* now, soon *Ch* 537, 956, *M* 293, 302, 763; ever *M* 317; already *M* 546; (emphatic particle) indeed *Ch* 695; **ne . . . ja,** never *Ch* 287, 291, *M* 857; **ja . . . ne** never *Ch* 545, *M* 98★, 194, 336, 372; **ja ne mes** never *Ch* 333, *M* 146, 230; **ja mes jor . . . ne** never again *M* 78; (as intensifying particle with temporal meaning weakened, negative sense) *Ch* 192; **ja soit ce que,** *conj.* although *Ch* 1008

jame, janbe, *sf.* leg *M* 152, 1052

je, *pers. pron.*; *nom.* **je** *Ch* 8, 147, *M* 61, **jo** *Ch* 507, **j'** *Ch* 327, *M* 888, **ge** *Ch* 143, *M* 649, **g'** *Ch* 950, (used disjunctively) **je** *Ch* 329, *M* 90, **je non** no (not I) *Ch* 671, *tonic form* **gié** *M* 338; *acc.* **me** *Ch* 610, *M* 1122, **m'** *Ch* 408, *M* 303; *dat.* **me** *Ch* 87, 714, *M* 86, **m'** *Ch* 409, *M* 80; *tonic form* **moi** *Ch* 288, *M* 669, (used after *prep.*) *Ch* 619, *M* 765, (as *dat.*) *M* 980, (as *acc.*) *M* 669; enclitic forms are entered separately

jent; *v.* **gent**

jerra, jerré, jeü, jurent, jut; *v.* **gesir**

jes=**je**+**les** *Ch* 1037

jeu, *sm.* game; *fere le j. certain* make love *Ch* 654; *tenir a jeus* consider as a joke, as something of little consequence or importance *M* 324

jeu parti, jeu *Ch* 1047, *sm.* choice (of two alternatives); *fere un j. p.* offer a choice *Ch* 956, 1041; *avoir j. p.* make a choice *Ch* 919★; *prendre un j. p.* accept a choice *Ch* 1040, 1047. (See Foulet in Roach, s.v. **partir**.)

joër *M* 70; *ind. pr. 6* **jeuent** *Ch* 804: *v.n.* play *Ch* 804; trifle, pass time frivolously *M* 70; make merry *M* 1010★. (See Foulet in Roach.)

joiant, *adj.* delighted *Ch* 224, 775

joïr, *v.a.* call encouragingly, welcomingly *Ch* 1062

jor, *sm.* day *M* 20, 212; daylight *Ch* 682, *M* 598; *toz jorz* still, continually *Ch* 67, 68; always *Ch* 569, *M* 196; *ne . . . a nul j.* never *Ch* 254; *ne . . . a j. de ma vie* never *Ch* 1025; v. also **ja** and **onques**

jou=jo+le *Ch* 609

jus, *adv.* down *Ch* 103

jusarme, *sf.* axe, gisarme *M* 512, 575. (The *jusarme* or *gisarme* was a weapon something like a pole-axe, double-headed, with a curved axe-blade on one side and a spiked point on the other.)

jusque, *conj.* (+ *indic.*) until *Ch* 378, *M* 668; *prep.* up to *Ch* 591; **jusq'a,** **jusqu'en** up to, until *Ch* 993, *M* 102, 718, 740; **jusc'a** from here to *Ch* 749

la, *def. art. f.* (with demonstrative force) *Ch* 820

laidece, *sf.* unworthy action; *fere l.* act ignobly *Ch* 998

laidir, *v.a.* ill-treat, injure *Ch* 163, 1139

laienz, *adv.* therein *M* 133, 196

lais(s)ier *Ch* 1084, **le(i)sser, laier;** *ind. pr. 3* let *Ch* 1143, **lesse** *M* 495, *5* **lessiez** *Ch* 1112; *impve. 2* **lesse** *M* 623, *4* **laisons** *Ch* 406, *5* **laissiez** *M* 720; *subj. pr. 5* **lessiez** *Ch* 1156; *subj. impf. 6* **laissassent** *M* 274; *v.a.* leave, leave alone, abandon, let go *Ch* 971, 972, *M* 274, 846; let, permit *M* 495, 720; (used absolutely) give up *M* 438★; *l. a* desist from *Ch* 587

lande, *sf.* open country *Ch* 1021

lant=lent *M* 484

laver *M* 544, *v.a. M* 544; *v.n. Ch* 349, *M* 942 wash

lé *adj.* wide *Ch* 209, *M* 170, 240; ample, large *Ch* 43, *M* 542

lecheor, *sm.* entertainer *Ch* 797

l'en=l'on *M* 400;=li en *M* 549

leu, *sm.* place *Ch* 730, *M* 213, 336; origin, family *Ch* 848; opportunity *M* 566; *de leu en leu* everywhere, all over *M* 881; *de leus en leus* everywhere (?), from time to time (?) *M* 853

lever; *ind. pr. 3* **lieve** *M* 600; *v.a.* lift, raise *M* 696; *v. refl.* get up *M* 600, 768

lez, *prep.* beside *Ch* 78, 297

li; v. **il** and **ele**

lices, *sf. pl.* lists, tilting-ground *Ch* 218

lié, *adj.* happy, joyful *Ch* 245, 775, *M* 307, 1068

lieement, *adv.* joyfully, merrily *Ch* 359

liepart, *sm.* leopard *M* 135, 158

lincel, *sm.* bed linen *Ch* 713

liue, *sf.* league *Ch* 122

liuee, *sf.* space of time (needed to go a league) *M* 816

lo *Ch* 32, **lou** *Ch* 50, *def. art. m. Ch* 32, 50; (with demonstrative force) *Ch* 1

lo, lou, *pron.*; v. **il**

loër, *v.a.* praise *Ch* 22, *M* 955; bless *Ch* 418

loge, *sf.* (small) room *M* 1062. (See Foulet in Roach.)

lor; v. **il**

lors, *adv.* then *Ch* 36, 557, *M* 106; **lors . . . que,** *conj.* when, at the time when *Ch* 675

louquel, *pron.* which *M* 581; **loquel que** (+*subj.*) whichever *M* 569; *dat.* **auquel** to which one *Ch* 312, 976, 1044

maaille, *sf.* coin of small value *M* 502

maille, *sf.* (coat of) mail *M* 732

mainne; v. **mener**

mains, *adv. comp.* less *M* 8

maint, *adj.* many, many a *M* 164, 1060

maintenant, *adv.* immediately, straightway *Ch* 441, 552, *M* 58, 101; **(tot) m. que,** *conj.* as soon as *M* 551, 795, 958

maintenir *M* 328, *v.a.* maintain, uphold *Ch* 4; *la parole m. a* continue talking of *M* 328

mais; v. **mes**

maisniee *M* 545, **mesniee** *Ch* 21, **mesnie** *M* 949, *sf.* servants, retainers *M* 545; company *Ch* 21. (The word is a collective noun=retinue, staff.)

mal, mau, *adj.* bad, evil *Ch* 919, *M* 644; evil, dangerous, baneful *M* 643; **ne ja mal,** *adv.* (emphatic negative) *Ch* 768; **m. dahez**; v. **dahez**

malaise, *sf.*; *a m.* ill at ease *Ch* 466

maleürté, *sf.* evil, misery *M* 204

malvaistié *M* 326, **mauvestié** *M* 198, *sf.* dishonourable action *M* 326; bitterness *M* 198

manace, *sf.* threat *Ch* 633

mander, *v.a.* request one's presence, summon *M* 57, 72

maniere, *sf.* way, fashion, kind *M* 655*, 865

mar, *adv. Ch* 160, 173; (with past tense=in an evil hour, inauspiciously) *tant m. fus* alas, lackaday *Ch* 160; (with *fut.* or *condit.*=emphatic negative) *ja m. seroiz* do not be, you must not be *M* 308; *ne ja m. feriez sanblant* you would be ill-advised ever to give a hint *Ch* 342

marri, *p.p. adj.* angry, indignant *Ch* 1003

martire, *sm.* anguish *M* 300

mau; v. **mal**

mautalant, *sm.* ill-will *Ch* 423, 946; rage *M* 704

mauvaisement, *adv.* wickedly *M* 80

mauvestié; v. **malvaistié**

meffet, *sm.* wrong, crime *Ch* 1137

meïsmes, *adj.*; *il m.* he himself *M* 224; *soi m.* herself *Ch* 579, himself *M* 446

mellor *Ch* 748, *M* 928; *f.pl.* **miaudres** *M* 11: *adj. comp.* better; **le mellor**;

nom. sg. m. **li miaudres** *Ch* 758; *obl. sg.* **lou miaudre** *Ch* 761, **le (lo) mellor,** *Ch* 763, 992; *superl.* best

mener *Ch* 1071: *ind. pr. 3* **moinne** *Ch* 137, *M* 72, **mainne** *M* 165; *fut. 3* **menra** *M* 93, *5* **menrez** *Ch* 1073; *v.a.* lead *Ch* 67, *M* 379; bring *Ch* 137, *M* 72; take away *Ch* 1034; **en . . . mener,** *v.a.* take away *Ch* 1028, 1071; *v.* also **orgoil**

mengier *M* 650; *p.p.* **mengié** *Ch* 367; *pret. 3* **menja** *M* 548, *5* **menjastes** *Ch* 440, *6* **mengierent** *Ch* 359; *fut. 1* **mengerei** *M* 313, *2* **mengeras** *M* 905; *subj. impf. 6* **menjassent** *M* 273; *impve. 2* **menjue** *M* 751, *5* **mengiez** *M* 307: *v.a.* and *n.* eat *M* 273, 751; *inf. subst.* food, meal *Ch* 346, *M* 31, 547

menuement, *adv.* finely; *m.* **ridee** with many small narrow pleats *Ch* 44

merci, *sf.* (as command) desist! stop! *Ch* 523, 608; *vostre m.* thank you *Ch* 695

mercïer, *v.a.* thank *Ch* 238, 292

mervelle, *sf.* wonder, astonishing thing *Ch* 1103; *avoir m.* marvel, be astounded *Ch* 614; *n'est m.* it is not surprising, it is no wonder *M* 416

merveller, *v. refl.* marvel, wonder *Ch* 166, 494, *M* 45

mes, mais, *conj.* but *Ch* 64, 215, *M* 12, 295, 488; *adv.* more *Ch* 122; henceforward *Ch* 573; now *M* 765; *ne . . . mes* never (referring to past) *Ch* 213, *M* 188; **mes que, ne mes,** *prep.* except *Ch* 144, *M* 43, 436; **mes que,** *conj.* (+ *indic.*) except that *Ch* 217, *M* 649; **(ne) mes que** (+ *subj.*) provided only that *Ch* 99, *M* 315, 337, 904; *v.* also **ja** and **onques**

mes, *sm.* dish, course *Ch* 356, *M* 956; food *M* 714*

mes, mi, m'; *v.* **mon**

meschief, *sm.* risk of peril, misfortune *Ch* 1205

mesconnoistre, *v.a.* fail to recognise, not to understand *M* 490

mesnie, mesniee; *v.* **maisniee**

mesprendre, *v.n.* act wrongly *Ch* 950

mesprison, *sf.* discourtesy *Ch* 301

messire; *v.* **Gauvain**

mestier, *sm.*; *avoir m.* need *Ch* 503, *M* 223; be useful, be of service *M* 2, 7, 649; *n'avoir m.* be of no use *Ch* 415, *M* 857

mestre, *adj.*, main, principal; *plus m. cuer* very heart *M* 197

metre; *pret. 3* **mist** *Ch* 84, *5* **meïstes** *Ch* 1042, *6* **mistrent** *Ch* 128; *subj. pr. 1* **mete** *M* 1083; *subj. impf. 3* **meïst** *Ch* 322: *v.a.* put *Ch* 84; lay, place *Ch* 350; *v. refl.* put oneself *M* 252; set out *Ch* 128; proceed, adopt (a certain pace) *Ch* 152; *se m. fors* go out, withdraw *Ch* 512; *se m. en* enter on, take *M* 426; *m. en brief* write down *Ch* 13; *m. a raison* address, speak to *Ch* 302

miaudre; *v.* **mellor**

miaus, miauz, *adv.* better *Ch* 766, 1109, *M* 178, 250; **venir m.,** *v. impers.* be better *Ch* 588, *M* 248

mie, *adv.* of neg.; *ne . . . mie* *Ch* 130, 284, 1073*, *M* 95; (used substantivally) *ne . . . mie de M* 123, 295, 401

mine, *sf.* kind of dice-game *Ch* 806

moie; *v.* **mon**

moillier, *sf.* wife *Ch* 991

moinne; v. **mener**

mois, *sm.* month; (in negative expression) *des m.* for months, for a long time, ever *M* 145, 659

moleste, *sf.* disaster, or *adj.* disastrous *M* 737

mon, *poss. adj.; m. sg. nom.* **mes** *Ch* 328, *M* 79; *obl.* **mon** *Ch* 929, *M* 88; *pl. nom.* **mi** *Ch* 838; *obl.* **mes** *Ch* 868; *f. sg.* **ma** *Ch* 929, *M* 81, **m'** *Ch* 924; *pl.* **mes** *M* 924; tonic forms *m. obl. sg.* **mien** *Ch* 941, *M* 1084; *pl. nom.* **mien** *Ch* 1085; *obl.* **miens** *Ch* 1039; *f. sg.* **moie** *M* 585, 970

monsaignor; v. **Gauvain**

mont *Ch* 83, **monde** *Ch* 990, *sm.* world, earth *Ch* 83, 753, 990

monter *Ch* 1111, *v.n.* avail *Ch* 1111; amount *M* 836*; mount *M* 115

Mor, *sm.* Moor *M* 515

morir *Ch* 588, *M* 719, *v.n.* die; *v.a.* (in past tenses) kill, slay *Ch* 334, *M* 925; **mort,** *p.p.* killed, slain *Ch* 616, *M* 302; dead *M* 723; distressed *Ch* 398

mors, *sf. pl.* manners *Ch* 315

mort, *sf.* death *M* 174; *trere a m.* put to death *Ch* 704

mostrer, montrer, *v.a.* show *Ch* 401, *M* 62

mot, *sm.* word *Ch* 113, *M* 96, 572; *a cest m.* at these words *M* 96; *ne mentir de m.* not to lie at all *M* 572; v. **soner**

mote, *sf.* mound *Ch* 207

mout, *adv.* very *Ch* 42, *M* 6; much *M* 46, 68; *m. de* many *Ch* 179, *M* 67; *m. tres* extremely *Ch* 42

mu, *adj.* speechless, dumb *Ch* 686

muele, *sf.* millstone *M* 441

muet, *ind. pr. 3* of **moudre,** *v.n.* grind *M* 441

mure *M* 18*, 37, 274, **mule** *M* 42, 92, *sf.* mule

nape, *sf.* overcloth (protecting the **doblier,** q.v.) *Ch* 350

navrer, *v.a.* wound *Ch* 665, 730, *M* 773

nc *M* 178, **n'** *M* 116, **nen** *M* 449, 476, *neg. adv.* (without and with *pas, mie* etc.) *Ch* 15, 17, 18*

ne, *conj.* or, nor *Ch* 7, 255, *M* 78; *ne ... ne ... ne* neither ... nor *Ch* 778-9, *M* 439

nef, *sf.* boat *M* 236

neiant, neient; v. **noient**

neïs, *adv.* even *M* 875

nel = **ne** + **le** *Ch* 168

nelui; v. **nul**

nen; v. **ne**

neporquant, neporcant, *adv.* nevertheless *Ch* 269, 274, *M* 984

nequedant, *adv.* nevertheless *M* 241

nes = **ne** + **les** *Ch* 15, 1071, *M* 382

nestre *M* 187*, *v.n.* be born

niés, *sm.* (*nom.* of **neveu**) nephew *Ch* 743

no, nou=**ne**+**le** *Ch* 192, 239, 284, *M* 52, 274, 324

noient *M* 253, **noiant** *M* 607, **neiant** *Ch* 318, **neient** *Ch* 590, *sm.* thing of
    little value *M* 253; nothing *Ch* 590, *M* 532; *neg. pron.* (without *ne*) of no
    avail *Ch* 1165; *por n.* on no account *Ch* 318; *por droit n.* quite in vain *Ch*
    723; *estre n. de* be useless *M* 654*; **ne . . . n.** *neg. adv.* not at all *Ch* 827, *M*
    382, 607; **ne . . . de noient** not at all, in no way *M* 612

non, *neg. adv. tonic M* 177*; *je non,* no, no I am not *Ch* 671; *v.* **se . . . non**

non, *sm.* name *Ch* 158, 737

norir, nor(r)ir, *v.a.* rear *Ch* 868, 1099

noter, *v.n.* sing (with instrumental accompaniment) *Ch* 801

nou; v. no

novel, *adj.* new *M* 9, 16; **de n.,** *adv.* newly, recently *Ch* 208

noveles, *sf. pl.* news *M* 1068

nu, *adj.* naked *Ch* 690; *nu a nu* both naked *Ch* 585

nuitiee, *sf.*; *a n.* a whole night through *Ch* 629

nul; *nom.* nus *Ch* 11, 190; *obl.* **nul** *Ch* 6, 280, **nus** *Ch* 180*, 213; *tonic obl.*
    nelui *Ch* 634, **nului** (used as *nom.*) *Ch* 1038: *pron. and adj.* no, none, nobody
    Ch 615; any, anybody *Ch* 439, 871, 1038, *M* 317

o, *conj.* or *Ch* 214, *M* 177; **o . . . o** either . . . or *Ch* 186, 339

o, ou, *prep.* with *Ch* 31, 99, 303, *M* 113, 161

o, ou, *rel. adv.* where *Ch* 64, 94, *M* 55, 168, 193; **la o** where *M* 363; **ou que,**
    conj. (+*subj.*) wherever *M* 318

o, ou=**en**+**le** *Ch* 152*, 515, 666, 1021, *M* 173, 378, 708

oblïee, *sf.* act of forgetfulness *Ch* 865

oblïer *Ch* 25, *v.a.* forget; *v. refl. Ch* 94

ocir(r)e *Ch* 187, 760; *p.p.* **ocis** *Ch* 542; *ind. pr. 3* **ocit** *Ch* 470, **ocist** *Ch* 195
    (see note to l. 184); *pret. 3* **ocist** *Ch* 540; *subj. pr. 3* **ocie** *Ch* 549; *inf.* (as
    neg. impve. 2) *M* 830: *v.a.* kill *Ch* 187, 470, *M* 828, 1022

oïl, *adv.* yes; *oïl voir M* 313, *oïl certes M* 524 yes, indeed

oïr *Ch* 188; *pres. p.* **oiant** *Ch* 290; *ind. pr. 3* **ot** *Ch* 314, *M* 1069*, *5* **oëz** *Ch* 998;
    pret. 3 **oï** *Ch* 53; *fut. 5* **orroiz** *Ch* 114; *subj. pr. 3* **oie** *Ch* 2: *v.a.* hear *M*
    1069, hear of *Ch* 2, *M* 794, *v.n.* hear *M* 330; *oiant vos* in your hearing *Ch*
    290; **oïr dire,** *inf. subst.* hearsay *Ch* 188

oirre, *sm.* journey across, traversing *Ch* 199*; journey *M* 508*; *grant o.* at
    great speed, in great haste *Ch* 147

oiseuse, *sf.* folly, trifle *M* 253

oisiaus, *m. pl.* of **oisel,** *sm.* bird *Ch* 50, 358, 810

ome; v. home

oni, *p.p. adj.* level *M* 692

onques, *adv.* ever *M* 1123; *ne . . . o., o. . . . ne* never *Ch* 14, 24, 517, *M* 110;

o. plus ne no further, not at all, *M* 536; *n' . . . o. nul jor* never at any time *Ch* 6; *o. mais* (*mes*) . . . *ne* never before *Ch* 576, *M* 142.

or, ore, *adv.* now *Ch* 330, 1054, *M* 346, 957; *des or en avant* henceforth *Ch* 595

ore, *sf.* hour *M* 187

orendroit, *adv.* recently *Ch* 440; straightway, now, here and now *Ch* 1112, *M* 53, 90; nowadays *M* 8

orer, *v.a.* wish, call down *M* 353

orgoil, *sm.* arrogant ferocity *M* 1029; *o. mener* show fierce arrogance *M* 680

oser; *subj. pr. 3* **ost** *M* 874, 875: *v.n.* dare, venture *M* 84, 108, 874

oste; *sg. nom.* **oste** *Ch* 228, **ostes** *Ch* 240, *M* 573; *obl.* **oste** *Ch* 420: host *Ch* 228, *M* 573; guest *M* 951

ostel, *sm.* lodging *Ch* 125, 139, *M* 322; house, dwelling *Ch* 426, 995, *M* 539

osteler, *v.a.* lodge, quarter *M* 541*; v. also **re-**

otroier *M* 104; *ind. pr. 1* **otroi** *Ch* 767, *3* **otroie** *Ch* 96, *6* **outroient** *M* 340: *v.a.* grant, undertake *Ch* 96; grant, accord *Ch* 767, 1046, *M* 104; (absolute use) grant favour to, favour *M* 425*

ou; v. **o**

outre, *adv.* through *Ch* 602, *M* 377, 997; across, over *M* 419

ovraingne, *sf.* business, purpose *M* 1025

ovré, *p.p. adj.* worked, patterned *Ch* 40; studied *M* 937

paier, *v.a.;* *se p. tieus cous* exchange such blows, inflict such blows *M* 812

paile, *sm.* precious cloth, brocade; *p. roé* cloth ornamented with a wheel design *M* 936

painne; poinne, peine, *sf.* difficulty, fatigue, hardship *M* 71, 166, 753; *por nule p.* at any price *M* 1125; *p. d'amors* love-sickness, toils of love *Ch* 322; v. also **quelque**

painne *Ch* 1176, *M* 540; v. **pener**

palefroi, *sm.* palfrey *Ch* 852

paliz, *sm.* palisade *M* 841

paor, peor, *sf.* fear *Ch* 1161, *M* 141, 375

par; par lui by itself, of its own accord *Ch* 565; *intensifying part. Ch* 953, *M* 684, 878, 950; (also with **tant** *Ch* 9, 194) greatly, exceedingly

parclose, *sf.* end *Ch* 1184

parfont, *adj.* deep *Ch* 209, *M* 170

parler *Ch* 721; *ind. pr. 3* **parrole** *M* 608, *6* **parolent** *M* 46: *v.n.* talk, speak

parmi, *prep.* through *Ch* 72, 219 on, full on *Ch* 657, *M* 710; by *Ch* 908; in *M* 33; across *M* 35

paroit; *impf. ind. 3* of **paroir,** *v.n.* appear *M* 69

parole, *sf.;* v. **tenir** and **maintenir**

parrole, parolent; v. **parler**

part, *sf.* direction *Ch* 74, *M* 111; share *Ch* 85; side, place *Ch* 234; *a une p.* on one side, aside *Ch* 395; *cele p.* thither, in that direction *Ch* 74, *M* 136; *de totes p.* everywhere *Ch* 526; *d'autre p.* on the other hand *Ch* 581; through to the other side *M* 383; *de sa p.* in his own direction *Ch* 961; *(conj. + subj) quele p. que* wheresoever *M* 111; *Dieus ... vos doint ... en lui grant part* (pious greeting) *Ch* 83–5

partir *Ch* 422, *v.n.* depart *Ch* 422; *se p. de* depart *M* 157; *v.a. partir un jeu* offer a choice *M* 565

partot, *adv.* everywhere *M* 881

pas, *adv.* of neg.; *ne ... pas Ch* 181, *M* 771, 1010; *pas ... ne M* 412, 614

pas, *sm.* pace *Ch* 152; *aler son pas* go slowly *Ch* 74; *perdre ses pas*, make a journey in vain, have a journey for nothing *M* 526

passer, *v.n.* (+ *dat.*) attack *M* 695

past, *subj. pr. 3* of **passer,** *v.n.* pass *M* 176

pastorel; *nom. pl.* **pastorel** *Ch* 197; *obl. pl.* **pastoriaus** *Ch* 155: *sm.* shepherd-boy, young shepherd

peçoier, *v.n.* shatter *Ch* 1120

pecol, *sm.* bed-post *M* 934

pel; *sg. nom.* **pieus** *M* 786; *obl.* **pel** *M* 838; *pl. obl.* **pieus** *M* 434, 435, **piez** *M* 782: *sm.* stake

pener, *v. refl.* strive *Ch* 1176; take pains, trouble *M* 540

penre *Ch* 1149 = **prendre**

pensé, *sm.* reverie, musing *Ch* 54, 93; *en p.* in mind *Ch* 400

penser, *sm.* reverie *Ch* 63

pensif, *adj.* dejected *Ch* 622

peor; *v.* **paor**

per, *sm.* peer, equal *Ch* 749; *p. a p.* on an equal footing, equal *Ch* 932

perillier, *v.a.* come to grief *M* 249

pes, *sf.* peace *Ch* 617, 900, *M* 95*, 562, 743

pesant, *pres. p. adj.* downhearted, apprehensive *M* 653

peser; *ind. pr. 3* **poise** *Ch* 449; *pret. 3* **pesa** *Ch* 1008; *condit. 3* **peseroit** *Ch* 573: *v. impers.* grieve

peson, *sm.* fish *Ch* 357

petit, *adj.* small *M* 160, 897; *adv.* little *M* 580*

piaus, *nom. sg.* of **pel,** *sf.* skin, hide *M* 706

pié, *sm.* foot *M* 414, 594; (unit of measurement) *Ch* 192, *M* 817; *p. de la sale* threshold, end of the hall *M* 320

piece, *sf.* period of time; *a pieces* fairly soon *Ch* 296

pieus, piez; *v.* **pel**

pitié, *sf.* sympathy, consideration *Ch* 1181*

piz, *sm.* breast *Ch* 1115

plaidier; *p.p.* **plaidié** *Ch* 116: *v.n.* talk, discuss *Ch* 116

plain *Ch* 192; *f.* **plainne** *Ch* 256; *adj.* full *Ch* 192, 256, 1066, *M* 817; broad *Ch* 641; ample *Ch* 648

plain, *adj.* flat, level *Ch* 132

plain(n)e, *sf.* plain *M* 208, 214, 384

plaisir *Ch* 580, **pleisir** *Ch* 587, *sm.* pleasure, will *Ch* 1089; *fere son p. de* make love to *Ch* 580; *venir a p.* please *Ch* 311

plait, *sm.* argument, speech *Ch* 1110; v. also **tenir**

planche, *sf.* footbridge *M* 237; beam *M* 240

plenté, *sf.* abundance, a great deal *Ch* 53; *a p.* copiously *Ch* 367, *M* 623★; *a grant p.* in abundance, lavishly *Ch* 237, *M* 549

plere, *Ch* 260; *ind. pr. 3* **plest** *Ch* 26; *impf. 3* **plaisoit** *M* 972; *subj. pr. 3* **plese** *Ch* 465; *v. impers.* please *Ch* 26

plesseïz, *sm.* enclosure *Ch* 148, 206

ploier; *ind. pr. 6* **ploient** *M* 150, **plïent** *M* 367; *impf. 3* **pleioit** *M* 418; *v.a.* bend *M* 150, 367, 1050; *v.n. M* 418

plusor, plusors, *pron.* and *adj.* many *Ch* 116, 417, *M* 865

poësté, *sf.* power, might *Ch* 953★

poi *Ch* 304, **po** *M* 190, **pou** *Ch* 268, *adv.* little; a little while *M* 36; *un poi* a little *M* 650; *ne trop ne poi* neither too much nor too little *Ch* 304; **a (bien) pou que . . . ne,** *conj.* very nearly, all but, be near to *Ch* 268, 658, *M* 190, 802

poin, *sm.*; *prendre as poinz* seize *Ch* 1133

poindre, *v.a.* spur *Ch* 921, *M* 465; **poignant,** *pres. p.* as *adv.* swiftly, at a gallop *Ch* 873

poinne; v. **painne**

point, *sm.* trace *Ch* 301; moment, opportunity, situation *M* 460★

pon, *sm.* pommel (of sword) *Ch* 535

pont, *sm.* bridge *Ch* 221; *p. tornoiant* drawbridge *M* 450★

pooir; *ind. pr. 1* **puis** *Ch* 15, *2* **puez** *M* 714, *3* **puet** *Ch* 667, *M* 6, *5* **poëz** *Ch* 364, *6* **püent** *M* 155; *impf. 5* **poïez** *M* 935; *pret. 3* **pot** *Ch* 1051, *M* 187★, *5* **peüstes** *Ch* 726; *fut. 1* **porrai** *M* 849, *2* **porras** *M* 636, *3* **porra** *Ch* 396; *condit. 1* **porroie** *Ch* 254, *3* **porroit** *Ch* 140; *subj. impf. 3* **poïst** *Ch* 320, *M* 138, **peüst** *Ch* 719, *6* **peüssent** *Ch* 755: *v. modal* be able; *inf. subst.* power *M* 966, 1090

por, *prep.* on account of *Ch* 16, 93, *M* 91, 137; on behalf of *M* 776; (+ *inf.*) in order to *M* 918; = **par** by *M* 153; **por ce que,** *conj.* (+ *indic.*) because *Ch* 53, *M* 122; (+ *subj.*) so that *M* 652; **por que** (+ *subj.*) in the event of, if perchance *Ch* 387

porchacer, *v.a.* seek *M* 231, 656

porfandre, *v.a.* cleave *M* 740, 822

porpenser *Ch* 61, *v.n.* and *refl.* reflect, think *Ch* 61, 581; ponder *Ch* 983

porpre, *sf.* material, fabric *Ch* 233

porreture, *sf.* filth, filthy matter *M* 893

pou; v. **poi**

praerie, *sf.* field, meadow *M* 280, 358

pré, *sm.* field, meadow *M* 35

pree, *sf.* field, meadow *M* 216

premerain, *adj.* first *Ch* 616, 1175

premier, *adj.* first *M* 726; *adj.* or *adv.* first *Ch* 27*, 119; **premiers,** *adv.* first, in the first place *M* 851; *a premiers* at first *Ch* 1201

prendre *Ch* 564; *p.p.* **pris** *Ch* 228; *ind. pr. 3* **prent** *M* 543; *impf. 1* **prenoie** *M* 831, *3* **prenoit** *Ch* 62; *pret. 3* **prist** *Ch* 34, *6* **pristrent** *Ch* 127; *fut. 1* **prendré** *M* 571, *3* **prendra** *Ch* 549; *condit. 1* **prendroie** *M* 973; *subj. pr. 1* **preigne** *M* 581, *6* **preignent** *Ch* 381; *impve. 2* **pren** *M* 567, *5* **prenez** *M* 986: *v.a.* take, seize *Ch* 127; catch *Ch* 549; *v.n.* choose *M* 567; **prendre a** *v.a.* accept as *M* 973; *v.n.* come upon *Ch* 34; begin *Ch* 62; **se prendre** *v. refl.* have it out with, pit oneself against *M* 493, 831

preu *Ch* 987, *M* 929; *nom. m.* and *f.* **preuz** *Ch* 308, 382: *adj.* valiant, worthy, valorous *Ch* 987, *M* 929; sensible *Ch* 308

preudon *Ch* 25, *nom. sg.* of **preudome,** worthy, estimable man

primes, *adv.* first *Ch* 979, *M* 100, 343

pris, *sm.* reputation, renown *Ch* 541, *M* 836*

prisier *Ch* 364, *v.a.* and *refl.* prize, esteem, praise *Ch* 10, 364, *M* 8, 502

proëce, *sf.* prowess *Ch* 997

proier *M* 1118; *ind. pr. 1* **pri** *Ch* 123: *v.n.* beg, pray *Ch* 123, 1155, *M* 1118

proiere, *sf.* request *Ch* 102, 517

prometre, *v. n.* (absolute use) make promises to, smile on *M* 425

prover; *ind. pr. 3* **prueve** *Ch* 1185; *v. refl.* show one's worth *Ch* 1148; show one's true character *Ch* 1185

pucele, *sf.* girl *Ch* 297, *M* 39. (See Foulet in Roach.)

puis, *adv.* thenceforth, thereafter *Ch* 1188; then *M* 227; *puis* (...) *que* then (...) when *M* 2–3, 245

puor, *sf.* stench *M* 186, 211

put, *adj.* evil, stinking *M* 263

q'; v. **que**

qoi, coi, *adj.* quiet, still *M* 1001; (used adverbially in) *tenir tot qoi* stand quite still *M* 997

quanque *Ch* 489, *M* 728, *indef. pron.* whatever

quant, *adv.* when *M* 105, 117

que, qu', c', *conj.*; (consecutive) in such a way that (*+subj.*) *Ch* 234, (*+indic.*) *M* 717; (causal) for *Ch* 111, 140, 252, 266*, *M* 6, 164, 640, because *Ch* 878, *M* 42; (temporal) when *M* 37; **que ... ne** (*+indic.*) without *Ch* 786, *M* 592, 817; **de ce que** because *Ch* 176, *M* 283; **por ce que** because *Ch* 53, *M* 10; **des que** seeing that *M* 766

que, *pron.*; v. **qui**

quel; *pron.* and *adj. rel.* and *interr. m.* **quel** *M* 306; *f.* **quel** *Ch* 167, **quieus** *M* 1015, **quele** *M* 111 which, what; v. **part**

quelque, *indef. adj.*; *a q. painne* with great difficulty *M* 179, 419; at whatever cost *M* 456, 1026

querole, *sf.* dance *M* 1110

queroler, *v.n.* dance *M* 1007

querre *Ch* 251, *M* 50; *ind. pr. 1* **quier** *Ch* 748; *fut. 1* **querrai** *Ch* 951: *v.a.* seek, look for *Ch* 251, *M* 97; *q. congié*; v. **congié; q. por,** *v.n.* look for *M* 290

qui, qi, *rel.* and *interr. adj.* and *pron.*; *m.* and *f. sg.* and *pl.*; *nom.* **qui, qi,** *Ch* 1, 3, 12, *M* 7, 25, 486, (*m.* or *neut.?*) *Ch* 529, (= *celui qui*) *Ch* 1170, *M* 125, 688, **qu'** *M* 19; *acc.* **que, qu', c'** *Ch* 693, *M* 63, 145, 301, 1022, **qui** *Ch* 190, **cui** *Ch* 143, (after *prep.*) *M* 275, (as *dat.*) *M* 282, 474, 999, 1055, (= *celui à qui*) *M* 425*; **qui** (= *si l'on*) (+ *condit.*) *Ch* 141, *M* 648, (+ *subj.*) *M* 507; *qui veïst!* you should have seen! *M* 300; *neut.*; *nom.* **que** *M* 447, 491; *acc.*, **que** *M* 59; *tonic obl.* **coi** *Ch* 114, 173, *M* 185, 895; **que que** whatever *Ch* 399

quidier; *ind. pr. 1* **quit** *M* 273, **qui** *Ch* 460, *M* 199, *3* **quide** *M* 230, *6* **quident** *Ch* 839; *impf. 1* **quidoie** *M* 832, *5* **quidïez** *Ch* 609, *6* **quidoient** *Ch* 834; *pret. 3* **quida** *M* 212, *6* **quidierent** *Ch* 1197: *v.a.* and *n.* think; *q. a* take for, consider *Ch* 460

quieus; v. **quel**

quil = **qui** + **le** *Ch* 185

quite, *adj.* scot free *Ch* 736; without obligation, question *M* 535

raconter, *v.a.* narrate, tell *M* 1113

raison, *sf.* reason *Ch* 167, good sense *Ch* 150; *par r.* rightly *Ch* 19, 1084; *metre a r.* address, talk to *Ch* 302, 305; *r. rendre* give an explanation *M* 494

randir *Ch* 1117, *v.n.* run rapidly, gallop

randon, *sm.*; *de r.* vigorously *M* 465

rapeler, *v.a.* remind *M* 611*

ratorner, *v.a.* get ready again *M* 387

ravoir, *v.a.* get back *M* 82, 88, 123

re- is a prefix, appearing as **r-** before a vowel, frequently used to make compound verbs, basically indicating repetition of the action of the verb. In some cases the prefix has completely lost its meaning, as in **raconter** (*M* 1113) which has become merely a formal variant of **aconter** (*M* 888) and **redouter** (*M* 244) alongside **douter** (*Ch* 299). From its basic use, as in **voir** 'see', **revoir** (*M* 365) 'see again', nuances have developed. Thus (i) if the same action is repeated but by another agent, the meaning is 'in his turn' or 'for his part', e.g. **venter** 'to blow' and **reventer** (*li autre vent reventent M* 202) 'blow in their turn', or **ferir** 'to strike' and **referir** 'to strike back' (*M* 697); (ii) the action may be repeated but in a different way or direction, and so **raler** (*M* 489) 'to go back'.

The prefix may attach itself to the auxiliary verb in a compound tense, e.g. *se resont acheminé* (*Ch* 887) 'they went on their way again', 'they resumed their journey' and *la mule ra ostelé* (*M* 541), the churl 'led the mule in its turn to its quarters' he having previously performed the same service for Gauvain. The same happens with the modal verb *voloir* e.g. in *Ch* 986.

recet, *sm.* lair (of animals); *estre a r.* dwell, lurk *M* 360

rechanter, *v.n.* sing for his part, sing in his turn *Ch* 801

recoillir *Ch* 1171, *v.a.* harvest, reap

reconter *Ch* 11*, 26, *v.a.* and *n.* tell *Ch* 11, 26, *M* 772, 1091

recovrer, *v.a.* attack again *Ch* 825*

recroire; *condit.* 2 **recreroies** *M* 664: *v.n.* and *refl.* (with *de*) turn back from, renounce *M* 453, 664; **recreant,** *pres. p.* as *subst.* coward, quitter *M* 449

redire, *v.a.* say in one's turn *M* 109; say for one's part *Ch* 959

redoter, *v.a.* fear *M* 244, 382

referir, *v.a.* strike back *M* 697, 710

refroidier *M* 224, *v.n.* refresh oneself, cool off

regarder *Ch* 1145, *v.a.* pay heed to *Ch* 1145; look at *M* 497; *v.n.* look *M* 34, 1004

remanoir *Ch* 383; *pret. 3* **remest** *Ch* 605; *fut. 6* **remandront** *Ch* 1050; *subj. impf. 3* **remansist** *M* 1026*: *v.n.* stay *Ch* 383, 605; remain, be left *M* 806; (used impersonally) remain, be left *M* 1026*

remetre, *v. refl.*; *se r. en l'anbleüre* ride on (off) at a brisk pace *M* 228, 259, 1133

remuant, *adj.* spirited, lively *Ch* 897

reoingnier, *v.a.* cut off *M* 886

reont, *adj.* round; *a la reonde* all around *M* 431. v. **Table Reonde**

repairier, *v.n.* return *Ch* 344; go away *Ch* 850

repost, *p.p.* of **repondre,** *v.a.* hide *M* 1020

reprendre *Ch* 650, *v.a.* take back *M* 894; blame, criticise *Ch* 650*

reprovier, *sm.* proverb *Ch* 416*, *M* 1

requerre, *v.a.* seek, need *Ch* 1152; attack *M* 725, 821, 883

res, *p.p.* of **rere;** *ferir res a res,* strike a glancing blow *Ch* 599

resalt, *ind. pr. 3* of **resaillir,** *v.n.* leap up again *M* 593

resanbler, *v.a.* resemble, look like *M* 515

resort, *sm.* remedy; *sanz r.* irremediably *Ch* 615

resnable, *adj.* reasonable, intelligent *Ch* 1006

respit, *sm.* delay *M* 90

respitier, *v.n.* delay *M* 536

restre (= **re** + **estre**), *v.n.* be likewise *M* 26, 484

retout, *ind. pr. 3* of **retoudre, retolir,** *v.a.* strike away again *M* 733

retrere *Ch* 15, *v.a.* give an account of, tell of, make known *Ch* 15, *M* 325

reva *M* 489, **revet** *Ch* 885, 909, *ind. pr. 3* of **raler** (= **re** + **aler**)

revel, *sm.* gladness, delight, bliss *Ch* 829

revenir, *v.n.*; *li revient a anui* is a trouble to him, presents him with trouble *M* 457

reventer, *v.n.* blow in their turn (of winds) *M* 202

revialt savoir = **vialt resavoir** wants next to know *Ch* 986; v. **re-**

riche, *adj.* splendid, magnificent *Ch* 211, 790

rien, riens, *sf.* anything *Ch* 183, 185, 239; thing *Ch* 310, 527, 894; *ne . . . de r.* not at all *Ch* 168, 1001, *M* 609, 675; not in anything *Ch* 291; *se nului i clainme r.* if anyone lays any claim to them *Ch* 1038

roé; v. **paile**

roïne, *sf.* queen *Ch* 31, *M* 26

roman, *sm.* romance *Ch* 803

ront, *ind. pr. 3* of **rompre** *v.a.* pull, tear out *M* 299

rosteler; v. **osteler** and **re-**

rote, *sf.* stringed instrument, rote *Ch* 802

rover, *v.a.* ask *Ch* 374

rungier, *v.a.* gnaw *M* 683

s'; v. **se, si, son**

sachier, *v.a.* pull, grab *Ch* 1115, *M* 701, 827

saignor *M* 973; *nom. sg.* **sire** *Ch* 85, 134, **sires** *Ch* 223; *sm.* lord, master *M* 487; husband *M* 973; (as vocative) Sir, my Lord *Ch* 452, *M* 966; (addressing King) Sire *M* 56

saillir; *ind. pr. 3* **salt** *Ch* 565, **saut** *M* 411, *6* **saillent** *M* 792; *pret. 3* **sailli** *Ch* 269: *v.n.* leap *Ch* 269, 598, *M* 351, 466

sain, *adj.* hale, in good health *M* 602; pure *M* 218

saisi, *p.p.* of **saisir,** possessed of, in possession of *Ch* 1026, 1068

sajement, *adv.* judiciously, discreetly *Ch* 305

sale, *sf.* hall, public living room (of a castle, but not necessarily the main hall; see Foulet in Roach) *Ch* 231, *M* 33

salu, *sm.* greeting, salutation *Ch* 158, *M* 485

samer, *v.a.* sow *Ch* 1170

sanblant, *sm.* appearance, aspect *M* 69; *par s.* in appearance *M* 11; to all appearances *M* 399*; *faire s.* make a show of *Ch* 223; give indications of *Ch* 342, 380, 559; *faire bel s.* make welcome *Ch* 409, 547*

sanbler = **sembler**

sarpant, sarpent, serpent, *sm.* snake *M* 182; dragon *M* 852, 877, 1100

saut; v. **saillir**

sauz, *sm.* willow *M* 932

savoir, *M* 448; *p.p.* **seü** *Ch* 200; *ind. pr. 1* **sai** *Ch* 532, **sé** *Ch* 330, *2* **sez** *Ch* 182, *3* **set** *Ch* 150, *4* **savon** *Ch* 188; *impf. 3* **savoit** *Ch* 55; *pret. 3* **sot** *Ch* 20; *fut. 1* **savré** *M* 580, *3* **savra** *Ch* 11; *impve. 2* **saches** *M* 856, *5* **sachiez** *Ch* 124; *subj. pr. 1* **sache** *Ch* 413; *subj. impf. 3* **seüst** *Ch* 401: *modal v.* know how to, be able to *Ch* 11; **savoir a** *v.a.* know to be *M* 646

se *Ch* 15, 246, *M* 83, **s'** *Ch* 136, *M* 48, *conj.* if; *se . . . non* except, if not *Ch* 183, 287, *M* 400, 781; *se* (+ *subj.*) in the expression *se Dieus me voie Ch* 1067; v. **veoir.**

sebelin, *sm.* sable *Ch* 487

secont, *num. adj.* second *M* 712

sejorner, *v.n.* stay, linger *M* 355, 388

sel=**si**+**le** *Ch* 106, 599, 1088

sen, *sm.*; *do s. issir* faint away *M* 190

senefiance, *sf.* significance, meaning *M* 370, 1015

senefïer, *v.a.* mean *M* 447

sente, *sf.* path *M* 1038

seoir *Ch* 374; *pres. p.* **seant** *Ch* 81; *impf.3* **seoit** *Ch* 896, *6* **seoient** *M* 933; *v.n.* sit *Ch* 81; **bien seant** *adj.* pleasantly situated *M* 94, 428; *inf. subst.* seat *Ch* 232

serjant, *sm.* servant *Ch* 243, 350

seror *M* 969; *nom. sg.* **suer** *M* 970, 1106: *sf.* sister

serre, *s.* safe place *M* 527; *graignor s.* place of greater safety *M* 527

serrer, *v.a.* hug, clutch *M* 826*; **serré,** *p.p. adj.* close (of texture), tough *M* 706

servise, *sm.* service, disposal *M* 967, 1084; service, respects *Ch* 306, *M* 903

set, *num. adj.* seven *M* 676

seür, *adj.*; *a s.* assured, certain *Ch* 391, 744

seürement, *adv.* in safety *M* 598, 1002; without fear *Ch* 247; for certain *Ch* 981

seus, *adj. nom. sg.* of **seul** alone *Ch* 88, 892, *M* 118, 561

sevre *Ch* 176; *fut. 5* **sivrez** *Ch* 192: *v.a.* follow *Ch* 176

si *Ch* 2, *M* 34, **s'** *Ch* 773, *conj.* and; (perhaps=and so, and therefore *Ch* 258; and yet, the fact remains that *M* 266, 922; (perhaps=*donc* and so *Ch* 708); as linking particle (not to be translated) *Ch* 349, 1057, *M* 74; (introducing impve.) *Ch* 247; **et si** *Ch* 236, *M* 236, 764, **et . . . si** *Ch* 269, **et se** *Ch* 106, 1088, **et si** *M* 23, and; **et si** (perhaps emphatic) and indeed *M* 11

si, *adv.* thus, in this fashion *Ch* 569; so (degree of comparison) *M* 98, 171, 195, 380; **si . . . con** as . . . as *M* 440; **si con** as, just as *Ch* 1125, 1198, *M* 22, 885; *conj.* although *M* 266; **si que** (+*indic.*) in such a way that, so that *Ch* 69, 95, 600, *M* 469, 713; **si que . . . ne** in such a way that . . . not, without *Ch* 631; **si . . . que, si . . . c'** (+*indic.*) so . . . that *M* 142, 429, 1018, (+*subj.*) *M* 194–6, 277, 1008

siecle, *sm.* world *M* 173

sil=**si**+**le** *Ch* 469

sire; v. **saignor**

sivrez; v. **sevre**

soe; v. **son**

soi, *pron. refl. tonic obl.* himself *M* 446, 867

sol, solement=**seul** *Ch* 586, **seulement** *Ch* 543; **sol** *n. adj.* as *adv.* *Ch* 929, 983; *sol a sol* in privacy, no one else being present *Ch* 628

solaus, *sm. nom. sg.* of **soleil** *Ch* 60, *M* 517

solaz, *sm.* pleasure, delight *Ch* 510

soloir; *ind. pr. 3* **suet** *M* 442: *v.n.* be wont, be accustomed *M* 22, 442

son, *poss. adj.*; *m.sg. nom.* **ses** *Ch* 400, *M* 349, 882; *obl.* **son** *Ch* 36, *M* 69; *pl. nom.* **si** *Ch* 833, **ses** *Ch* 833; *obl.* **ses** *Ch* 373, *M* 299; *f.sg.* **sa** *Ch* 21, *M* 42,

s' *Ch* 859, *M* 120; *pl.* **ses** *Ch* 12, *M* 544; *tonic forms m.sg. obl.* **suen** *Ch* 1101, *M* 5; *f.sg.* **soe** *Ch* 251, *M* 87, 91

soner, *v.a.*; *s. mot* say, utter a word *Ch* 1007

sor, *prep.* on *Ch* 126, *M* 37; on to *M* 412, 594; over, on top of *Ch* 39; *conquerre s.* gain victory over *M* 818

sorcil, *sm.* eyebrow *Ch* 642

sororé, *p.p. adj.* covered over, plated with gold *M* 935

sorquidé, *p.p. adj.* arrogant *Ch* 918

sou=**si**+**le** *Ch* 105

souef, *adj.* soft, smooth *Ch* 648

soufrir, soffrir *M* 807; *condit. 1* **souferroie** *Ch* 1045: *v.a.* suffer, permit *Ch* 1045; bear *M* 807

souper, *v.n.* to sup, have supper *Ch* 809, 812; *v.a.* sup on, have for supper *Ch* 436

soz, *prep.* under, beneath *Ch* 649, *M* 499, 833

suen; v. **son**

süer, *v.n.* sweat, labour *M* 940

sus, *adv.* up *Ch* 269; above *M* 936; *en sus* aside *Ch* 973

tables, *sf. pl.* backgammon *Ch* 804

taindre, *v.a.* strike, catch *Ch* 1119

taisant, *adj.* silent *Ch* 686

talant *Ch* 606, *M* 70, 630, **talent** *Ch* 386, *sm.* desire, inclination *Ch* 386, 606; *avoir t.* want *Ch* 386, *M* 70, 630; *a son t.* to his liking *Ch* 248; *prendre t.* be seized with a desire (to do something) *Ch* 34*; *fere son t. de* make love to *Ch* 530

taner, *v.a.* tan, brown *M* 517

tant *Ch* 22, **itant** *Ch* 504, *adv.* so much *Ch* 22, 285, 504, *M* 91, 129, 820; this much, to this effect *M* 332; **tant de,** *adv.* so much *M* 204; **a itant** now, meanwhile *Ch* 244; straightway *Ch* 341; **tant que, t. con** (+ *indic.*) *Ch* 49, 1093, *M* 30, 232, (+*subj.*) *Ch* 101, 757, *M* 79 until; **jusq'a t. que** (+*subj.*) until *M* 102; **par t.** by that means *Ch* 405; **por sol t. que** merely because *Ch* 1060; **t. seulement** alone, only *M* 120; **t. fere que** do so much that= go so far as to *M* 91, eventually *M* 120; **t. par,** v. **par**

tantost, *adv.* straightway *Ch* 129, 276; **t. con,** *conj.* as soon as *M* 73, 271, 761

tart, *adj.* late *M* 1131; *est t. que* (with *dat.* of person+*subj.*) longs to *M* 962, 977,

teche, *sf.* quality *Ch* 12

tel *M* 252; *f.sg.* **tel** *Ch* 88, *M* 725, **tele** *M* 774; *obl. pl.m.* **tieus** *M* 801, 812: *adj.* such

tenant, *adj.* long-lasting, durable *M* 859

tencier, *v.n.* compete, vie with one another *M* 1019

tenebre, *s.* darkness *M* 1033

tenebros, *adj.* dark *M* 172

tenir *Ch* 312; *ind. pr. 1* **taing** *Ch* 1037, **tieng** *M* 525; *pret. 6* **tindrent** *Ch* 1086; *fut. 3* **tendra** *M* 639; *condit. 3* **tendroit** *M* 618; *subj. pr. 5* **taigniez** *Ch* 955: *v.a.* hold, keep *M* 810; *v.refl.* pause *Ch* 716; *t. a* keep to, cleave to *Ch* 976, 1044; consider *Ch* 955, 1037, *M* 10, 153; **t. de,** *v. impers.* (with *dat.* of person) enter one's head to *M* 639; *t. conte* take account, tell, *Ch* 24; *t. lo chemin* follow the road *Ch* 48; *se t. a* choose, abide by *Ch* 312; cleave to *Ch* 1086, *M* 15; *se t. por* consider oneself, take oneself for *Ch* 658, *M* 604; *les paroles t.* converse *M* 30; *la parole t.* speak, say *M* 332; *son plait t.* plead *M* 349

tens, *sm.* time *M* 940

tere, *Ch* 16, *v.refl.* be silent *Ch* 16*

tierz, *ord. num.* third *Ch* 227, *M* 712

tieus; v. **tel**

toaille, *sf.* towel, napkin *M* 542, 944

tochier *M* 630, *v.a.* touch

toe; v. **ton**

toi, *tonic pron. 2nd pers.* (as direct *obj.*) *M* 751; (as *dat.*) *M* 844; (after *prep.*) *M* 831

toiere, *sf.* swamp, muddy pool *Ch* 1128

ton, *poss. adj.*; *m.sg. nom.* **tes** *M* 487; *obl.* **ton** *M* 745; *pl. obl.* **tes** *M* 526; *f.sg.* **ta** *M* 487; *tonic form f.sg.* **toe** *M* 577, 583

tor, *sm.*; v. **chief**

tor, *sf.* tower, keep *Ch* 231

torchier, *v.a.* rub down *M* 387

torner *Ch* 1159; *t. sor* make for, go towards *Ch* 660; *t. a declin* go down, set *Ch* 60; *t. a mal,* turn out badly *Ch* 621; *le me t. a mal* make me suffer for it *Ch* 1159; *s'en t.* go away *M* 356

tornoier, *v.n.* rotate, spin round *M* 440, 454, 1096

tost, *adv.* quickly, rapidly *Ch* 683, *M* 157; soon, easily, readily *Ch* 125*, 140, *M* 6, 298; v. also **par t.**; **si tost con,** *conj.* (+*condit.*) as soon as *M* 88; v. also **tantost con**

tot *Ch* 48; *m. nom. pl.* **tuit** *Ch* 787, *M* 354, 891, 935: *adj. and pron.* all; *adv.* quite, entirely *Ch* 27, 164, *M* 35, 54; (may agree with *adj.*) *toz abrivez Ch* 1033; *a toz* with *Ch* 884, 1018; *do tot* entirely *Ch* 249, 962; *tot a un mot* in a single word *Ch* 488; v. also **voie**

toudre; *p.p.* **tolu** *M* 80; *condit. 3* **toudroit** *Ch* 1053: *v.a.* take away *M* 80, (forcibly) *Ch* 1053; strike away *M* 711, 736

traï, *p.p.* of **traïr,** betrayed *Ch* 334; affected *Ch* 398

traïn, *sm.*; *se remetre en son t.* set off back *M* 259

traire, trere; *p.p.* **tret** *M* 695, *nom. sg. m.* **tres** *M* 96: *v.a. and refl.* draw *Ch* 785, *M* 695; withdraw *Ch* 973; *se t. avant* step forward *M* 96; *se t. vers* draw towards, draw closer to *Ch* 652; *p.p. adj.* drawn *Ch* 824; **t. a chief,** v. **chief; t. a mort,** v. **mort**

tranble, *s.* aspen M 932

trenchier M 707, *v.a.* cut M 707; cut off M 577; *v.n.* burst M 806

tres, *intensifying adv.*; *t. parmi* right across M 35

tres; v. **traire**

tresliz, *adj.* triple-meshed M 861

trespasser Ch 257, *v.a.* and *n.* pass, go past, go across Ch 159, 220, M 175; omit Ch 257, M 770*, 771*

trestot, *adj.* all, entire Ch 252, 753, M 87; *adv.* completely, utterly Ch 616; **trestuit,** *pron. nom. pl. m.* all Ch 988, M 63, 1019; v. also **delez**

trives, *sf. pl.* truce Ch 673

trompe, *sf.* top M 442

tronc, *sm.* block M 588, 621

trop, *adv.* very, very much M 162, 254; too, too much Ch 25; too long M 714; *ne t. ne poi* neither too much nor too little Ch 304

trover Ch 140; *p.p.* **trové** Ch 155; *ind. pr. 3* **trueve** Ch 1186; *subj. impf. 3* **trovast** Ch 75: *v.a.* find

tuit; v. **tot**

uis, us, huis Ch 500, M 439, 755, *sm.* door Ch 500, 513

umelïer, *v. refl.* make obeisance M 368

un, *indef. art.*; *un et un* one after the other Ch 757; **uns, unes** *pl.* a pair of Ch 38, 39, 41; v. also **armes**

usage, *sm.*; *l'avoir en u.* be thus Ch 1174

vaintre; *p.p.* **vaincu** M 779, 785; *subj. impf. 3* **vainquist** M 788: conquer, overcome M 779; *cil refust par lui vaincuz* he too had been conquered in his turn M 785

vair, *sm.* miniver, Ch 487; *adj.* lined or trimmed with miniver Ch 45

val, *sm.* valley Ch 149

valee, *sf.* valley M 169, 175

vaslet, *sm.* youth, serving-lad (of good birth) Ch 225*. (See Foulet in Roach, s.v. **vallet**.)

vassal, *sm.* knight M 826; *voc.* **vas(s)aus** (term of address, usually indicating annoyance, irritation, disdain etc.) Ch 722, 923

vellier, *v.n.* stay up, keep awake Ch 115, 681

venir Ch 875; *pres. p.* **veignant** M 483; *p.p.* **venu** Ch 218; *pret. 3* **vint** Ch 544, 6 **vindrent** Ch 1077; *fut. 1* **venré** Ch 846, 3 **venra** Ch 378, 6 **vendront** Ch 1049; *condit. 3* **vendroit** Ch 14; *subj. pr. 3* **viegne** M 51, 5 **venez** Ch 123; *subj. impf. 3* **venist** Ch 758; *impve. 2* **vien** M 587: *v.n.* come Ch 2, M 39; come back Ch 378, 689; *en v.* M 60, 587, *s'en v.* M 136, 481 come; *en v. a* come to, accrue to M 6*; *v. devant* (+ dat.) come up to M 897; *v. a plaisir* please Ch 311; *v. a chief* accomplish, succeed in M 672; *miaus v.* be better

Ch 588, *M* 248; *bien veignant!* welcome! *M* 483; *bien . . . venu(z)!* welcome! *M* 760, 921; **venir,** *inf. subst.* arrival *Ch* 224

ventaille, *sf.* ventail (part of helmet protecting mouth or chin) *M* 731

veoir *Ch* 373; *pres. p.* **veant** *Ch* 179; *p.p.* **veü** *Ch* 181; *ind. pr. 1* **voi** *Ch* 1027, *2* **vois** *M* 863, *3* **voit** *Ch* 206, *4* **veon** *Ch* 176, *5* **veez** *Ch* 144, *6* **voient** *M* 117; *pret. 1* **vi** *Ch* 1161, *3* **vit** *Ch* 73, *5* **veïstes** *Ch* 870, *6* **virent** *M* 37; *fut. 1* **verré** *M* 748, **verrai** *M* 667, *5* **verrez** *Ch* 149; *subj. pr. 1* **voie** *Ch* 413, *3* **voie** *Ch* 234, *5* **veoiz** *Ch* 511; *subj. impf. 3* **veïst** *M* 300; *impve. 5* **voiez** *Ch* 1095, **vez** *M* 987: *v.a.* see; *veant nos* before our very eyes *Ch* 179; *qui veïst!* you should have seen *M* 300; (in oath as expletive) *ja Dieus ne me voie* may God turn his face from me, God damn me *Ch* 1012; *se Dieus me voie* God bless me *Ch* 1067. (See Foulet in Roach, s.v. **se=si.**)

ver, *adj.* (stock epithet applied to eyes) bright, sparkling *Ch* 643. (See Foulet in Roach, s.v. **vair.**)

verité, *sf.* truth; *de v.* for a fact, for certain *Ch* 452

vermel, *adj.* crimson *M* 749

vermine, *sf.* reptiles *M* 263, 1044

vers, *prep.* towards *M* 38; compared with *Ch* 919*

vertu, *sf.* force, violence *M* 725, 801

vespre, *sm.* evening *Ch* 418, 1195

vespree, *sf.* evening *Ch* 808

vïele, *sf.* stringed instrument, fiddle *Ch* 799

viez, viés, *indecl. adj.* ancient, old *M* 3, 9, 13, 16

vilain, *adj.* base *Ch* 7, uncourtly *Ch* 263, 321

vilain, *sm.* villein, peasant, churl *Ch* 416*, 1184, *M* 1, 506

vilenie, *sf.* base conduct *Ch* 337, 550

vint, *num. adj.* twenty *Ch* 33, 543

vis, *sm.* face *Ch* 474, 644, *M* 892

vis; *ce m'est vis* it seems to me, in my opinion *Ch* 19

vis, *adj. nom.* of **vif** alive *Ch* 546, 700

vistement, *adv.* quickly *Ch* 169, 683

vo; *v.* **vostre**

voie, *sf.* road *Ch* 71; way *Ch* 95, 960, *M* 128; (metaphorical) *M* 9; journey *M* 85, 144, 925, 969; *tote(s) voie(s)* nevertheless *Ch* 17, *M* 926; always, continually *M* 15; *chemine t. v.* journeys on *M* 390

voir, *sm.* truth *Ch* 113; *de v.* of a truth, truly *Ch* 567, 947, *M* 1036

voir, *adv.* truly *M* 313, 928

voisin, *adj.* near *M* 1057

volenté, *sf.* intention *Ch* 399; wish, desire *Ch* 332, 451; *a sa v.* as he wishes *M* 550, *a ta v.* as you wish *M* 567; *fere sa v. (ses volontez) de* make love to *Ch* 522, 724; *faire vostre v. de* do what you wish with *Ch* 773

voloir; *ind. pr. 1* **voil** *Ch* 198, *2* **viaus** *M* 585, *3* **vialt** *Ch* 283, *M* 99 **viaut** *Ch* 293, *M* 616, **vuet** *M* 492, *5* **volez** *Ch* 191; *impf. 1* **voloie** *M* 939, *3* **voloit** *Ch* 717, *5* **volïez** *Ch* 1040; *pret. 3* **voust** *Ch* 239, **vost** *Ch* 403, *M* 101,

5 **vousistes** *Ch* 724; *fut. 3* **voudra** *M* 500, 5 **voudroiz** *Ch* 976; *condit. 3*
voudroit *Ch* 12; *subj. pr. 3* **voille** *Ch* 387, 6 **voillent** *M* 59; *subj.impf. 1*
vousisse *Ch* 610, *3* **vousist** *M* 85: *v.* wish, want, be willing; *a son voloir*
as one wishes *M* 769, 906; *voille o non* whether he will or no, willy-nilly
M 177
vostre, *Ch* 936, **vo** *Ch* 1035, *poss. pron.* yours
vuel, *sm.; mon v.* if I had my way *M* 302

INDEX OF PROPER NAMES

References are exhaustive, except where indicated by †.

Artu *M* 19, **Artu[r]** *Ch* 743, **Artus** *Ch* 29, *M* 21, **Artuz** *M* 282, (King) Arthur

Cardoil, Carlisle *Ch* 30, *M* 22
Champaigne, Champagne *M* 516
Crestïen de Troies, Chrétien de Troyes *Ch* 18

Damedieus, the Lord God *M* 1122
†**Dieu** *Ch* 158, *M* 354, **Dé** *M* 624, **Dieus** *Ch* 83, **Deus** *M* 571, God

Fortune *M* 425, 762

†**Gauvain** *Ch* 31, *M* 50, **monsaignor G.** *Ch* 8, *M* 918, **messire G.** *Ch* 119, *M* 716, Arthur's nephew (= Eng. Gawain)
Girflez, Girflet (one of Arthur's knights) *M* 286
Gringalet, lou, Gauvain's horse *Ch* 226★
Gueherïez, Gueheriet (one of Arthur's knights) *M* 285
Guenievre, (Queen) Guenevere *M* 1116

Inde Major, India *Ch* 993

†**Keu,** Kay (Arthur's seneschal) *Ch* 32, *M* 50

Logre, Arthur's kingdom *Ch* 750
Loire, River Loire *M* 392

Maisieres; v. Paiens de M.
Maïsté, li Sires de, Lord God *Ch* 1078
Maogre, Majorca *Ch* 749
Marcel, saint, *M* 510★
Moretaigne, Mauretania *M* 515

Nature *Ch* 259

Paiens de Maisieres, Paien de Maisières (named as author of *M*) *M* 14*
Palerne, Palermo *Ch* 485
Pantelïons, sainz, Saint Pantelion *M* 666*
Pavie, Pavia *M* 279
Pentecoste, Pentecost, Whitsun *M* 20
Pere, saint, Saint Peter *M* 746

Romenie, Romagna (?) *Ch* 485

Table Reonde, Round Table *M* 1121

Yvain *Ch* 32*, **messire Y.** *M* 286, one of Arthur's knights

TWO OLD FRENCH GAUVAIN ROMANCES

PART II

PARALLEL READINGS WITH
SIR GAWAIN AND THE GREEN KNIGHT
by
D. D. R. OWEN

INTRODUCTION

There exists a relationship of some kind between *Le Chevalier à l'épée* (=*Ch*) and *La Mule sans frein* (=*M*) on the one hand and *Sir Gawain and the Green Knight* (=*GGK*) on the other. This has long been recognised and can be strikingly demonstrated if we select and combine elements from the two French romances to produce the following story:

King Arthur holds court one festival time, with Guenevere and his lords and ladies all assembled (*M* 20–9). A shock-headed giant appears, of remarkable hue and armed with a great, broad-headed axe (*M* 504–17). As he has heard of Gauvain's high reputation, he will propose a 'game': Gauvain is to cut off his head with the axe on condition that he himself will later suffer a return stroke. Gauvain accepts and repeats the terms of the pact. The giant stretches out his neck; and when the hero has beheaded him with a single blow of the axe, the huge man at once takes up his head and departs (*M* 564–95).

Taking leave of the king, Gauvain arms and sets out from the court to pursue the adventure he has claimed (*M* 338–57). His steed is 'lou gringalet' (*Ch* 226). He proceeds through wild regions peopled with savage beasts and fire-breathing serpents (*M* 129–88, 358–83). Worse still is the bitter wintry cold he encounters as he travels through a valley (*M* 189–205). But emerging from the perilous country, he comes before a splendid, moated castle surrounded by a palisade of sharp stakes (*M* 425–34; *Ch* 206–17). He enters, to be civilly received by an underling (*M* 471–83). Servants take his arms and stable his horse; and he is led into the hall, where a fine fire burns (*Ch* 225–37). A man of stupendous size greets him (*M* 509–10, 518–19), and he is taken to a richly-furnished bed-chamber (*Ch* 472–93).

In the hall he is well feasted and too well wined (*Ch* 346–61); and the host learns with satisfaction that his guest is the peerless Gauvain (*Ch* 732–51). Then, from the moment when the hero finds himself in the presence of the young lady of the house, each is filled with admiration for the great beauty of the other. The knight greets the lady briefly and courteously (*Ch* 250–75) and offers her his service (*Ch* 306).

A light meal is served, and the wine flows free (*Ch* 434–45). Seated beside the lady, Gauvain exchanges courtly conversation with her, both taking delight in the other's presence (*Ch* 297–325). The host bids him not to leave the castle yet, and Gauvain agrees (*Ch* 376–8, 385–7). He is to sleep in the castle (*Ch* 455–7); and the lady will keep him company after dinner until the host returns from his woods (*Ch* 372–5).

The fair one joins him in his bed uninvited, and kisses and embraces are exchanged. More than once Gauvain, very conscious that his honour is at stake, is on the point of possessing her; but this he does not do (*Ch* 514–682). When he spurns the lady's offer of her person and of another rich gift, she bids him at their parting to take a bridle that she has (*M* 966–89). The host returns from the woods (*Ch* 426); and some time later Gauvain asks leave of him (*Ch* 835–41) and quits the castle with the bridle in his keeping (*M* 991–1002). He is warned of the perils that lie ahead: for the man who has called him to his dwelling has slain all who have gone there before, and Gauvain will stand in danger of his life. But, thinking of the injury to his reputation should he turn aside, the hero rides on (*Ch* 154–205).

Reaching his goal, he discovers an underground chamber that he decides to investigate, whereupon there emerges the giant from whom he is to receive the axe-blow (*M* 497–512). After an exchange of courtesies (*M* 518–23), Gauvain is told to prepare to take the stroke. He consents, and bends his neck. The giant brings down the axe but feints with it (*M* 608–30): Gauvain suffers no more than a slight flesh wound (*Ch* 598–601, 659–61). He has not been struck in earnest on account of his loyalty in keeping faith with the giant (*M* 631–3). Moreover the latter, by putting Gauvain to the seduction test, has proved him the best knight in the world; and he has fully assayed his merit with his weapon (*Ch* 746–63).

The hero refuses to have further dealings with the lady of the castle and indulges in a misogynistic outburst, complaining of woman's deceit since the time of Eve (*Ch* 1168–91). It remains for him to return to the royal court, where he is greeted by Arthur, Guenevere and the company of knights (*M* 1056–67), and there is general jubilation (*Ch* 1196). He has brought the bridle with him (*M* 1068 ff.), and tells his adventures from first to last, the good and the bad (*M* 1091–1112; *Ch* 1198–1202).

This, of course, give or take a little is the essential story of *GGK*. No doubt is possible about the existence of a relationship: its nature is the only point of debate, and the main alternatives can perhaps be reduced to four:

1. There has been common use of what some would call 'folklore motifs' or traditional elements taken from widely circulating popular tales. No direct line of transmission would be traceable between the French and English texts; and the *Gawain*-poet would probably have received his material by word of mouth (as indeed he claims at the beginning of his romance).

2. The Englishman has used as his primary source a text (presumably French) to which *Ch* and *M* were collaterally related. At its simplest, this would assume the existence of a story that was the common source for *Ch* and *M*, and a late version of which provided the model for *GGK*.

3. The *Gawain*-poet used a text in which the stories of *Ch* and *M* had already been conflated.

4. He knew and used *Ch* and *M* directly, along with a number of subsidiary sources.

I have elsewhere examined at some length the points where *GGK* recalls and those where it differs from the French romances.[1] They will all be scrutinised again in the Commentary that follows, so I shall not detail them here. But before deciding which of our feasible relationships has the most to commend it, it will be as well to look at the nature of those parallels and differences. Let us then start with the parallels.

Firstly there are many striking similarities of situation, as may readily be seen in the reconstruction above. Then within these situations we find numerous identical or very similar details that tend to occur in 'runs' as first one and then the other of the French texts offers a series of elements that is matched by a series in *GGK*. Some of these details are the commonplace of medieval romance, as when they relate to festivities at court, a knight's arrival and reception at a castle, his feasting there, well intentioned warnings of perils in store, a misogynistic tirade (less common in the romance, of course, than in other branches of medieval literature), or the hero's return and account of his adventures. In themselves they cannot be considered significant, but their occurrence in runs does give them some value as evidence.

In a different category are the many less conventional details, and

[1] 'Burlesque Tradition and *Sir Gawain and the Green Knight*', *Forum for Modern Language Studies* IV (1968), pp. 125–45.

among them a number that are probably unique to these texts. There is, for instance, the appearance of the challenger: his great size, shaggy hair, amazing colour (not the same, admittedly, in *M* and *GGK*, but in both texts it inspires wonder). Despite various circumstantial differences, the proposal and acceptance of the grisly 'game' are couched in strikingly similar terms; and the same may be said of the two bouts of axe-play, especially when one takes into account parallels with the sword-testing in *Ch*, and the emergence of the challenger in both *M* and *GGK* from underground, a feature for which neither story offers an explanation. Consider too the sequence of the hazards faced by the hero on his journey to the castle in *M* and *GGK*, or the detailed description of the bedchamber and fireside seat common to *Ch* and the English romance. Accounts of feasts are one of the staples of romance, but not references to Gauvain/Gawain's over-indulgence in wine. Then we find, in both *Ch* and *GGK*, the host offering his guest the pleasure of the lady's company until his return from his woods; Gauvain/Gawain's earnest but unwonted concern for his honour when alone with the fair one at night; the host's admission of having tested him with his weapon; the uncharacteristic indulgence by Arthur's nephew (of all people!) in anti-feminist railing; and the hero's avowal at the close of both *Ch* and *GGK* of the unfortunate side of his adventures, neither tale ending on that note of triumph which is sounded at the finish of most romances. None of this is banal; all (and many subsidiary points that I omit) is shared by the English and French poems.

One or two small details may be mentioned which, while they are perfectly at home in their French context, are less well motivated when they appear in the English poem. The offering in *M* of an option (*jeu parti*, with the idea of 'game' lost or much reduced) matches better, one might think, the frightful nature of the beheading test than does the craving in *GGK* of a Christmas 'game', however skilfully the Englishman has developed the yuletide atmosphere of the occasion. Less debatable, perhaps, is the fact that whereas the hero's recapitulation of the terms of the agreement has, as we shall see, a real function in the narrative of *M*, in *GGK* it is somewhat gratuitous. More striking still is the strained logic of the sight of Gawain's limbs beneath his robe in *GGK* 868 by comparison with the parallel reference in *Ch* 511.

A wealth of parallel situations and within those situations runs of matching details that range from the conventional to the otherwise unique—what more does our comparative study have to offer? Surprisingly, in view of the vastly different styles of the French and English poems, it reveals a number of close verbal resemblances such as the following:

> Al watz hap vpon heȝe in hallez and chambrez   (GGK 48)

... li baron ... / Furent alé esbanoier / Parmi la sale amont as estres.   (M 31-3)

> 'Bot for þe los of þe, lede, is lyft vp so hyȝe ...'
> ' ... I passe as in pes, and no plyȝt seche ...'
> 'Þou wyl grant me godly þe gomen þat I ask
>   bi ryȝt.'   (GGK 258, 266, 273-4)

'Ice te demant tot en pes: / ... / Por ce que t'ai oï prisier, / Te partis orendroit un jeu, / Et por ce que je voi mon leu.'   (M 562, 564-6)

Gawain and the lady indulge in

> ... clene cortays carp closed fro fylþe.   (GGK 1013)

Tant l'ot cortoisement parler / Et tant lo voit de bones mors ... (Ch 314-15)

The lady's beauty is described:

> Wyth chynne and cheke ful swete,
> Boþe quit and red in blande,
> Ful lufly con ho lete
> Wyth lyppez smal laȝande.
>
>   (GGK 1204-7)

Et fres et coloré lo vis, / La boche petite et riant,   (Ch 644-5)

And later, the reasons given for the feinted strokes are identical:

> ' ... þou trystyly þe trawþe and trwly me haldez.'   (GGK 2348)

... Por ce que mout loiaus estoit, / Et que bien tenu li avoit / Ce qu'il li avoit creanté.   (M 631-3)

Further word for word correspondences can be cited. The testing weapon, for instance, is referred to as a 'giserne' in GGK (288 etc.) and as a 'jusarme' in M (512 etc.). Remarkably, when the hero approaches the scene of his ordeal, the description in GGK of what he sees contains in three lines (764-6) four terms ('a won', 'in a mote', 'loken', 'diches') that appear in three lines (207-9) of the parallel account in *Ch* ('sor une mote', 'chastel', 'fermez', 'fossé'). Even less to be expected is the information in both the English and the French that the hero lights on a 'cave' (*GGK* 2182, *M* 498); but his curiosity as to what it might be is never satisfied, since his deliberations are cut short by the emergence of the challenger.

Worthy of mention is another type of correspondence, namely that in which we find an 'echo' from one of the French romances interrupting in *GGK* a run of parallels with the other. One such intrusion occurs when, within the temptation sequence with all its reminiscences of *Ch*, the lady's words recall those of the damsel in *M*:

> 'ȝe ar welcum to my cors,
> Yowrc awen won to wale,
> Me behouez of fyne force
> Your seruaunt be, and schale.'
>
> (*GGK* 1237–40)

'Sire,' fait ele, 'il est bien droiz / Que je mete tot a devise / Lo mien cors en vostre servise.'   (*M* 1082–4)

Similarly, though the dealing of the axe-blow reminds us essentially of *M*, the hero's flesh wound is exactly paralleled in *Ch*:

> . . . he . . . hurt hym no more
> Bot snyrt hym on þat on syde, þat seuered þe hyde.
>
> (*GGK* 2311–2)

Sel fiert res a res do costé / Si qu'il li a do cuir osté, / Mes ne l'a pas granment blecié.   (*Ch* 599–601)

Reserving our judgment for the moment on all these parallels between *GGK* and the French poems, let us turn to the almost equally striking differences, and first to certain important features of the English romance that are quite foreign to *Ch* and *M*. Chief of these are the information carried in the prologue, the pentangle passage, the exchange of winnings motif, and the sinister presence of Morgan the Fay. The exchange of winnings, it is true, is admirably linked to the central theme; nevertheless none of these elements can be considered vital to the plot, and it is no coincidence that they are often supposed to have been derived by the Englishman from secondary sources. Indeed, if we are to credit him at all with the ability to assemble material from more than one place, then here are very clear instances where the possibility must be allowed.

Are we also to believe him capable of embellishing and expanding his chief matter from the resources of his own imagination as well as from a knowledge of other literature? This is surely more prudent than to reduce him in our view to a skilful translator and metrician, denying him any creative power. It follows that an event, a scene tersely depicted in *Ch* or *M* may have sufficed to inspire a more elaborate and richly detailed version of the same thing in *GGK*. The most striking example may be the dashing descriptions of the hunt in the English poem, standing in place of a single line in *Ch*; but some subsidiary source could well have made its contribution here. So the fact that the length of *GGK* well exceeds that of *Ch* and *M* together cannot properly be held as evidence against a close relationship.

More significant, it may be thought, is the very different way in which certain episodes are treated. In particular, whereas in *M* only one night separates the two parts of the beheading test, in *GGK* a whole year intervenes; and secondly, there is a wealth of difference between the seduction scenes in *Ch* and in the English romance. One could, of course, argue that if the Englishman was free to combine and restructure earlier material, he must also be granted the liberty to follow his own caprice in modifying what he found there. But in these two cases it is interesting to find strong indications of the influence of subsidiary sources. In the Caradoc story a year elapses between the striking of the two blows, and there is good reason to suppose the Englishman familiar with this tale.[2] And as regards Gawain's relationship with the lady of the castle, we shall see that his knowledge and use of Chrétien's *Lancelot* at this point is equally probable.

There is another kind of discrepancy between *GGK* and the French texts which may be illustrated by three examples: in *GGK* the challenger is green, in *M* black; in *GGK* the hero shows a great depth of humility when he volunteers to undertake the adventure (ll. 343–61), and this is in strong contrast to Gauvain's cocksure attitude in *M* (ll. 304 ff., 568 ff.); the quest in *M* is for a bridle, whereas in *GGK* it is a girdle that is brought back to court. Common to each of these examples is the fact that the French work provides an element that could have prompted a deliberate change on the Englishman's part: the challenger's astonishing colour; Gauvain's utter self-confidence coupled with his hypothetical reference to his witlessness (we shall

---

[2] See especially Larry D. Benson, *Art and Tradition in 'Sir Gawain and the Green Knight'*, New Brunswick, N.J. (Rutgers U.P.), 1965.

study this later); the bridle surrendered to him by the lady and brought back from his adventure.

Lastly, there is a good deal of episodic matter in the two French romances that does not appear in any form in *GGK*. But it would be idle to suggest that in view of this the Englishman must have been working from a simpler model. Anybody wishing to conflate the stories of *Ch* and *M* is forced into some degree of selection: will the hero ride a mule or his own steed, 'lou Gringalet'? will his testing occur in a revolving fortress or a more orthodox castle? will he leave that place alone or in the lady's company? There are, to be sure, some episodes that might be taken into a composite version but which are absent from *GGK*; on the other hand, one has only to consider the possibility of the *Gawain*-poet performing this operation to see valid artistic reasons for their exclusion.

*　　*　　*

When all these facts are taken into account, what kind of relationship do they imply? For a start, no argument can, I think, be derived from the differences between the English and French texts. If the relationship is distant, no further explanation is needed; if it is close (as direct derivation), the reason for them can only be that the English poet rehandled his material extensively, selecting some episodes and discarding others, modifying certain elements to accommodate them to his new narrative pattern and others simply as the fancy took him, calling upon further sources from time to time in order to enhance the structure or texture or tone of his work. No one, I imagine, would claim that he invented the bulk of the romance. Therefore he either built it up from a body of source material (known or unknown) or performed a task of translation and limited redaction, working from a text now lost. In the latter case, we have to assume that most of the differences between his poem and *Ch* and *M* were in his lost French model, and so his role is virtually reduced to that of a talented translator. In the former case, he would emerge as a more independent, creative literary artist, with powers of invention and organisation beyond those of a mere redactor. Either is theoretically possible; but there is in *GGK* an imaginative range and especially a verbal richness not characteristic of surviving French romances, but speaking rather in favour of the first possibility.

The least one can say is that, in the absence of any indication that the Englishman was not capable of making such changes as would explain the differences between his poem and the French, the question of their relationship can be approached only through the similarities they show. As far as the general thematic developments are concerned, almost all can be accounted for by reference to *Ch* and *M* or to other surviving texts or traditions; so we are again thrown back on the possibilities that either the *Gawain*-poet did the assembling himself or he transposed a lost text where it had been done for him. It may be noted that there is no evidence at all that the beheading and seduction tests were associated in a single story antedating *Ch* and *M*; and indeed it is likely that the author of *Ch* invented his seduction episode by combining elements from Chrétien's *Lancelot* and *Gauvain*.

When we turn to the similarities of detail, we find that these must preclude any distant relationship. Even allowing for the fact that they include a number of the stereotypes of medieval romance, when considered together they do demand, by the manner of their occurrence as well as by their substance, a very different explanation. There are present in great quantity parallels which it would be hard to find elsewhere, and which appear in matching sequences or runs. The more conventional details, by occurring within such runs, acquire a value as evidence which they would not have in isolation. It might be claimed that resemblances are of little significance when they concern a knight's coming to a castle and passing over the bridge, having his horse stabled and being led into the hall where a fire blazes, being welcomed by the host and told to do there as he pleases. But when that knight is Gauvain/Gawain and he is arriving at the place of his nocturnal testing, while in both accounts he had already met the welcoming host, the correspondences of detail are all the more telling. And when they are prefaced, as we have seen, by lines (describing the castle's situation) that show precise verbal parallels in unusual combination, only by pinning one's faith on extreme coincidence can one avoid accepting a very close relationship.

Indeed it is verbal correspondences such as those I have quoted that would seem to clinch the case for a not merely close, but direct connection between the texts. Along with the less logical appearance in the English of perfectly reasonable details from the French, they make it hard to conceive the use by the *Gawain*-poet even of an intermediate text. Of course, one can never deny the ultimate possibility that some Frenchmen combined *Ch* and *M* into a single story, retaining not only all those events common to them and *GGK* but also the original phraseology virtually intact. But why strain after some unknown and unknowable French redactor and his imagined text in order to belittle the Englishman's achievement?

My conclusion, therefore, is that the *Gawain*-poet made systematic use of his direct and detailed knowledge of *Ch* and *M* in much the same form as we have them today. I maintain that on those who would contest this lies the onus of providing a simpler and more plausible explanation, based on close study of the texts, for every correspondence of incident, detail and expression. Since I doubt whether this can be done, I shall base my investigation of *GGK* on the assumption of the author's direct indebtedness to the French romances as his principal and essential sources. So in the comparative study that follows, I shall not be attempting to establish or re-argue my case, though it may be that further relevant evidence will emerge.

No doubt some of the parallels I shall suggest will seem at first sight venturesome, even capricious. But before passing judgment, the reader will, I hope, carefully review all the relevant circumstances: for me to reiterate them at every turn would unnecessarily lengthen my study and prove dull preaching to the already converted. So let a single example serve now to make my point.

In my earlier paper, I proposed that a line from *M*, ' "Mout savré," fait Gauvains, "petit" ' (580), may be seen as 'prompting the Englishman to make Gawain indulge in an excess of humility: "I am the wakkest, I wot, and of wyt feblest" (354)'.[3] To the cursory reader this must appear an extremely dubious proposition; but some reflection will perhaps temper his initial scepticism.

The terms of the beheading challenge and a description of the first blow are given in *M* 574–94 and, with much expansion and some circumstantial differences, in *GGK* 288–432. Despite the dissimilar presentation of the events in *GGK*, a first examination will show that all but three of the twenty-one lines of *M* find an echo there, and in the same sequence as in the French. Of those three lines, 588 contains a reference to the block which, in his context, the Englishman would have perfectly good reasons for discarding. The others are 590–1, where Gauvain states that his mind is made up regarding the challenge:

> 'Mout savré,' fait Gauvains, 'petit,
> Se je ne sai louquel je preigne.'

Now if the *Gawain*-poet did use these lines as he used the rest of the

[3] Op. cit., pp. 131–2.

French passage (except for 588), keeping the original sequence, we would expect to find them recalled somewhere between the Green Knight's statement of his terms and Gawain's recapitulation of them (i.e. somewhere within ll. 301–80). And what do we find?—This is precisely the passage in *GGK* where Gawain declares his desire to accept the challenge (in place of Arthur); and he prefaces his request with the words:

'I am the wakkest, I wot, and of wyt feblest.' (354)

The plea of coincidence may once more be entered, especially perhaps in view of the tense of *savré* in *M* 580, which makes the sense of Gauvain's remark quite the opposite of Gawain's: 'I will show myself very feeble-minded if . . .' against 'I am the most feeble-minded'. Yet the fact remains that when due account is taken of all the circumstances, when the same character at the same juncture in virtually the same train of events refers to his own (hypothetical or actual) extreme lack of 'wyt', I at least would not be prepared to rate the chances of coincidence or even of vague recollection on the Englishman's part very high.

For the purposes of the following commentary, then, I have to assume from the start that the whole of my case for a direct relationship is made. When more corroborative evidence is introduced, this will be a by-product of the exercise, not its purpose. My aim henceforth will be to discover what light a knowledge of the *Gawain*-poet's chief sources can throw on his working methods. I shall not attempt any systematic or overall interpretation of *GGK*. At best my observations may encourage a few new lines of enquiry and evaluation; but even in provoking disagreement they may serve to bring into sharper focus certain problems that have to be faced by the student of the English romance, not least in connection with the extent and nature of the indisputable French influence. Subsidiary sources will be mentioned from time to time, but will not be comprehensively examined. In brief, my intention is simply to offer a set of working notes in the hope that, directly or indirectly, they may make some contribution towards a fuller appreciation of a very remarkable work of literature.

The English poem will be considered section by section, my divisions being governed more by the author's use of his models than by the phases of the narrative, though the two aspects often coincide. When this has been done, I shall try to draw together the principal lessons that have been learned and offer a general view of the poet's narrative craft as revealed by his use of the primary sources. Some readers may prefer to turn first to this summary conspectus before embarking on the detailed enquiry to which I now proceed.

COMMENTARY

GGK ll. **1-36**[1]   *Prologue.*

This opening has no parallel in *Ch* or *M*. The author's reference to an oral source may be purely conventional. The nature of some of the parallels that follow suggests a closer knowledge of the French texts than mere hearsay would allow. He seems either to have had access to them in manuscript or to have committed them to memory in most of their detail.

37-59   *Arthur's Christmas court at Camelot.*

The initial setting of the scene is conventional, but is probably elaborated from *M* 20-33. It is noteworthy that the passages have seven elements in common: King Arthur—at (named town)—on (named feast-day)—with many knights—indulging in recreation—with fair ladies—in halls and chambers. Compare in particular *GGK* 48 with *M* 33, where *vpon heȝe* is paralleled by *amont* and could therefore be interpreted as 'above', 'upstairs' rather than 'to the highest pitch' (TGD).

60-135   *The king will not join the banquet until he learns of an adventure.*

This passage has no significant parallel in the French texts (apart from the introduction of Guenevere, *GGK* 74, *M* 26, *Ch* 31). The poet adopts the motif found in other Arthurian romances, including *Caradoc*,[2] of the king not eating until some adventure presented itself (cf. TGD, p. 76). But apart from introducing this note of expectancy, his chief purpose here seems to be to create an atmosphere of rich living and carefree happiness against which to set the sudden change of mood at the Green Knight's arrival.

[1] All references to *GGK* are to the text of J. R. R. Tolkien and E. V. Gordon, 2nd edn. revised by Norman Davis, Oxford, 1967. I refer to this edition as TGD.

[2] For the Caradoc story see W. Roach and R. H. Ivy, *The Continuations of the Old French 'Perceval': The First Continuation* (Philadelphia, 1949-52), Vol. I, pp. 90 ff., Vol. II, pp. 210 ff., and Vol. III, i, pp. 142 ff.

136-231 *The Green Knight enters.*

M 504–17 provides the essentials: There suddenly appears—a terrible figure—of enormous height.—His unusual complexion—evokes wonder.—He has a mane of hair—and carries an axe—that is huge—and broad. The Englishman has, however, decided to replace the churl (*vilain*) of *M* with a more noble personage (a necessary step, since he will later be equated with Gawain's lordly host), and for this he had a likely model in *Caradoc*, where the intruder is a knight, is richly dressed, and rides his steed into the hall (the *vilain* of *M* is not mounted). From these two sources, and using his descriptive gifts to great advantage, he has elaborated this memorable scene. The challenger's strange greenness is an invention prompted, it would appear, by the churl's remarkable hue (blackness) in *M*, but not otherwise motivated in the French texts.

In making the challenger burst into the royal court and not merely turn up, as in *M*, in the course of Gawain's later adventures, the poet doubtless had the Caradoc story in mind. With his eye for symmetry, he saw moreover that of the two encounters in the beheading game, one could be used to initiate the action and the other to provide its climax. To this end he was also to appropriate the year's delay between them that figures in *Caradoc*. Already we have an inkling of his great talent for organising his material.

232-57 *Arthur greets the intruder.*

No parallel in the French texts. The court's reaction to the Green Knight's arrival is used to build up dramatic tension; and Arthur's courteous greeting serves to introduce the dialogue leading up to the newcomer's outrageous request.

258-300 *The Green Knight's challenge.*

As in *Caradoc*, the terms of the challenge are addressed to the king, but the Green Knight's preamble is much the same as in *M* 559–67: Because of your reputation—(I come in peace, seeking no hostility)—I ask a game—as it is appropriate. The Englishman fills out the scene a little by making Arthur mistake his intentions, then he returns to the details of his model: With this *giserne* (*jusarme*, *M* 574)—I shall suffer a blow—on condition that I may return the stroke—on a later occasion. —Now what will the answer be? (*M* 574–9)

The points I have enumerated are contained in fifteen quite bald lines of M. Emphasising his peaceful intentions, the churl says that because of Gauvain's renown he proposes a *jeu parti*, since the time is propitious.[3] At this point (*M* 567–73) he calls upon Gauvain to choose, and the hero agrees. Then the 'choice' is offered:[4] 'Behead me with this axe on condition that I will cut off your head in the morning when I return. Now make your choice.'

The Englishman's method in expanding this passage is easy to follow and will be found typical of his use of source material throughout the romance. First he takes up the motif of the renown of the person addressed by the challenger and deals with it in seven lines, extending the compliment paid to Arthur to cover in particular the quality and chivalry of his knights. This prepares us for the issuing of the challenge not to the king himself but to his entourage. Next there is the challenger's profession of his peaceful intentions, likewise taken over and expanded. On the face of it, Arthur's subsequent assumption (*GGK* 275–8) that he comes seeking a fight (and this is still part of the expansion of the 'peace' motif) is uncalled for; but perhaps the poet wishes to suggest that the intruder's fierce appearance outweighs the mildness of his words, and Arthur's declaration does give the Green Knight an opportunity to reiterate that, despite his ability to vanquish all comers, he craves in fact only a game.

It may be that the *Gawain*-poet was unfamiliar with the French expression *partir un jeu* (in any case in *M* it is not altogether appropriate in this context) and that this gave rise to his rather bizarre notion of the challenge being a game. It is also possible that his imagination simply played about the word *jeu*, leading him to the idea of a sport that could be accommodated to the setting of yuletide revelry. Or again, it is by no means out of the question that, under the influence of the French idiom, he conceived the beheading test as a game when he was still planning his romance, and that it was this idea that moved him to substitute Christmas for the Pentecost of *M* as the festival when the test was to take place. It is far from easy to assess his command of French: there are places, as we shall see, where he seems to have mis-

[3] *Ieu* is glossed by Orłowski as 'droit' in his edition of *M*. This would make the correspondence with *GGK* even more exact; but we find this hard to justify.

[4] No alternative is stated; and Orłowski, following Gaston Paris, supposed that there is a lacuna in the text at this point. As there is no other evidence for this, it is likely that the alternative was left implicit. In *Caradoc* the intruder requests a *don*, which is more appropriate. The illogicality in *M* may simply stem from the author's arbitrary choice of the phrase *partir un jeu*.

interpreted a word or two; yet who can say that these are not instances of his playing with associations rather than misunderstanding the literal meaning?

Gauvain's acceptance of the *jeu parti* comes in *M* (568–73) before the churl proposes its terms. The author of *GGK* has not yet brought the challenger into confrontation with Gawain, since his court setting demands that it should be the king who is first addressed; and so his postponement of the hero's acceptance follows naturally. It may be noted that Gauvain refers to the churl as 'mon bon oste' (*M* 573), and one might wonder if it was this that gave the Englishman the idea of identifying the Green Knight with Gawain's host at the castle where he undergoes the seduction test, and thus adroitly linking the two originally independent stories. This may seem far-fetched, but it will emerge ever more clearly as we proceed that we are dealing not with a mere line-by-line composer, but with a man who had a gift for organising his material into a tightly-knit and harmonious whole, and whose powers of invention were apt to be set in play by the smallest detail in his models.

Though worded differently and more rhetorical in their expression, the terms of the game in *GGK* are very similar to those in *M*, with the exception already mentioned that a year's respite is substituted for that of a single night. The Englishman does add the detail of the Green Knight's offering his axe as a gift to any who takes up the challenge: indeed, it is retained by Gawain as a marvel among men. Although there is nothing of this in *M*, we are told there that when Gauvain has taken the weapon and delivered the blow, the *vilain* catches up his head and makes off. Were it not for his reappearance some lines later carrying his axe, the natural inference would have been that it had been left behind in the hero's hands. In *GGK* inference has become stated fact.

The passage ends, as in *M*, with the challenger calling urgently, though in different terms, for a reply. In the French, of course, his words are addressed to Gauvain alone, in *GGK* to the court at large, since Gawain has as yet been glimpsed but briefly at the queen's side.

301-74   *Gawain is granted the 'game'.*

Having located the scene at the royal court, the Englishman now has to bring Gawain forward as the one to confront the challenger. This could have been simply done in a couple of lines, but he prefers to insert a tensely dramatic scene: the silence; the intruder's taunts (following ironically upon his earlier complimentary address); Arthur's shame and forthright acceptance of the challenge; Gawain's courteous intervention and claim that his more humble person, not the king's should be put at risk; Arthur's surrender of the axe to his nephew.

For the *Gawain*-poet Arthur was no 'roi fainéant', as his predecessors had often portrayed him. So he thought it appropriate that it should be he who made the first move, especially as the request for the 'game' had been first addressed to him. The transference of the honour to Gawain then had to be contrived, and this he managed with admirable tact and no bruising of royal dignity.

At first sight there appears to be nothing of the French texts in all this. Yet, as I suggested in my introductory remarks, it seems to have been a single line in *M* that prompted the Englishman to make Gawain indulge in his almost excessive show of humility: ' "Mout savré," fait Gauvains, "petit . . ." ' (*M* 580). This immediately follows the *vilain*'s call to Gauvain to choose his course of action, and has a direct echo in GGK 354: 'I am þe wakkest, I wot, and of wyt feblest.' Here we have the kind of correspondence of small verbal detail within a run of parallels that, when found so often throughout the English romance, convinces us that its author had his models virtually word-perfect and was not using some vague memory of tales once heard.

375-416 *The terms of the 'game' are rehearsed, and Gawain asks the knight's name.*

In *M* Gauvain makes his choice by repeating the terms proposed by the *vilain* (580–5). There is no need for such recapitulation in GGK: the challenge has been issued in the full hearing of the court and of Gawain, who now comes forward to meet it, axe in hand. It would not, perhaps, have been surprising had the Green Knight reiterated his terms and demanded Gawain's agreement before any blow was struck; but to make the hero repeat them is a less obvious device and plainly taken over from *M*. Indeed at this point we are very near to direct translation: The hero will deal the first blow 'quat-so bifallez after', GGK 382 ('conment qu'il aviegne', *M* 582); and after a lapse of time will 'take at þe an oþer / Wyth what weppen so þou wylt', GGK 383–4 ('te renderai / La moie [teste], se vjaus que la rende', *M* 584). In both texts the challenger thereupon exclaims his complete satisfaction at the response.

But around this passage the Englishman has added something new, namely the challenger's asking his opponent's name, his demand that he shall be later sought out by Gawain, the latter's request that the intruder's identity and dwelling be divulged, and the reply that he shall learn it when the blow has been struck. In this addition we have a good example of the *Gawain*-poet's care for proper motivation. In *M* there is an air of mystery about the *vilain*. Not only is he never named and his position and function never satisfactorily elucidated, but from the first he shows knowledge of Gauvain's errand (526 ff.) and a little later of his name (559), seemingly without being told. Whether this is careless composition on the part of the author or some vestige of the churl's supernatural origin we are left to surmise. At least it did not satisfy the Englishman. So first he effected in a logical way the disclosure of Gawain's identity; then, with the hero committed to go after a year in search of the challenger, he made preliminary provision for the divulgence of the latter's name and dwelling too.

The Englishman returns to his source with the intruder's call to action (412–4), corresponding to the 'or en vien donc!' of *M* 587.

417-61 *The Green Knight is beheaded, summons Gawain to the tryst at the Green Chapel, and departs.*

Now the Green Knight takes up his stance, bending and exposing his neck. Gawain lays hold of the axe and severs the head with one blow. All this is in *M* where, however, we find a further detail: the *vilain* lays his head on a block, to which he has led Gauvain. Perhaps the Englishman deemed this superfluous; more likely he thought the block would be incongruous in the royal court. But the brilliant visual touches he adds more than compensate for his omission; and many more follow as he replaces the two bald lines of *M* ('Li vilains resalt maintenant / Sor ses piez, et sa teste prent', 593–4) with a scene containing this information, but in much more vivid terms. Then, whereas the *vilain* simply returned with his head to the *cave*, the Green Knight holds his aloft so that, when he has mounted his steed, it may speak his fateful summons to Gawain. Like many of his compatriots, this English poet shows a power of imagination and a particular taste for weird and grisly detail such as is seldom encountered in medieval French writers, and certainly not in the author of *M*.

I hope that at this point I may be allowed a moment of unsupported speculation. The Green Knight gives his identity thus: 'Þe knyȝt of þe grene chapel men knowen me mony' (454); and it is at the Green Chapel that Gawain must find him. Now I proposed earlier that the knight's strange hue was suggested by the remarkable pigmentation of the *vilain*: but why green? *M* gives us no help. I suspect, though can offer little evidence, that here the Englishman was influenced by another French text he knew, a text that told of a knight dressed all in green, or at least with a green hat on his head. I fancy that this knight was referred to, even if he had another name, as 'li chevaliers au vert chapel'. The *Gawain*-poet might have misunderstood the meaning of *chapel*, 'hat', or else deliberately mistranslated it in order to give the Green Knight a mysterious and unlikely abode. That, it seems to me, would be in keeping with his methods as we see them operating throughout the romance. But until such a text is produced, of course, the possibility must remain in the realm of hypothesis.[5]

462-90 *The feast is resumed.*

No parallel in the French texts. In *M* at this point Gauvain retires to bed to sleep soundly. The Englishman, on the other hand, breaks the tension by making Gawain, Arthur and the court return to their good humour; and, with the axe hanging as a trophy above the dais, the feast is resumed. It is inevitable now that the 'run' of borrowings from *M* must be interrupted, since the second beheading follows directly there, whereas the Englishman has elected to postpone it until much later.

491-565 *A year passes.*

No parallel in the French texts. The *Gawain*-poet has chosen to indicate now the passing of a year; and this he does with great felicity as well as logic by describing the passage of the seasons. He leads back into the action by showing Gawain resolved to leave in order to keep his pledge, despite the sorrow of the court.

566-618 *Gawain arms.*

The first part of the description of Gawain's arming shows some possible debt to *Ch*, but a much clearer one to Chrétien's *Erec*, though naturally enough the Englishman describes his dress in terms of the fashion of his own day.

In *Ch* Gauvain, though not unarmed as we later discover, does not equip himself, when he leaves court, for some knightly foray or

---

[5] In view of other correspondences with the romance of *Boeve de Haumtone*, it is interesting to find that in one of the Continental versions the hero is furnished with 'un vert chapel' (see A. Tobler & E. Lommatzsch, *Altfranzösisches Wörterbuch*, under *chapel*).

expedition, but simply for a pleasant ride in the country. The richness of his costume, however, may have prompted the *Gawain*-poet to elaborate on his own hero's accoutrement. Reminiscences of detail may be the fine silk of the doublet (*GGK* 571, cf. *Ch* 40), the fur-lined *capados* (*GGK* 572-3, cf. the *mantel vair* of *Ch* 45), and the golden spurs (*GGK* 587, *Ch* 38). But there is nothing here singular enough to clinch the case.

More certainly, however, the Englishman had in mind the arming of Erec as he composed his scene.[6] The following common features are found: the hero asks for his armour; a rich carpet (*tapit* is the word in both texts) is spread on the floor; there his gear is placed and he goes to be armed; his feet and legs are clad in steel; he dons a hauberk of fine chain-mail with an undergarment beneath, and there is mention of a rich surcoat; he takes his sword and a brilliantly shining helmet adorned with a gemmed circlet. In *GGK* Gawain mounts Gryngolet, which (as 'le Gringalet') is also his steed in *Erec* and *Ch*. Remembering the lapse of two centuries between Chrétien's romance and *GGK*, and in view of the Englishman's clear concern to evoke contemporary military fashion, we may think it remarkable that the descriptions tally in so many respects. So here is a readily identifiable instance of how he called upon his acquaintance with subsidiary texts to furbish up the rather lustreless material of *M* and *Ch*.

619-69 *The pentangle on Gawain's shield.*

This celebrated pentangle passage is quite foreign to *Ch* and *M* and, it might seem, to their spirit. Here the Englishman proclaims his hero's virtues: he is free of all *vylany*, magnanimous and compassionate in his love of his fellow men, honest and noble in speech, valiant in battle, and above all committed to piety, *trawþe*, *clannes* and *cortaysye*. Now whilst in *M* little concern is shown for the inner Gauvain, this is not entirely true of *Ch*. There the poet opens by lauding the virtues of the

> .. bon chevalier qui maintint
> Loiauté, proëce et anor,
> Et qui n'ama onques nul jor
> Home coart, faus ne vilain.
>
> (*Ch* 4-7)

Gauvain is as polished in manners as he is valiant in arms. Throughout the romance we are reminded of his *cortoisie* (274, 300, 314, 382, 571,

---

[6] Ed. M. Roques, Paris (C.f.m.â.), 1955, ll. 2621-57.

1006), and we see in action his concern for loyalty and truth (e.g. 111, 716–7, 1198–9). Moreover, his 'bones mors' are recognised by the maiden (315); but this, it would appear, is the sum of his *clannes* so far as sexual relations are concerned.

By comparison with *M*, we might in fact feel a certain 'inwardness' about *Ch*, with its frequently introspective hero and its apparent pre-occupation with moral values. It is notable that the word *cortois* and its derivatives appear thirteen times there, but never in *M*. In *Ch* Gauvain even goes slightly beyond the baldly conventional in his use of God's name (e.g. 83–5, 1078–9), and his host recognises the divine hand in his success (764). Yet in all this one is conscious of the social, moral, and even religious values being displayed not for themselves but as part of a rather cynical probing of Gauvain's character and possibly of the whole convention of *courtoisie* and *amour courtois*. In particular, Gauvain's courtly virtues cannot hold firm against his sexual drive (590–3), and the sense of honour that most obviously obsesses him concerns his reputation as an active lover (575–68, 622–40).

The Englishman would hardly have failed to notice the moral im-plications in *Ch*. He could have chosen to ignore them and concentrate on the adventurous action offered by both French romances; he could have retained the set of values offered by *Ch* with their perceptible flaws; or he could have substituted a less fragile ethic of his own largely illustrated through the behaviour of his hero. He opted for the latter course and, it seems to me, devised this pentangle passage as a declaration of intent, with an eye both to the values he found but rejected in *Ch* and to the later developments he planned for his own story. His Gawain was to be a less superficial character, inspired by a *cortaysye* that was deepened and fortified through its association with pious observance. But at the same time, the hero was to keep some of the attributes so prominent in *Ch*: above all, his concern for truth and loyalty and rejection of *vylany*, and his bouts of morose introspection revolving primarily around questions of personal honour.

670–90   *Gawain's departure from Arthur's court.*

Gawain's impetuous departure from Camelot leaves its inhabitants lamenting what they fear will be his permanent loss. In both *Ch* and *M*, of course, Gauvain leaves the royal court, though in circumstances not strikingly similar to those in *GGK*. But there are other parallels to be drawn.

In a following section we shall see how the Englishman uses features of Kay's perilous ride as described in *M* and later to be duplicated by Gauvain. Now when Kay rode forth, the damsel whose mule he bestrode was left in tears at the sight of him departing alone and ill-equipped on what she realised would be an unsuccessful mission (*M* 117–23). I surmise that these lines suggested the flowing tears of *GGK* 684 (though tearful leave-takings are hardly rare in life or romance). But if so, the English poet, wishing further to darken the scene with hints of mortal dangers to be faced, called to mind the shepherd's grim warnings to Gauvain in *Ch* 160–3 and 194–5.[7] If I am right, here is another admirable instance of the *Gawain*-poet sensitively responding to small details in one source, developing them with an eye to coming events, and drawing in elements from another source to enrich his narrative still further.

691-712   *The hero's route.*

No parallel in the French texts. The Englishman has chosen to introduce some geographical precision at the beginning of Gawain's ride. Its function, as I understand it, is purely artistic and not to provide a signpost to any particular location of the Green Chapel. It supplies realistic amplification (as, for example, do the later hunting scenes), and excites the audience's curiosity with a glimpse of the familiar before they are led beyond the bounds of the known world into a region of fantasy and peril.

It may be mentioned that the phrase 'þaȝ hym no gomen þoȝt' (*GGK* 692) could have been modelled on *M* 324 'no tient mie a jeus', though the French expression is common enough in other texts.

713-39   *The wintry journey.*

This passage is a rehandling of material found in *M* 132–205, itself derived from some account of an infernal journey. The common or comparable elements are as follows: The knight finds hostile creatures before him—and so many strange perils (*maleürté M* 204)—that the tenth (half, *M* 205) could not be told.—Fierce beasts are detailed,— and dragons.—The knight is pursued,—but is not harmed because of supernatural protection (God's in *GGK*, the mysterious lady's in *M* through the intermediary of her mule; later, when Gauvain makes the journey, he invokes God's aid).—Worst of all—was the great wintry cold.

As usual, if the two passages were taken in isolation, coincidence

---

7 The first of these passages is cited as a parallel in TGD, p. 96.

might be pleaded as the cause of their similarity; but when they are seen in their total context, this view is hardly tenable. There are not enough close verbal parallels to settle the matter without the broader considerations, though on the other hand the knight's encounters occur in a sequence (first beasts and dragons, then bitter cold) that it might be hard to find elsewhere. The occurrence in *GGK* of a refreshing fountain and a perilous bridge would have been conclusive, but they do not appear.

In fact, the most striking thing to notice about the Englishman's use of this episode from *M* is that he has removed all traces of its Christian eschatological inspiration, notably the valley itself, its darkness and stench, the fire breathed by its denizens, the fountain, and the bridge over 'the devil's river' (cf. *M* 390–400). He could not have failed to recognise these features for what they were. But, whether from qualms of religious or artistic conscience, he has preferred to substitute a more realistic picture of an English winter, unless one sees in the *wormez*, *wodwos* and *etaynez* the half-brothers of the infernal reptiles and devils. At the same time, however, it has been suggested that the *Gawain*-poet has given the episode certain more subtle eschatological overtones, such as are afforded, for instance, by his hero's choice of All Souls' Day for his departure.[8] One might perceive here, as in the pentangle passage, a tendency for him to hint at a deeper, spiritual significance attaching to Gawain's adventures than is found in the French sources.

740-62 *Gawain prays for shelter.*

The Englishman pursues the theme of the wintry ride and takes the opportunity to reinforce our impression of Gawain's devout attitude to his quest, once more going beyond his source in pictorial and psychological representation. In l. 748, as if to signal his return to *Ch* for inspiration, he names for a second time Gawain's steed Gryngolet.

763-806 *He comes to a splendid castle.*

Now an important run of borrowings from *Ch* begins, though reminiscences of *M* may not be entirely absent. There, of course, we have two perilous journeys, by Kay and by Gauvain. Each leads directly (as indeed we might expect) to an arrival at a castle. That reached by Gauvain is enclosed by a palisade of sharpened stakes (*M* 433–4). Kay, as Gawain in *GGK*, emerges from the wood into

[8] Cf. J. A. Burrow, *A Reading of 'Sir Gawain and the Green Knight'*, London, 1965, pp. 54–5.

the *praerie* (*M* 280); and it may well be significant that the same word *prayere* occurs at this point in *GGK* (768). Again, the English poet could have been prompted to linger over the fact of Gawain's crossing himself immediately before his discovery of the dwelling in the wood by the assertion in *M* 425 that fortune is on the hero's side when his road leads him to the castle.

For the rest, however, the debt to *Ch* (206–21) appears clearly enough in both the sequence and the nature of the parallels: The hero sees before him a castle—on a mound (?),*—shut about*—and moated: —the finest ever owned by knight.*—There is a large enclosure without,—and the good lodging within is mentioned.—The hero goes to the main approach (*lices, Ch* 218)—and reaches the end of the bridge.—Never had he seen a finer barbican (*herberjage . . . el baille, Ch* 210–11).

As he has done elsewhere, the Englishman has taken a brief passage from his model and extended it with picturesque detail: the chalk-white chimneys and painted pinnacles that speak of the architectural designs more of his own than of the Frenchman's day. The elements I have asterisked above are, however, of a more particular interest, since they enable us to peer closely over the adaptor's shoulder as he works.

Though TGD gloss *mote* as 'moat' at *GGK* 764, the phrase 'he watz war . . . of a won in a mote' appears rather to be the direct translation of *Ch* 206–7: ' . . . voit / Sor une mote (='mound') un bel chastel.' Straightforward transposition here, then, from the French into English. Then comes a curious circumstance.

In each text the next line contains a word normally meaning 'shut': *loken, GGK* 765; *fermez, Ch* 208. But in the French phrase 'fermez de novel' the meaning is not 'shut' but 'fortified'. It looks suspiciously as if the *Gawain*-poet is here guilty of a mistranslation and goes on to say that the building is 'loken vnder boȝez . . . aboute bi þe diches' as a way out of the difficulty in which he has landed himself. Yet we must always admit the possibility that his understanding was not at fault, but that he deliberately chose the alternative sense to allow for a brief, graphic addition that it evoked in his imagination.

The third element I have singled out is perhaps an instance of the same thing being said in different words. Whereas in *Ch* the building is more splendid than any except the property of a prince or king (213–14), the Englishman describes it as the fairest ever owned by a knight (767), which means precisely the same.

These three instances, then, reveal different aspects of the *Gawain-*

poet's technique. He may sometimes translate directly; or he may render an idea faithfully but in different terms; or again, whether through faulty translation or a flash of motivated inspiration, a detail of the French may prompt him to introduce an entirely fresh notion with which to add new colour to his narrative.

807-41   *Gawain is made welcome at the castle.*

After introducing the civil porter who answers Gawain's call, the Englishman proceeds to put *Ch* (see ll. 222-47) to further extensive use. People come to greet Gawain—and they pass over the bridge.—His steed is stabled,—and he is led into the hall.—There is joy at his coming. —He is disarmed.—A fine fire blazes in the hall.—The lord of the place welcomes him[9]—and tells him to do here as he pleases.—The hero thanks him.

Once more it is less the nature of these fairly conventional details than their number and the general context in which they appear that puts the Englishman's debt beyond debate. Yet still we see him busily sifting, selecting, and often rearranging the features that best suit his design. So the host is not brought forward to meet Gawain at the beginning of the scene, but produced like a smiling spider in his courtly web once the knight has been escorted with ceremony into the hall. This is in keeping with the total scheme he has devised, with the hero not, as in *Ch*, being lured into his castle by the host, but going there in deliberate furtherance of his quest and being received rather than sought by that personage.

842-74   *He is taken to a bedchamber to be richly robed.*

In *GGK* the seduction scenes still lie over 300 lines ahead. But now the Englishman gives further evidence of his organisational skill. He decides, as it were, to give us a preview of the bedroom where the testing is to take place. And his description takes the form of an elaboration of the scene in *Ch* 472-87. After a portrait of the host, the borrowings begin.

He takes Gawain—to a bright room (the source of the brightness is unspecified in *GGK*; in *Ch* twelve candles provide the *grant clarté*)— with fine bedding.—There are splendid curtains,—coverlets—and fur adornments,—and hangings of silk from distant parts (Toulouse [?] and Tharsia in *GGK*, Palermo and Romagna in *Ch*).

Now Gawain is richly robed in a passage added by the English poet

9 It may be observed that in both texts the two men had met earlier.

to emphasise further the splendour and warmth of the hero's reception. But from *Ch* he does seem to appropriate one small detail. There the host instructs his daughter not to extinguish the candles in the room where she will be with Gauvain, so that 'vos veoiz son gent cors' (511). Here we are told that Gawain's handsome body is seen beneath the material of his robe: 'Lowande and lufly alle his lymmez vnder' (868). The passage has given rise to some debate,[10] for a robe might be supposed to hide rather than reveal a man's limbs. However, when we consider the line in the context of this run of borrowings, we can scarcely dodge the conclusion that the *Gawain*-poet has taken over a small effect with less congruity than it had in the French, though using it as a vivid introduction to a further encomium of the hero's physical beauty.

875-900   *The meal.*

Now we see Gawain seated by the hall fire and then handsomely plied with food and wine. Passages from *Ch* still guide the poet's invention. First he returns to the French description of Gauvain's reception at the castle, with the 'settel semlych ryche' of l. 882 and its fine covering corresponding precisely to the fireside 'mout riche seoir . . . covert d'une porpre de soie' of *Ch* 232–3.

Then the Englishman passes to the lines in *Ch* (349–61) in which the laying of the tables and serving of the meal are recounted in much the same terms: the clean, white tablecloth, overcloths, salt-cellars, silverware are all there. The preparatory washing is mentioned, as is the fish that is served in plenty. The delighted hero makes merry, but (and these are the most significant of all the parallels) he is encouraged still further and drinks overmuch wine.

A noteworthy change by the Englishman is to omit the meat, roast birds and venison that are offered to Gauvain. His motive is plain: as this is Christmas Eve in his story, it is a fast-day and no meat is taken. Over-indulgence in wine might be thought less fitting at such a time; and indeed, despite critical attempts to see some subtle justification in the reference, the most likely explanation is that the poet was loathe to let slip such a lively, human touch. In the French romance it had its function; for there the host, one might argue, was concerned with dulling Gauvain's wits so that he might offer his daughter and not be

---

[10] See H. L. Savage, *The Gawain-Poet. Studies in his Personality and Background*, Chapel Hill, 1956, pp. 176–90.

suspected by his guest of any ulterior motive. In *GGK*, however, it is safer to regard the feature as picturesque rather than functional.[11]

Another important change made by the *Gawain*-poet is to show the hero apparently eating alone, whereas in *Ch* both host and daughter feast with him. I would suggest that he does this in pursuit of a better dramatic structure than is found in his model. There the sequence is as follows: Gauvain is welcomed into the castle; the host fetches his daughter to keep him company while dinner is being prepared; the girl warns Gauvain of possible peril; all three eat together; Gauvain and the girl are once more left alone and discuss the danger of the situation; after a further light meal the hero is taken to the bedroom where he is to be tested.

The Englishman has decided to exclude from the castle scenes the mortal peril of the sword. Gawain will undergo only a moral testing. He therefore virtually deletes all hints of physical menace, such as are given in *Ch* by the daughter, and accordingly deems a second private conversation to be superfluous. First he concentrates on the lavish quality of the hero's welcome (reception, robing, feasting), and post-pones for greater dramatic impact his first meeting with the lady of the house. Had the lord feasted with Gawain, the lady would also have been present. But the poet prefers to reserve their encounter for the next scene and provide for its setting, ironically enough as will appear, the innocent celebration of evensong in chapel. Thus he betrays a feeling for progression as well as dramatic irony finer than is evident in the more matter-of-fact, episodic structure of the French romance.

901-27 *Gawain discloses his name.*

In this section Gawain names himself in response to the attendants' questioning, and the host and all those in the castle rejoice in the presence of Arthur's nephew. At the corresponding point in *Ch* the hero's identity is still unknown to the people in the castle and is not, in fact, disclosed until his testing is over (ll. 735–51). Then it comes to us as no surprise to find the customary crop of common details: On being questioned—Gawain gives his name,—associating it with that of King Arthur.—His host shows his pleasure.—Gawain is peerless among knights.—There is great rejoicing in the castle at the news (cf. *Ch* 788–9).

[11] It is interesting to find the motif taken up, apparently from the same source, by the author of the *Queste del saint Graal*, and thence by Malory (see in Part I our note 22, p. 9).

Why has the Englishman brought forward this scene? There are good reasons, of course, why he should. It is hardly likely that a knight would be received unheralded at a noble court and feasted and cosseted for a full week without his identity being asked or made known. Not that it was a mystery for his host, Sir Bertilak, though that will only appear later. But more than this, the *Gawain*-poet doubtless already has in mind the smoothing of his hero's path to the lady's affection, and even her future taunts at his unwonted lack of initiative in the 'lel layk of luf'. Indeed, those in the castle are made to look forward eagerly to a lesson from such a celebrated expert in the art of 'luf-talkyng' (927), and this in a passage unprompted by the French. The poet is plainly taking advantage of this early disclosure to lead up to what the informed public as well as the lady will see as Gawain's almost paradoxical reticence in the bedchamber scenes.

928-69 *The hero meets the young lady and her old companion at evensong.*
Gawain's first meeting with the future temptress is much modified from the corresponding episode in *Ch* (252-73). The host seems to pluck him aside as he makes for her, instead of virtually thrusting her into his arms; the meeting takes place in the austere setting of the chapel instead of the castle hall; and another figure (later revealed as Morgan the Fay) appears in the lady's company.

Yet there are common features: the lady looks admiringly at Gawain, and he in turn is struck by her beauty and quality (*costes, GGK* 944; *valor, Ch* 253), which surpasses that of all others.

The reason for the introduction of Morgan from some other source is not my concern here. The important point is that the circumstances of this first encounter have been radically changed, almost reversed in fact, by the English poet. Instead of the lady being expressly fetched for and literally handed over to the hero for his delectation as in the French romance, she now is presented as initially aloof, inaccessible and accompanied by an old hag who recalls the typical duenna. Nevertheless glances are exchanged like a discharge across a spark-gap, and soon the meeting is effected. The Englishman has a sure eye for such devices as will bring more dramatic tension into his tale; and here too, with hindsight, we can appreciate the irony of Gawain's eagerness to pursue the acquaintance of this vision of female beauty.

970-94 *Greetings are exchanged and the evening is spent in revelry.*
Reminiscences of *Ch* continue. The brevity and courtliness of the initial

salutation is mentioned in both texts (*GGK* 973–4, *Ch* 274–5), and the hero's offer of his service duly follows (*GGK* 975–6, *Ch* 306).

Then the Englishman postpones for a while the *tête-à-tête* between Gawain and the lady, using instead a later passage in *Ch* (427–55): The hero is led by the ladies (hand in hand with the maiden in *Ch* 428),— and the servants are asked to bring a light meal (spiced cakes, *GGK* 979; fruit and wine, *Ch* 438).—The wine flows free;—and the host calls for good cheer and bids Gawain make merry,—before giving the word to retire for the night.

So we find further proof of the *Gawain*-poet's mastery in rearranging and fusing elements from his source, forever adding his own bright touches of colour (as here the host's hanging of his hood on a spear to launch the festivities). We note too that he avoids throughout any hint of boorishness on the part of the castellan, or in this case a suspicion of gluttony (in *Ch* the man calls for supper, and his daughter is quick to remark that fruit and wine will suffice, since he ate well but a short while ago). The refinement of manners in *GGK* contrasts with the brusque and altogether odd behaviour of the host in *Ch*.

995–1019 *Next day, Gawain enjoys the young lady's company.*

The passing of that night and the following day is briefly recounted (in *Ch* the night of testing is the first that Gauvain spends in the castle). Then, over dinner, a scene is enacted that matches closely the events preceding the meal in *Ch* (297–317): Gawain and the lady are seated together—and hold conversation that is courtly—and refined ('clene cortays carp closed fro fylþe'. *GGK* 1013; 'Tant l'ot cortoisement parler / Et tant lo voit de bones mors', *Ch* 314–15).—They are engrossed in mutual dalliance.

For once, the *Gawain*-poet has been more succinct than his model. Though there is no open declaration in *Ch*, the reader is left in no doubt that the couple have fallen in love; indeed the girl's reluctance to lead Gauvain further is due only to her awareness of the peril of the situation. In *GGK*, however, we are given rather more freedom to make what we will of the relationship: the seduction episode is being subtly prepared, but not so blatantly that its dramatic impact will be lost when it comes.

I might add that details from the description of the feast in *Ch* which the Englishman had not used in his account of the previous day's dinner are pressed into service at this juncture, as the following quotations show:

Þer watz mete, þer watz myrþe, þer watz much ioye,
Þat for to telle þerof hit me tene were.

(GGK 1007–8)

Mes je ne voil plus demorer
As mes un a un aconter,
Mes mout orent char et peson,

.   .   .   .   .   .

Et mout mengierent lieement.

(Ch 355–7, 359)

1020-78 *On the following day, Gawain wishes to leave, but is urged to stay until New Year's Day, since the Green Chapel is close by.*

Having brought Gawain to Bertilak's castle on Christmas Eve, the Englishman has to detain him there until it is time to leave for his New Year tryst. So in this passage he sees the Christmas festivities out, and shows Gawain eager to depart and his host persuading him to stay, since his goal, the Green Chapel, is but a short distance away.

This is all additional to his source, except for the general situation of the castellan desiring his guest to remain at his court against the latter's inclination. It gives the poet further opportunity to stress the gaiety of the court and the warm courtesy of its lord, in continued contrast to the more bluff and sinister behaviour of the host in *Ch*.

1079-1104 *The lord will go hunting and leave Gawain in the lady's company.*

The castellan's anxiety not to let Gawain leave is again strongly emphasised, this time in a passage modelled directly on *Ch* 372–87. The following common points may be noted (as usual the sequence is rather different in *Ch*): The host has Gawain sit—in the company of the ladies (his daughter in *Ch*).—He asks Gawain to stay—and the hero agrees—since the lord is giving him lodging.—He is to sit with the lord's wife (daughter)—and enjoy her company—until his return;—for he is going hunting ('ses bois veoir', *Ch* 373).

The sworn agreement in *GGK* shows what importance the castellan attaches to Gawain's staying in his stronghold, and thus reflects the urgency of the host's bidding in *Ch* (reinforced there by an instruction to a servant to hold him under duress if necessary). In both cases, of course, there is a hidden motive beyond mere hospitality, for Gawain's testing will soon take place within these walls.

1105-25 *Gawain and his host agree to exchange any 'winnings'.*

No parallel in the French texts. At this point the *Gawain*-poet begins to introduce the subsidiary 'exchange of winnings' motif from another source. At least part of his aim could have been to fill out this part of his story so as to bring the whole romance to the desired length. With his usual skill he will expand the brief mention in *Ch* of the castellan's visit to his woods into a trio of hunting scenes and link to them this further element of interest which, finally, he will associate with the main adventure in the castle, the attempted seduction of Gawain. The poet may be thought almost the prototype of the 'sporting Englishman' in his evident preoccupation throughout the romance with games and contests. And here he has contrived to set a sport within a sport, the bargain over the winnings within the wider context of the hunt.

1126-77 *The hunt.*

The first day's chase: no parallel in the French texts other than the single line in *Ch* (373) that seems to have inspired the three hunting scenes.

1178-1207 *The lady approaches Gawain's bed at dawn.*

Now the first of the seduction scenes is reached; and before any detailed comparisons are made with the French, some more general observations are called for.

To create his essential story the *Gawain*-poet has chosen to combine the most striking adventures found in *M* and *Ch*. In each of the French romances the hero is subjected to a supreme and unusual physical trial —in one to the beheading 'game', in the other to the interventions of the automatous sword. By his survival in either case the hero gives proof of his preeminence among mortal knights. So the Englishman has a choice between two climactic episodes, unless of course he decides to include both.

His preference went to the beheading test, and he planned his material so that it would provide the high point of his romance, not being resolved until near the end of the story. Now as I have already suggested, he has a fine feeling not only for the balance and unity of his work but also for a controlled progression towards the climax of the narrative. If he included the sword episode as well, he would have two momentous physical tests coming in fairly close succession, and there would be a danger of the thunder of the beheading scene being stolen by the previous ordeal by sword.

On the other hand, he doubtless appreciated the dramatic qualities of the bedchamber episode, and especially the irony implicit in the sore frustration of Gauvain the amorist. So he decided that he would retain the essentials of the bedroom scene with the exception of the menacing sword. But what, then, is there to prevent his hero from taking full advantage of the situation in which he finds himself alone at night with a charming bedmate? The Englishman has his solution ready: moral scruples will hold Gawain back. However, he must be pressed hard in this moral testing. The lady implicated should not be involved half-heartedly and against her better judgment as in *Ch*: she must play the role of the ardent seductress forcing Gawain to the very brink of capitulation.

In this way, I imagine, the poet worked out his scene of moral testing to anticipate that of the physical trial. And it may have been with this in mind that he had earlier left us with an impression of the hero's moral strength and 'clannes'. We shall see, moreover, how cleverly he links the episode with the beheading test, to which it now appears not as a rival but a significant preliminary. And we shall also find that he had not after all totally discarded the sword-motif, for he recalls an element from it when Gawain goes through his final ordeal.

So this is how the seduction episode probably evolved; and I feel it would have taken much the same shape even if the Englishman had had no other model for this part of the story. But in fact there is good evidence that he knew, and was significantly influenced by, the *Lancelot* of Chrétien de Troyes. That is the text from which the author of *Ch* had combined elements to form his own bedroom scene,[12] so we are here faced with a curiously circular piece of transmission: the *Ch*-poet used features from Chrétien, though with an interesting reversal of situation; the Englishman takes *Ch* as his primary source but, with likely knowledge of *Lancelot*, he moves back some way towards the sense he finds there.

In the opening passage a number of features suggest that *Ch* 513–17 is uppermost in his mind: Gawain is in bed—when the lady secures the door—and takes her place unbidden beside him. The description of the temptress in *GGK* 1204–7 is virtually a direct translation of two lines

[12] See in Part I our notes to *Ch* 454 ff., 588–9, 598–603. References to *Lancelot* are to the edition by M. Roques (*Le Chevalier de la Charrete*), Paris (C.f.m.â.), 1958.

that come somewhat later in *Ch* (644–5): her complexion is white mingled with red ('fres et coloré', *Ch* 644), her lips small and laughing ('La boche petite et riant', *Ch* 645).

At the same time there is a most vital difference in which *GGK* and *Lancelot* (1202 ff.) agree against *Ch*. This is the hero's acute and almost comical embarrassment at the prospect of the lady's company and the way in which he counters her initiative by lying like a log.[13] Moreover, in *Lancelot* the 'dameisele' wears a *chemise*, and the lady in *GGK* is presumably clothed (as in the third of the seduction scenes); but the girl in *Ch* is naked.

1208–40   *The lady pledges her service to Gawain.*

The Englishman proceeds to elaborate his scene by introducing a dialogue between lady and hero. There is dialogue in *Ch* too, but quite contrary in sense and savour. Thus, whereas the girl had warned the ardent Gauvain that, despite appearances, 'Je ne sui pas o vos sanz garde' (*Ch* 525), the lady in *GGK* dwells on the fact that they are quite alone and cannot be surprised (1230 ff.). Knowing as we do that the *Gawain*-poet still has *Ch* very much in mind (mention of a truce in *GGK* 1210 and *Ch* 673 may be a slight indication of this), we are entitled, I think, to consider such instances as deliberate reversals of details in the French rather than as independent invention.

But if in this part of his romance he is relying very largely on scenes and episodes in *Ch* for his inspiration, he has not entirely abandoned *M*. There has been much critical comment on the lady's frank declaration:

> '3e ar welcum to my cors,
> Yowre awen won to wale,
> Me behouez of fyne force
> Your seruaunt be, and schale.'
>
> (*GGK* 1237–40)

Frank this certainly is, but not so brutal as to conflict as much with courtly parlance as some have suggested. TGD are certainly right in interpreting 'my cors' as 'me' or 'myself',[14] and the relative innocence of the words is revealed by comparison with their very probable

---

[13] In a rather similar situation Boeve de Haumtone feigns sleep, as does Gawain in *GGK* (see A. Stimming, ed., *Der Anglonormannische Boeve de Haumtone*, Halle [Bibliotheca Normannica VII], 1899, ll. 752 ff.).

[14] TGD, pp. 108–9; cf. Burrow, op. cit., pp. 81–2.

source in *M*. There the maiden whose bridle Gauvain has restored
grants him an embrace and many kisses:

> 'Sire,' fait ele, 'il est bien droiz
> Que je mete tot a devise
> Lo mien cors en vostre servise . . .'
>
> (*M* 1082-4)

It will be noticed how closely the elements of these two declarations
correspond: The lady places her person at the hero's disposal—to do
with as he will.—It behoves her—to put herself at his service. Chance
agreement to this extent must surely be ruled out, even granted the
rather conventional nature of the utterance. But why should the
Englishman momentarily abandon *Ch* for *M* at this point? We can, I
think, hazard an explanation.

Firstly, as I have said, he is here consciously reversing the situation
in *Ch*. So the girl's refusal there to give herself to Gauvain (e.g. 'Et si
vos gardez desormés / De tochier a moi . . .', 618–19) suggests to him
the opposite inclination in his own seductress. Perhaps he recalls the
scene in *M* (930 ff.) where Gauvain, having sat with the mysterious
châtelaine on a costly bed, meets with a rebuff the offer of her lands and
her person ('Mon pooir / Et moi met en vostre servise', 966–7). This
in turn could have reminded him of the later passage I have quoted.

In any case it is worth observing that in *M* 1082-4 there is no question of the damsel's total surrender to Gauvain. For though earlier she
had vowed that if a knight restored her bridle to her she would be
'trestote soe' (87), and even accord 'li baisiers et l'autre chose' (107),
she now wastes little time in quitting Arthur's court.

To return to the lady's words in *GGK*, I see in them no lack of
courtoisie since, depending on circumstances and the frame of mind of
her companion, they could be taken as a somewhat florid expression
of innocent devotion. In short, they are deliciously ambiguous[15] and
leave on Gawain the entire onus of the next move in this courtly
contest of words.

1241-89   *The hero rebuffs the lady's advances.*

Gawain continues deftly to parry the lady's verbal advances, showing
the humility to which we were introduced early in the romance (see
GGK 301–74), but not swerving an inch from the path of virtue.

In the end, like the damsel in *Lancelot*, the lady recognises that she

---

15 Cf. Burrow, loc. cit.

will progress no further on this occasion, so she speaks of leaving. Lines 1283–7 in *GGK* have given commentators some trouble. Are these thoughts all passing through the lady's mind, or do some represent the poet's comment?[16] A passage from the *Lancelot* episode will, I believe, help to clarify this point.

After the damsel has lain long enough with the unresponsive hero to realise that she has nothing to expect from him that night, she speaks of leaving so that he may be 'plus a eise' (1251). Indeed, she returns to her own room,

> Et lors a dit a li meïsmes:
> 'Des lores que je conui primes
> Chevalier, un seul n'an conui
> Que je prisasse, fors cestui,
> La tierce part d'un angevin;
> Car si con ge pans et devin,
> Il vialt a si grant chose antendre
> Qu'ainz chevaliers n'osa enprendre
> Si perilleuse ne si grief;
> Et Diex doint qu'il an veigne a chief.'
>
> (*Lancelot* 1269–78)

These, then, are thoughts that run through the damsel's mind, and it appears that the *Gawain*-poet has taken the burden of them into his romance. The first half of the quoted passage he has paraphrased and put into the lady's mouth as part of her blandishments of Gawain (e.g. *GGK* 1268–75); but the gist of the remaining lines, with the foreboding of dangers the hero must face, he has rendered as thoughts that 'þe burde in mynde hade' (1283). Perhaps there is some inconsistency in the way in which the poet seems to have given the lady foreknowledge of the blow. Yet I think we must accept this, with the reflection that here is another of the rare instances where the Englishman allows his source to dominate his expression a little too much for the requirements of mere logic.

1290–1318 *After a kiss the lady leaves, and Gawain rises.*

As she prepares to leave, the lady taunts Gawain with his backwardness in craving a kiss. He feels bound to make good his omission, and on this note they part. To kiss, it appears, is not to overstep the bounds of 'clannes' in Gawain's eyes. Nor, in *Ch*, did kisses and chaste embraces

[16] Cf. TGD, p. 110.

provoke the fury of the guardian sword: this much the texts have in common.[17] At the same time, it is amusing to find the hero's honour being impugned in this way by the lady, when in *Ch* Gauvain himself was distraught at the idea of his ardour as a lover being called into question (581–9, 624–36). And the English poet will make more of this later.

1319–1475 *The hunt and exchange of winnings, followed by the second day's hunt and the lady's second visit to Gawain's bed.*

No parallel in the French texts. The description of the first day's hunt is concluded, to be followed by the agreed exchange of winnings. On the morrow the lord and his men take up the chase once more, and again the lady approaches Gawain's bed. It may well be, as has often been suggested, that the Englishman is using the erotic connotations of the hunt in symbolic counterpoint to the lady's pursuit of the hero.

1476–1557 *After a further unsuccessful attempt at seduction, the lady leaves.*

Taking up again her theme of Gawain's uncourtly reticence, the lady urges him on to a further kiss. Once more the hero's sense of honour is being exploited; and his fear of being refused if he took the initiative is mentioned by him in self-defence (1492–4). In all of this, a knowledge of *Ch* helps us fully to appreciate the irony of the situation. For there, despite the very different circumstances, it was precisely Gauvain's fear of being frustrated that whipped him on to further endeavour (cf. *Ch* 575 ff., 622 ff.). And we recall with a smile the enforced abstinence in *Ch* when we read the lady's words in *GGK*:

> '3e may not be werned,
> 3e ar stif innoghe to constrayne wyth strenkþe, 3if yow lykez,
> 3if any were so vilanous þat yow devaye wolde.'
>
> (*GGK* 1495–7)

How the English poet must have enjoyed playing with the sense of his model as he shaped his own polished and admirably subtle dialogue! After the kiss the lady returns to the assault, still seeking to shame Gawain into activity:

---

[17] We may again recall the scene in *Boeve de Haumtone* where Josiane comes with love-talk to the hero's bed and overcomes his scruples: 'Par mult grant amour se sunt entrebeisé. / Mes mar le besa Boefs le sené, / Ke il se repenti, ainz ke l'an fu passé' (ed. Stimming, ll. 772–4).

'For schame!
I com hider sengel, and sitte
To lerne at yow sum game.'

(*GGK* 1530-2)

But all in vain. This is not the gallant who, in *Ch*, preferred the thought of perishing in amorous embrace to that of a long life of shame, with his failure to profit from the same situation common knowledge. He indeed was one of those truly chivalrous knights referred to by the lady, who

' . . . for her lele luf hor lyuez han auntered,
Endured for her drury dulful stoundez'

(*GGK* 1516-17)

and who eventually won through to bring 'blysse into boure' (1519). We may be sure that the Englishman was here slily and deliberately contrasting Gawain with his *alter ego* in the French romance.

1558-1732 *The second hunt is followed by the exchange of winnings and revelry in the castle. Gawain is persuaded not to leave yet, and the third day's chase begins.*

We return to the hunting and subsequent exchange of winnings, and there follows an account of the feasting, singing and merry-making (1648-57) that seems to catch an echo or two of the celebrations in *Ch* 788-813. But otherwise no parallels are found in the French texts, and the Englishman is plainly concerned at this stage more with enriching his canvas with extraneous descriptive detail than with advancing his plot. At the same time, however, he now and then rekindles our suspense with a hint or a recollection of Gawain's approaching ordeal (1670 ff.; cf. earlier 1283-7).

1733-91 *The lady's third attempt at seduction almost succeeds.*

For the third time the lady comes to Gawain's room to stir him from sleep and try him once again with her seductive speech and behaviour. Her efforts almost meet with success, for she 'nurned hym so neȝe þe þred' (1771) that he was on the brink of capitulation. In *Ch* Gauvain is twice at the very point of possessing the girl when the sword intervenes (596-7, 652-4; cf. 521-2); here in *GGK* it is a last-minute resurgence of his sense of honour that holds the knight back. Yet, just as in *Ch*, Gawain is plagued by the thought that his 'cortaysye' is at stake if he refrains (*GGK* 1773; *Ch* 581-9, 622-36). One might think that the Englishman is concerned here with exposing the lusty con-

ception of courtly honour expressed by the hero in *Ch* by contrasting
it with the more responsible, though equally courtly, feeling for social
obligations that carries the day with Gawain.

When the lady suggests that Gawain has a more cherished 'lemman'
to explain his coolness towards her (*GGK* 1782–7), we recall that it
was Lancelot's infatuation with Guenevere that had motivated his
churlish conduct towards the damsel in Chrétien's romance. It is very
likely that the English poet, too, had this in mind as he put the words
into the lady's mouth.

1792-1871 *Gawain refuses the lady's offer of a ring, but accepts her girdle,
which will protect him in combat. She withdraws.*

Having brought his hero through his ordeal by seduction with virtue
intact, the *Gawain*-poet now has to prepare for the physical testing.
Naturally his thoughts revert to *M*, which will provide his model for
the sequel to the beheading bargain. But this cannot take place yet:
Gawain has first to take leave of the lady and her lord and quit the
castle. So it is easy to see how his attention may have been drawn to
that scene in *M* which shows Gauvain abandoning against her wishes
the mistress of the castle where his opponent in the beheading game
dwells. And this I believe did happen.

Let us compare this section of *GGK* with *M* 974–89. In both texts
the lady has just offered herself to the hero.—She wishes to press a rich
gift on him (a ring in *GGK*, a castle in *M*),—but he declines, saying
that he must pursue his journey.—Instead he will take something of
less value (a girdle in *GGK*; a bridle in *M*, which in 253 had been
referred to as 'tel noient'),—which he gladly accepts from the lady.—
They part.

A less obvious but perhaps more significant parallel lies in the nature
of the object that the knight takes with him. The girdle has magic,
protective qualities, as the lady herself explains. Of the bridle we know
very little, except that it was highly prized by the maiden who started
the whole quest, and that it belonged to the mule whose presence
guarded its rider from the perils of the journey. It would seem, then,
to have some talismanic properties. At the end of both *GGK* and *M*,
of course, this will be the only trophy carried back by the hero to
Arthur's court.

In the light of other similarities I have noted between *GGK* and
Boeve de Haumtone,[18] it is worth mentioning too that Josiane, who had

[18] See above, footnotes 5, 13 and 17.

pressed her love on Boeve, made for herself a silken girdle, which she wore to protect her virginity during her unwelcome marriage to another man. It is certainly not impossible that the *Gawain*-poet, who is likely to have known this popular romance, borrowed from it the idea of the lady's protective girdle. It would assuredly have appealed to his sense of irony to devise such a very different use for the same piece of apparel.

In this section, then, we find the Englishman as usual varying his techniques to suit both an immediate and a long-term purpose. He has turned to an appropriate passage in one of his chief models and drastically adapted it in detail (a ring for a castle, a girdle for a bridle), while at the same time retaining the basic elements in their sequence. And he has filled out the scene by adding features of his own (the lady's request for a gift from Gawain, the bright descriptive touches), and by conveying this slight step forward in the action through the give-and-take of an animated dialogue.

1872-1997   *The last day's hunt is followed by the exchange of winnings. That night Gawain takes his leave.*

Here we see Gawain being shriven, the lord's return from the chase, the final exchange of winnings, and Gawain's leave-taking. The only parallel with the French texts is the host's assigning a servant to set the knight on his road, which perhaps recalls the lady's instruction to the *vilain* in *M* that he shall see Gauvain safely out of the castle. For the rest, the Englishman is rounding off motifs that he has introduced into the basic story: the hero's piety, the hunt, and the exchange of spoils.

So ends the third 'fitt', which has been so artfully expanded by the poet from the economical and rectilinear narrative of his chief source. The result is to balance the lively events at Bertilak's court, including the seduction scenes, against the framing story of the beheading game. At the same time, the Englishman has tempered the crudity of the French with a delicate display of courtly manners and expression and an emphasis on his hero's somewhat solemn virtue, which was quite absent from his model.

1998-2090   *In the morning, Gawain sets out with a servant as guide.*

Gawain sets forth with the servant for his tryst, bearing the girdle with him. No significant parallel with the French texts, except for the hero's taking the girdle (bridle in *M*) with him when he leaves the castle.

2091-2159 *Gawain is not deterred by the warnings of the servant, who directs him to the Green Chapel and then leaves him.*

The servant tries to dissuade Gawain from proceeding to the Green Chapel. This little scene is directly inspired by Gauvain's dialogue with the shepherd in *Ch* 175–202. The following parallel details may be noted: The person who warns the hero has his good at heart.—The man he is intent on finding slays all who go to his dwelling,—and he too will risk death.—So he should go some other way.—The hero replies rather curtly—that he will not turn aside,—for this would be a disgrace.

The servant's unworthy offer to keep quiet about Gawain's recreancy should he take another route was in all likelihood suggested to the Englishman by *Ch* 200–2, where we are told that if it became public knowledge that Gauvain had turned aside, he would never live it down.

So now we see the *Gawain*-poet returning to a more direct use of his source material, while continuing to enliven it with touches of his own. Thus, he gives the servant's instructions on the direction of the Green Chapel verbatim (it is at the bottom of a wild valley), whereas the author of *Ch* simply states that Gauvain rode to the valley that had been pointed out to him (203–5).

2160-88 *The arrival at the Green Chapel.*

When Gawain comes to the Green Chapel, the poet naturally has *M* in mind once more, and so we find features recalling Gauvain's arrival at the spinning castle (*M* 496–503). The hero dismounts,—and decides to search around.—He looks through a hole (*arche*, *M* 497)—to discover a *cave*.

These few facts have been transformed in masterly fashion by the Englishman to produce as eerie a scene as one could wish. However he may have hit upon the notion of the Green Chapel, it is no chapel that he shows us (*M*'s picture comes closer to one, with its archway and cellar or crypt). With his hint that this could be the Devil's lair, he brings a further touch of that grotesque atmosphere which had such an appeal for his compatriots.

2189-2238 *The Green Knight appears.*

Most of this section appears to be the fruit of the *Gawain*-poet's vivid imagination as he sets the scene for the encounter, though the idea of whetting the weapon may have been taken from another of his familiar texts.[19] As at the first meeting in *M*, however, the challenger emerges from a 'hole' (the deep *cave* in *M* 498), and there is specific mention of the breadth of the axe (*M* 512). Moreover, in both texts the point is made that he is perfectly hale (*GGK* 2229 ff., *M* 602). In having Gawain face up to the knight without a respectful bow, the Englishman was probably remembering *M* 607: 'ne lou redota noiant'.

2239-83 *Gawain flinches from the first axe-blow and is reproved.*

Now we find a run of borrowings from *M* 610-28: The challenger addresses the hero—and reminds him of his covenant.—The latter replies that he will not gainsay him,—but submit—without resistance. —He bends his neck,—and the challenger raises the axe.—Had it struck him, he would have perished.

Here the Englishman introduces a novel twist: Gawain flinches from the blow, and the Green Knight reproves him for his fear. Although this does not happen in *M*, the hint is there for the English poet to develop in his own fashion; for we are told when the challenger heaves up his axe that 'il lo fet por lui esmaier' (*M* 629).

We must, I think, assume that the *Gawain*-poet had his sources memorised, rather than imagine him turning from place to place in a manuscript. If so, it is remarkable how, while keeping their details in clear focus and using them as it suits his plan, he is capable at the same time of imaginative creation around those details.

2284-2330 *After a second feinted blow, Gawain is slightly wounded by a third.*

In this section he springs another surprise on us. The Green Knight lifts his axe twice more and the third time catches Gawain a glancing blow with it. In *M* we are never told that the weapon is brought down at all, yet for the snick we read of in *GGK* the poet did have his model —in *Ch*.

From *M* we learn that the challenger 'n'a talant de lui tochier' (630). The Englishman appears to take over this detail when he says that the Green Knight aims his second blow, 'bot not þe mon rynez' (*GGK* 2290), since he stays his hand. The third stroke, however, 'hurt hym no more / Bot snyrt hym on þat on syde, þat seuered þe hyde' (2311-2); and this is a faithful translation of *Ch* 599-601 ('Sel fiert res a res do costé / Si qu'il li a do cuir osté, / Mes ne l'a pas granment blecié'),

[19] *Perlesvaus* (ed. W. A. Nitze & T. A. Jenkins, Vol. I [Chicago, 1932], p. 284). Cf. TGD, p. 126.

which describe how Gauvain is snicked by the descending sword (cf. *Ch* 659–61). In both texts it is made clear that the hero's blood is spilt —on the snow in *GGK* (2315), on the sheets in *Ch* (713).

We are already familiar with the English poet's technique of fitting a reminiscence of one of the French romances into a run of borrowings from the other (cf. my comments on *GGK* 1208–40). Here is a further instance of how he raises the quality of his accomplishment far above mere adaptation and elaboration. And again we are impressed by the fact that he is not simply stirring his ingredients into a fresh mixture; for this concept of the graze received from the testing weapon is admirably integrated into the new plot, as appears in the next section. Having carried the feature over in his mind from its original place in the bedroom scene, he now relates it both to the present 'beheading' theme (derived from *M*) and to the recent assaying by the lady of Gawain's virtue (inspired by *Ch*).

Another characteristic feature of his art well illustrated here is his ability to bring some psychological depth into situations which, in his sources, proceed on the purely narrative and factual plane. His characters think and feel their way through the events that befall them: in the French romances one feels that they react for the most part instinctively and with little independence of spirit.

2331–88 *The Green Knight has twice feinted as Gawain has kept his bargains. The snick was for the girdle he took, and which Gawain wishes to return.*

The Green Knight reassures Gawain that his trial is at an end and explains the reason for his three strokes. In *M*, of course, there had been only one; but the Englishman, having made artistic capital of the threefold temptation in the bedroom scenes, balances against it the triple physical test of the axe-blows and, as I have said, cunningly relates both ordeals.

For the explanation of the two feints he has recourse to the author's comment in *M* 629–33; The challenger menaced the hero with a pretended blow, not touching him—because of the agreement— loyally kept. The agreement referred to in *M* is the *jeu parti*, in *GGK* the exchange of winnings. Thus the *Gawain*-poet has succeeded in tying this thread too into the Green Knight's revelation. His skill at harmonising the diverse elements he has selected continues to earn our admiration.

The third stroke Bertilak associates more directly with the seduction test and Gawain's acceptance of the girdle; and now the poet's thoughts move back to *Ch* for a while. With *GGK* 2362–5 we may compare *Ch* 746–63: the host admits to having contrived the seduction test and announces that it has shown the hero to be the best knight in the world. Again, however, the Englishman provides a novel and more serious touch by substituting Gawain's movement of anger and shame for the joyful acceptance of the compliment in his source. In *Ch* we shall find Gauvain becoming embittered at the subsequent turn of events, but in neither of the French romances does he evince the feelings of guilt and insufficiency of which the *Gawain*-poet makes such great play, especially towards the end of his romance.

2389-2406 *Gawain has done his penance and shall keep the girdle and be reconciled with the lady.*

This section is based on *Ch* 759–73, with appropriate modifications: The lord tells the hero that he has been put to penance (been assayed, *Ch*)—by his weapon.—He offers the hospitality of his castle (its *saignorie*, *Ch* 772),—and says he will be fully reconciled with his wife (makes over his daughter, *Ch* 767).

2407-28 *Gawain rails against women's wiles.*

In *Ch* Gauvain took good advantage of his host's benevolence, gladly accepting his union with the daughter and long enjoying the castle's hospitality, though declining to take over its possession. But the introspective Gawain of *GGK* is less compliant and launches into a somewhat ungallant tirade against women and their wiles.

For this passage the Englishman has looked a little ahead in *Ch*, to the point in fact where Gauvain has suffered the humiliation of being abandoned by his newly-won 'bride' for an entire stranger. Though this kind of misogynistic outburst is a commonplace of medieval literature (the author of *Ch* may well have been thinking of Chrétien de Troyes's *Conte du Graal*, ll. 5855–65), it would hardly be reasonable to look further than this for his source of inspiration. We compare *GGK* 2414–26 with *Ch* 1168–88 (and cf. 1096–1109): Foolish man— has been brought to grief—by women's deceitful nature—since the time of Adam (Eve, *Ch* 1175).

The gist of both speeches is the same, though as we have come to expect, the Englishman has not been slavish in his imitation. Their artistic function, on the other hand, I take to be rather different in the two romances. I suspect the author of *Ch* of a humorous intention as he makes Gauvain, of all people, rail against womenkind. But the English poet has long been preparing us to accept this kind of rueful comment from a Gawain whose moral scruples have been so severely exercised in his dealings with Bertilak's wife. He has turned, I believe, purposeful incongruity into the perfectly congruent expression of his more deeply reflective hero's feelings of self-reproach at having been lured into the snare of sex.

2429-78 *The Green Knight names himself as Bertilak and the old lady as Morgan. Gawain leaves for Arthur's court.*

No parallel in the French texts. The host in *Ch* never names himself and perhaps the *Gawain*-poet felt this as an omission. He may even have been prompted to what is, for the modern reader, an unfortunate exposition of Morgan's part in the affair by his own ponderings on the identity of the mysterious *châtelaine* in *M*. Or perhaps he merely wished to exonerate the otherwise very civil and civilised Bertilak from the blame of devising such an outrageous trick to play on Arthur and his court.

2479-2504 *Gawain's welcome at court and his shame.*

Gawain's return carries reminiscences, appropriately enough, of both *Ch* and *M*: He rides back to court—unscathed 'in vale' (*M* 1042-5).— There is jubilation at his coming (*Ch* 1196),—and the king and queen are there to receive him (*M* 1058 ff.).—He tells of his adventures (*Ch* 1198-9, *M* 1091-2),—the good and the bad (*Ch* 1201-2), including the love of the lady (*Ch* 1203).

So, though neither of the French texts shows its hero burdened by shame as is Gawain, we do read in *Ch* 1193 that 'De s'aventure a mout pensé', and that romance does leave him under something of a cloud. For the last time in his story we find that though the Englishman's handling of the situation is commendably original in its detail and psychology, even here there is something in the French to trigger off his final suggestive development.

2505-30 *Gawain will always wear the girdle in penance; his companions adopt a green baldric for his sake.*

No parallel in the French texts. Whereas in *M* the bridle is almost ignored in the elation of Gawain's return, in *GGK* the girdle becomes the focus of attention. And if both of the French romances conclude on something of a dying fall, the English poet has contrived an ending to lift the spirits not only of Gawain, but of us all.

CONCLUSIONS ON THE
GAWAIN-POET'S TECHNIQUES

Our anonymous Englishman set himself the task of creating an entirely new romance from a store of narrative material, in French for the most part, that he had at his disposal. His imagination had been stirred in particular by the two short Gauvain romances that have been the chief subject of this study; and he decided that by selecting, rearranging, adapting and amplifying he could produce the kind of story he wanted and of a length he considered suitable.

This was a task to tax his powers of organisation to the utmost, and from it he has emerged triumphant. For he was not content simply to stitch together translated sections of his sources, tricked out with the ornaments of the English alliterative tradition. He was determined to produce a true work of art, having its own system of balances and symmetries, and an overall unity at every level—narrative, poetic, moral. This meant seeing in his mind's eye the whole structure of the romance before he set about the actual work of composition.

A rough description of his ground plan would be to say that he has framed the central episodes of *Ch* within the beheading theme inherited from *M*. But this is altogether too simple. For we find runs of borrowings from his main sources broken by passages of his own invention, designed to intensify a certain atmosphere or deepen the meaning of the story by introducing moral or psychological considerations, or in other cases supplied to make a smooth transition between the main stages of the plot. Sometimes a sequence from a primary source will be interrupted by a sub-theme (such as the hunt, or exchange of winnings), partly inspired by other texts but amplified, no doubt, by the poet's own skill. Elsewhere we may find a reminiscence of one of the main texts inserted into a run from the other; or a feature such as the arming of Gawain or the whole seduction episode elaborated and modified by the introduction of material from a secondary source. Even within an extended run of borrowings from one of the main models one may notice (as in the case of the use of the central episodes in *Ch*) that there is no slavish following of the order in which the events are recounted.

The extent to which the *Gawain*-poet has manipulated and re-structured his material is, then, a most striking aspect of his art. Moreover, every move has its own logic and makes a positive contribution to the progress of the story and to the harmony of the total design. Time and again he has achieved a more striking balance of elements than is seen in his models: the placing of Gawain's sojourn at the Green Knight's castle between the two parts of the beheading game; the three hunting scenes set against and throwing into relief the three phases of the attempted seduction, with the three strokes at the Green Chapel being related to both; the raising of the stature of Bertilak and his court to provide a truer counterpoise to Arthur and his company, and at the same time giving Gawain an opponent who matches him in courtesy as well as might. These are a few of the more obvious structural refinements to the credit of the English poet, but each scene contains its share of smaller effects tending in the same direction.

With a lesser artist, a quest for symmetry and proportion might have led to some structural rigidity, with a stemming of the flow of the narrative between the high points of the action. This the *Gawain*-poet has in the main avoided. We have seen how he kept the whole of his story in his mind as he composed, now recalling a past incident, now adding a detail that we realise will have future relevance. Consequently he conveys a sense of progression, even during the more static scenes. The pace does, inevitably, vary, but it never lags. The course of the story is less headlong than in the French romances: there are reflective or descriptive passages (the pentangle, for instance, or the passing of the seasons) that are brought in to modulate the tempo. We have found the poet, perhaps to achieve his desired length, adding certain motifs (notably the hunt and the exchange of winnings) that seem almost superfluous: they are linked to the main plot, but do not advance it. But there is an especial liveliness in the telling here, and in the hunting scenes even a breathlessness, that sweeps us on without our feeling that we have been side-tracked at all.

As well as the poet's fine sense of progression, he shows a greater feeling for dramatic tension than is discernable in his sources. There are his well-timed hints of impending hazards that keep us forever on the alert. And there is his ability, by means of silence as well as dialogue and description, to electrify the atmosphere at significant moments such as the Green Knight's abrupt invasion of the gay Arthurian world, or the mute exchange of glances between Gawain and the lady at their first encounter. Equally he is capable of quickly releasing the tension again by returning to a relaxed mood or perhaps introducing a passage of bland dialogue, as when Bertilak emerges from his hole at the Green Chapel.

For those who know the French romances there is another kind of tension to be savoured: the tension of irony as the reader or listener expects a situation to develop or a character to behave in a particular way, only to find the mischievous poet giving a novel twist to his inherited material. We think especially of Gawain's attitude to the lady, but there are other instances too where familiarity with the earlier stories would not fail to enrich the contemporary public's appreciation of the new situations just as it does our own.

Taking the broad view, then, we can wonder at the *Gawain*-poet's fine craftsmanship as he works his material into a new shape that has the aesthetic virtues of overall unity and balance. His narrative may be less direct than in his principal sources, but it is never wayward, and progresses with a pace that is interestingly varied though always under control. Never does his story run the risk of becoming diffuse in the telling: indeed, despite his general policy of expansion, he is prepared to compress a scene from a model when he feels the need for greater dramatic density (there are instances of this in the account of Gawain's first days in Bertilak's castle). And throughout he regulates the emotional charge in a way that never permits our interest to flag.

Turning now from his main structural achievements to the more detailed aspects of his composition, we scarcely find less to admire. Occasionally, but only occasionally, he comes near to direct translation (examples are in ll. 381-4, 764, 1204-7, 1237-40). This we would scarcely expect, when his chosen verse-form is so different from the French: other considerations apart, his quest for alliteration is bound to lead him away from the 'one-for-one' substitutions of the literal translator.

His characteristic method is to take a passage from his source and convey the gist of it in his own words, often changing the order of its constituent elements, and usually elaborating to a greater or lesser extent in the process. Let us see a typical case.

Ch 222-47 presents the following elements: (1) Lord (and servants) come to greet G.—(2) with joy.—(3) Servants take arms and horse.— (4) G. led by host—(5) over bridge.—(6) Fine fire—(7) in hall.—

(8) Richly draped seat round it.—(9) Horse stabled.—(10) G. thanks host.—(11) Host says meal being prepared.—(12) Tells G. to enjoy himself at his ease,—(13) and say if anything fails to please him.

The *Gawain*-poet has rearranged these features as follows (ll. 815–38): (1) (people, not lord)—(5)—(9)—(4)—(2)—(3) (arms)—(7)—(6) —(1) (lord comes to greet G.)—(12), (13)—(10). He has postponed (8) for later use (ll. 875 ff.); and (11) he has omitted, though a meal is in fact served once Gawain has been robed (ll. 884 ff.). The passage has been paraphrased rather than translated, and some elements have been elaborated, in particular the details of the greetings afforded the hero.

The Englishman's amplification of his received material works in several directions. There is his immense enrichment of the verbal texture, the use of words for their sound as well as meaning, the synonyms and wealth of epithets. Then there are the colourful details conjured from the poet's own imagination, and which so often bring a more vivid, visual quality to a description (a good example is the evocation of the castle in ll. 785–802), as well as intensifying the atmosphere of a scene, whether it be of care-free festivity or of dreadful foreboding. The expansion and invention of dialogue must also be mentioned as one of the poet's more valuable contributions throughout the romance. In these ways he adds substance and not infrequently a greater degree of realism to the more terse and matter-of-fact narration of his sources.

His methods of amplification would repay an extensive study. So often a single word or phrase in the French will stimulate him to a shorter or longer development in which some play of associations may be detected. As he set out more to transform than to translate, it is difficult to assess the accuracy of his knowledge of the French language. It may be that on a couple of occasions we can catch him out: his rendering of the *jeu parti* as a game, and his apparent mistranslation of *fermez* as 'loken' (l. 765). But it is impossible to be sure. These too may be instances of new creation through verbal associations.

In the case of 'loken' it may be doubted whether the resulting image is altogether successful—the steepling castle 'loken vnder boȝez' seems a little incongruous, even if one relates the participle to 'aboute bi þe diches'. And there are other instances of a close adherence to a source leading to a somewhat illogical circumstance: Gawain's repetition of the terms of the beheading agreement (ll. 381–5); the vision of his limbs beneath the robe (l. 868); his over-indulgence in wine (ll. 899–900): the lady's apparent foreknowledge of the blow to be struck (ll.

1283–7). But these are very slight blemishes amid so much excellence.

I have been speaking of the *Gawain*-poet's main sources as though they were the texts of *Ch* and *M* as presented to us in the sole surviving manuscript. This is hardly likely to have been the case; but the assumption is not, I think, fatally rash. We have seen a number of examples of almost exact translation that suggest a model very close to what we know; and even behind the more amplified renderings in *GGK* it is usually possible to detect an exemplar essentially the same as the surviving texts.

Whether or not the poet had them on parchment in front of him is, however, a more difficult question to answer. Sometimes the closeness of the readings suggests that he did. But against this must be set the extreme flexibility of his adaptation, as he culls from first one text and then the other (not to mention his sporadic use of subsidiary sources) and moves backwards and forwards, even within a single romance, in his search for inspiration. Add to this the fact that he seems to have arranged the whole pattern of his story in his mind before he began the task of actual composition and we must, I think, conclude that he had all of his romances firmly set in his memory, in detail as well as in outline. This does not mean, though, that the texts may not also have been available to him within the covers of one or more manuscripts (there is no reason why all his French models should not have been bound together: *Ch* and *M* are only two of the many offerings in Berne 354). If he did have them virtually by heart, indeed, it is likely to have been through close acquaintance with them in some no longer identifiable English library. And there speculation must rest.

This survey has been restricted to the *Gawain*-poet's techniques of adaptation as they have emerged from the preceding comparative study. In conclusion, I must mention one other feature that has a vital bearing on his whole attitude to his work and on any interpretation that may be put upon it. This is the radical change he has wrought in the personality of Gawain himself. From the impetuous pursuer of *aventures*, chivalric and amorous, that was Gauvain he has produced a far more serious and mature figure. That courtesy of which Arthur's nephew was the traditional embodiment survives not merely unimpaired but reinforced, with the surface polish and politeness backed by a more genuine humility than our French romances show. The heroic resolve, firm as ever, springs now rather from a pious sense of duty than from recklessness. And in matters of the heart, Gawain gives only a glimpse of that gay initiative that had won him such a reputation among the ladies of his circle, as other poets confirm.

Not only has the Englishman re-formed Gawain's character, he has reformed it too. The honour this prince of knights now craves is not simply to avoid being bested in any of the chivalric or sexual activities. It is a standard of conduct prescribed not by his vanity but by his conscience; and a deep sense of guilt assails him with the thought that he has fallen short of that standard. The lady provocatively plays on the weaknesses of the old Gauvain: the new, self-critical Gawain just manages to hold firm.

Though this deepening and spiritualising of the hero's psychology is, I believe, one of the most significant developments of his source material the Englishman has achieved, I have no intention here to consider its meaning in the total scheme of the romance. Suffice it to say that whereas in his French models the main emphasis lay on physical prowess and a somewhat superficial concept of chivalric and courtly behaviour, this brilliant and thoughtful poet has chosen rather to present us, mainly through the person of Gawain, with a demonstration of high-principled chivalry and certain lessons in social as well as individual morality.

One final remark. Far from detracting from the English poet's merit, knowledge of his sources and a study of his own romance beside them has served to expose his talent in all its complexity and, paradoxically, its originality. A heavy use of sources so often produces nothing but plagiarism. Between plagiarism and such an achievement as this there is a vast difference. And that difference we may call genius.